"Levit's important book proposes that legislative restrictions on speech enacted during times of emergency are more likely to be democratically legitimate if the legislature has deliberated fully and well. Where Levit advances the argument is by developing a multi-faceted model we can use to determine if that sort of deliberation has occurred in specific cases. One of the book's strengths is its close historical inquiry in several case studies to illuminate how his model of legislative deliberation works in practice. In so doing, Levit furthers our understanding of both the meaning and the possibilities of deliberative democracy."

—*John E. Finn, Professor of Government Emeritus, Wesleyan University*

"This book has significant implications for recent developments in democratic theory as applied to the momentous decisions of wartime. As attention turns from deliberative democracy, the careful, informed consideration of alternatives by mass publics to democratic deliberation, most likely to occur within democratically authorized institutions, Levit's case studies initiate the development of the much-needed relevant norms."

—*Daniel DiLeo, Penn State Altoona*

"What makes laws legitimate? Levit shows us legitimation in practice, examining how Congress restricted freedom of speech during modern crises. We learn how democracies deliberate to realize the common good while preserving fundamental rights, even in dark times."

—*Michael Kochin, School of Political Science, Government and International Affairs, Tel Aviv University*

Legislative Deliberative Democracy

Freedom of speech is a basic right in a democracy. During war, however, national legislatures tend to enact laws that restrict this basic right. Under what circumstances can such laws be democratically legitimate?

Avichai Levit argues that the degree of democratic legitimacy of laws that restrict freedom of speech during war depends on the extent of legislature deliberation on such laws. The more law makers in both chambers of the legislature seriously consider information and arguments, reason on the common good and seek to persuade and decide the best legislative outcome, in committees and on the floor, the more democratic legitimacy can be associated with such laws. This book fills a gap in the scholarly literature regarding the evaluation of the democratic legitimacy of laws that restrict freedom of speech during war, by bridging different theoretical perceptions and presenting an alternative normative account of deliberative democracy which focuses on the deliberations of a national legislature. Using the United States as a case study, Levit delves into the details of Congressional deliberation during World War I, World War II and the Cold War, as well as the political histories that brought about such laws.

Legislative Deliberative Democracy will be of interest to academics and students alike in the fields of political theory, American politics and political history.

Avichai Levit is a civil service professional and former diplomat. He is currently Deputy Department Director for Audit of the Ministry of Defense at Israel's State Comptroller's Office, directing oversight activities of the national security sector. He is a visiting lecturer at Tel Aviv University's School of Political Science, Government and International Affairs.

Routledge Innovations in Political Theory

Aesthetics and Political Culture in Modern Society
Henrik Kaare Nielsen

Post-Fukushima Activism
Politics and Knowledge in the Age of Precarity
Azumi Tamura

Reconstructing Nonviolence
A New Theory and Practice for a Post-Secular Society
Roberto Baldoli

Rethinking Positive and Negative Liberty
Maria Dimova-Cookson

The Problem of Value Pluralism
Isaiah Berlin and Beyond
George Crowder

On Biopolitics
An Inquiry into Nature and Language
Marco Piasentier

Democracy, the Courts, and the Liberal State
A Comparative Analysis of American and German Constitutionalism
David J. Miles

Legislative Deliberative Democracy
Debating Acts Restricting Freedom of Speech during War
Avichai Levit

For more information about this series, please visit: https://www.routledge.com

Legislative Deliberative Democracy

Debating Acts Restricting Freedom of Speech during War

Avichai Levit

Routledge
Taylor & Francis Group
NEW YORK AND LONDON

First published 2021
by Routledge
52 Vanderbilt Avenue, New York, NY 10017

and by Routledge
2 Park Square, Milton Park, Abingdon, Oxon, OX14 4RN

Routledge is an imprint of the Taylor & Francis Group, an informa business

Library of Congress Cataloging-in-Publication Data
A catalog record for this title has been requested

ISBN: 978-0-367-56998-3 (hbk)
ISBN: 978-1-003-10056-0 (ebk)

Typeset in Times New Roman
by codeMantra

For Limor,
Bara, Ori, Yotam and Yaheli

Contents

Introduction

Freedom of speech is a basic right in a democracy. During war, however, there is a tendency to curb freedom of speech. In the face of external threats, governing institutions restrict it. The United States is such a case.

In June 1917, eight weeks after Congress declared war on Germany, it passed the Espionage Act[1] (still in effect until this day), which prohibits, when the United States is at war, for anyone: to make "false statements" with an intent to interfere with the operation or success of the armed forces or to promote the success of its enemies; to attempt to cause insubordination, disloyalty, mutiny or refusal of duty in the armed forces; to obstruct the recruiting or enlistment service of the United States; and to mail any letter, pamphlet, publication or thing of any kind, in violation of any of the provisions of the Act.[2]

During World War I over 2,000 people were prosecuted under the Espionage Act and approximately half were convicted.[3] A number of cases reached the Supreme Court which upheld the convictions of lower courts. Other indictments under the act were made during World War II.

In 1918 Congress legislated the Sedition Act,[4] an amendment to the Espionage Act, which in addition prohibited during war any "disloyal, profane, scurrilous or abusive" expression about the form of government, the Constitution, the armed forces or the flag of the United States (or use of any language intended to bring the latter "into contempt, scorn, contumely, or disrepute"); or use of any language intended to "incite, provoke or encourage resistance to the United States"; as well as expression urging, inciting or advocating any curtailment of production of products necessary to the prosecution of war.[5] The Sedition Act was repealed by Congress in 1921.[6]

This book is concerned with the phenomena of legislation by a national legislature restricting freedom of speech during war. Under what conditions can the legislation of such laws be considered democratically legitimate?

By democratically legitimate I mean that people consent to obey the law, even if they have reservations. People do not view the law as unconstitutional, and in general, government has no need to force obedience.[7]

There is limited scholarship regarding an answer to this question. First, although the literature of war and emergency powers shows that governmental war powers, including the abridgment of rights during war, should be legitimized in law by the national legislature after deliberation,[8] the literature does not explain the conditions under which the legislation of such laws can be considered democratically legitimate.

Second, while deliberative democracy theory offers an answer to the question of legitimacy of legislation in democratic political systems – a democratically legitimate law is produced in a process of public discussion and debate in which participants reason on the common good – the theory of deliberative democracy put forward by theorists such as Jürgen Habermas[9] is poorly suited for the real world: we live in large-scale democratic countries, and it is impossible for all the citizens in a country to participate in an ideal deliberative process.

Third, while libraries contain collections of epics on war, on domestic and legislative politics, and on civil liberties, there are only very few works that connect these subjects, and when they do, they are subjective analyses since they use values as a yardstick. Such substantive reasoning is problematic because of its subjective nature. Zechariah Chafee's classic study of free speech in the United States,[10] for example, weighs values and interests to understand the First Amendment[11] and to find "the true meaning of freedom of speech" and the "boundary line" of free speech in wartime.[12] Geoffrey Stone's comprehensive narrative on free speech in wartime also analyzes values and principles and, reviewing six episodes in U.S. history, concludes that in each of them "the United States *excessively* sacrificed the freedom of speech" although over time Americans "*have* made progress" (emphases in the original).[13]

I agree with many of the arguments Chafee and Stone put forward; however, we live in large-scale democratic nation-states and our democracy is representative – our representatives are the ones who enact the laws that govern us – therefore we should look in the realm where actual decisions (laws) are made and examine arguments made by our representatives when legislating laws restricting freedom of speech during war. To use Michael Kochin's words (drawing on Bruno Latour): facts are made by people, and made somewhere; therefore, to understand a policy (or a law), we need to follow actors into the sites where they produce it.[14] In this case we need to follow politicians into the legislature.

Thus, while different fields in academia have touched upon the question of the democratic legitimacy of legislation restricting freedom of speech during war, explanations have been incomplete – whether they are in the realm of war and emergency powers, deliberative democracy or law.

I fill the above-mentioned gaps in the scholarly literature regarding the evaluation of the democratic legitimacy of laws restricting freedom of speech during war, by bridging different theoretical perceptions and presenting an alternative normative account of deliberative democracy that focuses on the deliberations of a national legislature.

I regard deliberative democracy as an aspect of representative democracy and not as a substitute for it[15] and therefore argue that legislation restricting freedom of speech during war can be considered democratically legitimate if members of a national legislature deliberated well; that is, during the process of discussion and debate, they reasoned on the public good, seriously considered information and arguments and sought to decide and to persuade as to the best legislative solution. I term this "Legislative Deliberative Democracy."

My claim is that laws restricting freedom of speech during war carry a higher degree of democratic legitimacy when members of a democratic government's national legislature, the representatives of the people, duly deliberate on them, that is, if information and arguments are put forward in a collective reasoning process on the merits of the legislation and on the greater public good (e.g., arguments in regard to the constitutionality of the proposed legislation or in regard to protecting the welfare of the nation during war) and persuasion takes place. The higher the extent of deliberation, the more legitimacy is attached to the legislation.

The matter of deliberations in a national legislature on laws restricting freedom of speech during war, and thus the degree of their democratic legitimacy, is particularly important because most legislation does not raise fundamental issues of democratic legitimacy; that is, in general, laws enacted by the national legislature do not undermine civil liberties. On the other hand, historically, wars have had the effect of undermining civil liberties in democracies, including laws enacted by the national legislature that restricted freedom of speech.

I propose using the following criteria to measure legislative deliberation: committee hearings, debate in both chambers, exchange of information and arguments on the floor, framing arguments in terms of the public good and persuasion.

This book also addresses a lacuna in scholarly literature in regard to empirical analysis of deliberative politics. Over the past three decades, noteworthy contributions have been made in the realm of political philosophy, but very few studies have analyzed real political deliberation. The book meets this void by assessing the extent of actual deliberation in the U.S. Congress when legislating restrictions on freedom of speech during war. As a result, it uses empirical evidence to illustrate theory.

An analysis of deliberation in legislature, in this study the U.S. Congress, requires an understanding of how such laws came about in the first place. Therefore, a political-historical inquiry is in place: what was the purpose of laws restricting freedom of speech during war; what and who did they serve, and how?

Employing a structural functionalist research approach, I propose that in times of crisis in the United States, and in order to protect and unite the nation, certain restrictions on speech were deemed necessary: different input functions in the political system – political socialization processes, elements in the administration (e.g., the Department of Justice) and in Congress, as well as groups and associations in society (e.g., extensive anticommunism articulation by groups in the late 1940s) – claimed and demanded it; as a result laws restricting freedom of speech were legislated; and the courts fulfilled their function by judging according to those laws.

This book is both normative and empirical, or descriptive: I propose an alternative normative conception relating to the question of the democratic legitimacy of legislation restricting freedom of speech during war (Legislative Deliberative Democracy) and illustrate how it was realized in political history, by assessing the extent of deliberation in the U.S. Congress. In addition, it employs a functional approach to explain how restrictions on freedom of speech came about. Therefore the qualitative case-study method is the most appropriate research methodology.[16]

While there were many ways freedom of speech was restricted in the United States in times of crisis, including state statutes,[17] there were four instances when the American national Congress enacted federal acts restricting freedom of speech, and these are the focus of the book. (I deal only with the portions of the statutes that restricted speech, and not with the parts that regulated matters of espionage, military secrets and classified information, foreign commerce, aliens and the like.) The federal acts discussed are the Espionage Act of 1917, the Sedition Act of 1918, the Alien Registration Act of 1940 (the Smith Act) and the Internal Security Act of 1950 (the McCarran Act).[18]

The Espionage Act of 1917 is still in effect, and it not only restricts specific speech when the United States is at war but also declares nonmailable items in violation of the act. The act was enforced during both world wars and was upheld by the Supreme Court.

The Sedition Act of 1918, actually an amendment to the Espionage Act, prohibited during war language provoking resistance to the United States and was also upheld by the Supreme Court (however, repealed by Congress in 1921).

The Smith Act of 1940, introduced in Congress on the eve of World War II to "prohibit certain subversive activities," prohibited advocating the necessity of overthrowing the government by force and was enforced both in World War II and in the course of the Cold War. The act was initially upheld by the Supreme Court in 1951 (*Dennis v. United States*).[19]

The McCarran Act of 1950, legislated at the height of the Cold War to "protect the United States against certain un-American and subversive activities," required communist organizations to register with the attorney general and established the Subversive Activities Control Board. Passed into law over President Truman's veto, it too was initially upheld in 1961 by the Supreme Court (*Communist Party of the United States v. Subversive Activities Control Board*).[20]

This book has four main parts. Initially I will introduce a normative framework concerning the democratic legitimacy of laws restricting freedom of speech during war. In it, I shall review literature of war and emergency powers, the background and fundamental elements of deliberative democracy theory, deliberative democracy as an aspect of representative government and criteria on how to measure legislative deliberation.

The next three parts look at the United States as a case study, starting with World War I and the Espionage and Sedition Acts, followed by World War II and the Cold War, including the Smith Act of 1940 and the McCarran Act of 1950.

As illustrated throughout Parts II–IV, the afore-mentioned acts' main purposes were, during times of crisis, to:

1 Prohibit inciting disloyalty in the armed forces and obstruct enlistment (the Espionage Act): by making it unlawful, when the United States is at war, to "willfully cause or attempt to cause insubordination, disloyalty, mutiny, or refusal of duty," in the armed forces of the United States, or "willfully obstruct the recruiting or enlistment service of the United States";
2 Prohibit provoking resistance to the United States (the Sedition Act): by making it unlawful, when the United States is at war, to "willfully utter, print, write, or publish any language intended to incite, provoke or encourage resistance to the United States";
3 Prohibit certain subversive activities (the Smith Act): by making it unlawful to "willfully advocate" the necessity of overthrowing or destroying any government in the United States by force or violence, organize any group who does so, or conspire to do so;
4 Protect the United States against certain un-American and subversive activities by requiring registration of communist organizations (the McCarran Act): the act required communist-action organizations, organizations which are substantially directed, dominated or controlled by the foreign government or foreign organization controlling the world communist movement, whose purpose is to establish a communist totalitarian dictatorship, to register with the attorney general and report names of their officers and members and an accounting of moneys received and expended.

Each of the empirical parts (Parts II–IV) begins with an account of the enactment and enforcement of and judgment on the acts, which analyzes processes in the political system, including processes of political socialization, interest articulation and aggregation, communication and adjudication. Afterward, on the basis of the normative conception concerning the democratic legitimacy of laws restricting freedom of speech during war that I develop in Part I ("Legislative Deliberative Democracy"), I assess the extent of deliberation on the different statutes in the

U.S. Congress, among other things: congressional committee hearings, and the extent of deliberation on the floor, including the presentation and the consideration of information and arguments.

I conclude with a summary of the main arguments and findings of congressional deliberations; point out the relevance of the normative framework to constitutional democracies besides the United States, as well as to legislation restricting civil liberties during war other than freedom of speech; and highlight policy implications regarding the war on terror which are relevant in our times.

Notes

1 65th *Congress*, 1st Session, *Congressional Record – Senate*, Vol. 55, 3259–3264, June 5, 1917.
2 Act of June 15, 1917, chap. 30, title I & title XII, Espionage, *Statutes at Large of the United States of America*, Vol 40, Part 1, 219 & 230 (Washington: Government Printing Office, 1919). The Espionage Act is actually concerned with espionage matters and the protection of military secrets, but two parts have to do with free speech during war.
3 Geoffrey R. Stone, *Perilous Times: Free Speech in Wartime from the Sedition Act of 1798 to the War on Terrorism* (New York: W.W. Norton & Company, 2004), 593, ft. 136.
4 65th Congress, 2nd Session, *Congressional Record – Senate*, Vol. 56, 6057, May 4, 1918; 65th Congress, 2 nd Session, *Congressional Record – House*, Vol. 56, 6186–6187, May 7, 1918.
5 Act of May 16, 1918, chap. 76, *Statutes at Large of the United States of America*, Vol 40, Part 1, 553 (Washington: Government Printing Office, 1919).
6 Joint Resolution of March 3, 1921, chap. 136, *Statutes at Large of the United States of America*, Vol 41, 1359–1360 (Washington: Government Printing Office, 1921). There were relatively few prosecutions under the Sedition Act since it was enacted so late in the war; Stone, 191.
7 Here I assent to Gianfranco Poggi's observation that legitimacy in the modern constitutional state – citizen's compliance to the State's authority –is based on the citizens' understandings of Weber's legal-rational type of legitimacy; that is, laws are valid if produced according to the procedural rules vested in the State's constitution and are the product of reason. Gianfranco Poggi, *The Development of the Modern State: A Sociological Introduction* (Stanford: Stanford University Press, 1978), 107.
8 See for example Clinton L. Rossiter, *Constitutional Dictatorship: Crisis Government in the Modern Democracies* (Princeton: Princeton University Press, 1948), 296, 300, 302.
9 Jürgen Habermas, "Three Normative Models of Democracy," *Constellations* 1 (1994): 1–10; Jürgen Habermas, *Between Facts and Norms: Contributions to a Discourse Theory of Law and Democracy*. Trans. William Rehg (Cambridge: The MIT Press, 1996), especially 296–308 (originally published in German in 1992).
10 Including during World War I and through 1941, Zechariah Chafee, *Free Speech in the United States* (Cambridge: Harvard University Press, 1967).
11 To the Constitution of the Unites States – "Congress shall make no law... abridging the freedom of speech, or of the press." Chafee, vii–xiii, 8–9, 31–35.
12 Chafee, 31, 35.

13 Stone, 530, 533, 3–14 (cited in ft. 3).

14 Michael S. Kochin, "What Political Science Needs to Learn from Science Studies," *2009 Annual Meeting of the American Political Science Association*, Toronto, Canada.

15 See similar perspectives in Joseph M. Bessette, *The Mild Voice of Reason: Deliberative Democracy & American National Government* (Chicago: The University of Chicago Press, 1994); and in John Uhr, *Deliberative Democracy in Australia: The Changing Place of Parliament* (Melbourne: Cambridge University Press, 1998).

16 Steenbergen et al. developed a discourse quality index as a quantitative measure of discourse in deliberation (Marco R., Steenbergen, André Bächtiger and Jürg Steiner, "Measuring Political Deliberation: A Discourse Quality Index," *Comparative European Politics* 1 (2003): 21–48.) Disadvantages for using a quantitative research methodology for explaining the phenomena of legislation restricting freedom of speech during war include: (1) Quantitative coding captures only what is said and fails to notice what has not been discussed. For example, it would fail to notice a lack of substantial arguments regarding limiting freedom of speech, in the case that they were absent. (2) The index developed measures only speech that makes demands, clarifying questions are not coded (Steenbergen et al., 27), yet such questions are part of deliberation, indicating that a member of the legislature is listening, and therefore they should be measured. This book looks at the entirety of the exchange between members of Congress on a bill. (3) Quantitative research is not fit to capture the context and background conditions of legislature deliberation, such as presidential attempts to influence Congress or constituent pressures.

17 See Stone, *Perilous Times* (cited in ft. 3). Self as well as imposed censorship of the press was also employed –for example see Michael S. Sweeny, *Secrets of Victory: the Office of Censorship and the American Press and Radio in World War II* (Chapel Hill: University of North Carolina Press, 2001).

18 The Sedition Act of 1798, which was enacted during the "Half War" with France (which made it a crime to publish "false, scandalous, and malicious writing" against the government of the United States, and expired by its own terms in 1803), is excluded from this book because the environment of its legislation was very different, thus making it a unique case, which is incomparable to the others. To note just two examples: (1) Characteristics of mass society of the late modern era, pertinent to the periods of World War I, World War II and the Cold War –such as mass media (magazines, radio, film), diverse associations and interest groups –were not yet developed. (2) The inner workings of Congress as a legislative institution were different. For example, initially Congress relied on temporary select committees. The Senate Judiciary Committee was established only in 1816, and it played an important role –including from a deliberative aspect –with respect to the Espionage, Sedition, Smith and McCarran Acts of the twentieth century.

19 In 1957 the Court adopted a narrow interpretation of the Smith Act (*Yates v. United States*) and prosecutions ceased. Geoffrey R. Stone, "Civil Liberties in Wartime," *Journal of Supreme Court History* 28 (2003): 236–238.

20 In a case in 1965, the Supreme Court held that registration violated the Fifth Amendment privilege against self-incrimination (*Albertson et al. v. Subversive Activities Control Board*). David Caute, *The Great Fear: The Anti-communist Purge Under Truman and Eisenhower* (New York: Simon and Schuster, 1978), 172, 38. And in a later ruling, the Court held a provision of the Act unconstitutional (*United States v. Robel*, 1967). Stone, *Perilous Times*, 416*n*.

References

Bessette, Joseph M. *The Mild Voice of Reason: Deliberative Democracy & American National Government*. Chicago: The University of Chicago Press, 1994.

Caute, David. *The Great Fear: The Anti-Communist Purge Under Truman and Eisenhower*. New York: Simon and Schuster, 1978.

Chafee, Zechariah. *Free Speech in the United* States. Cambridge: Harvard University Press, 1967.

Congressional Record: Containing the Proceedings and Debates of the First Session *of the Sixty-Fifth Congress of the United States of America*, Vol. LV, Parts 1–3. Washington: Government Printing Office, 1917.

Congressional Record: Containing the Proceedings and Debates of the Second Session *of the Sixty-Fifth Congress of the United States of America*, Vol. LVI, Parts 5–7. Washington: Government Printing Office, 1918.

Habermas, Jürgen. "Three Normative Models of Democracy." *Constellations* 1 (1994): 1–10.

Habermas, Jürgen. *Between Facts and Norms: Contributions to a Discourse Theory of Law and Democracy*. trans. William Rehg. Cambridge: The MIT Press, 1996.

Kochin, Michael S., "What Political Science Needs to Learn from Science Studies." *2009 Annual Meeting of the American Political Science Association*. Toronto, Canada.

Poggi, Gianfranco. *The Development of the Modern State: A Sociological Introduction*. Stanford: Stanford University Press, 1978.

Rossiter, Clinton L. *Constitutional Dictatorship: Crisis Government in the Modern Democracies*. Princeton: Princeton University Press, 1948.

Statutes at Large of the United States of America, Vol. 40, Part 1. Washington: Government Printing Office, 1919.

Statutes at Large of the United States of America, Vol. 41, Chapter 136. Washington: Government Printing Office, 1921.

Steenbergen, Marco R, Bächtiger, André, and Steiner, Jürg. "Measuring Political Deliberation: A Discourse Quality Index." *Comparative European Politics* 1 (2003): 21–48.

Stone, Geoffrey R. "Civil Liberties in Wartime." *Journal of Supreme Court History* 28 (2003): 215–251.

Stone, Geoffrey R. *Perilous Times: Free Speech in Wartime from the Sedition Act of 1798 to the War on Terrorism*. New York: W.W. Norton & Company, 2004.

Sweeny, Michael S. *Secrets of Victory: The Office of Censorship and the American Press and Radio in World War II*. Chapel Hill: University of North Carolina Press, 2001.

Uhr, John. *Deliberative Democracy in Australia: The Changing Place of Parliament*. Melbourne: Cambridge University Press, 1998.

Part I

Normative Framework

1 The Democratic Legitimacy of Laws Restricting Freedom of Speech During War

When can we say that laws passed by a legislature restricting freedom of speech during war – which are later enforced and judged by the employment, or threat of employment, of nothing less than physical force by the executive – are legitimate in a democracy?

In this chapter I will introduce a normative framework concerning the democratic legitimacy of laws restricting freedom of speech during war. It has five sections. Initially, I shall review literature of war and emergency powers, including the normative claim that abridgment of individual rights during war should be legitimized by the national legislature after deliberation. In the second section, I look into the meaning of deliberation and discuss deliberative democracy theory, including a critique, which leads to the third section, in which I argue that deliberative democracy should be regarded an aspect of representative government. In the fourth section I address the question, is the United States a representative deliberative democracy, and how so? Finally, in regard to the circumstances in which legislation restricting freedom of speech during war can be considered democratically legitimate, I propose an alternative normative account of deliberative democracy that focuses on the deliberations of a national legislature and point out criteria on how to measure legislative deliberation.

War Powers and Deliberation

There is a tension between "basic" freedoms, such as freedom of speech, and the need to protect the existence of the nation in time of war. To use Carl Friedrich's words, for any community that is committed to a faith in which its members receive a substantial amount of freedom and work together effectively, the task of survival "becomes one of defending the inner-most self as well as that of defending the outer-most boundary."[1]

Clinton Rossiter pointed out in his well-known study on war and emergency powers that "wars are not won by debating societies."[2] Historically, in times of crisis, democratic constitutional governments are altered to overcome threats; that is, government has more power and the people fewer rights.[3] For example, governments abridge the rights of citizens to speak freely.[4] However, the purpose of this strong government (or "constitutional dictatorship") is the defense of democracy, of the political and social liberties of the people.[5]

Both Rossiter and Friedrich begin their review on war and emergency powers with a discussion on the Roman dictatorship, in which absolute power was granted temporarily to a citizen, in order to overcome a threat and defend the republic and its constitution.[6] Under modern conditions the actual practices of constitutional dictatorship are often of legislative nature;[7] that is, emergency legislation is introduced or existing laws are modified.

Hence, when discussing the dangers of constitutional dictatorship, Rossiter stated that any particular step in encroachment of the state upon the liberties of its citizens should be instituted as a permanent policy "only by the elected representatives of the people and only after full deliberation."[8] In addition, among the criterions to judge a constitutional dictatorship, Rossiter listed legitimizing powers in the constitution or in law and he discussed the importance of the national legislature, for example in relation to any demands for the abridgment of rights.[9]

John Finn offers a theory of constitutional maintenance and constitutional crises with the task of "defending the inner-most self."[10] Taking into account that democratic governments will take whatever action necessary to ensure survival, including overriding individual rights,[11] Finn deems that in times of crisis, the written words of a specific constitution that limit the powers of government aren't what are important, rather it's "why we initially thought such limitations desirable."[12] He refers to "constitutive or preconstitutional principles"[13] that democratic constitutional governments must abide to and that bind, whether or not they appear in any particular constitutional document.[14] They include reason and deliberation in public affairs:[15] "for questions of constitutional emergencies, constitutionalism should be understood not in terms of limited government but rather as a commitment to a public life premised upon the public articulation of reasons in support of particular actions taken for the public welfare."[16] Hence, "constitutional maintenance demands not substantive limitations on emergency power"[17] but rather articulation of reasons that can persuade others – the reasoned justification of the need for emergency powers.[18] Concurrently "good" reasons are those that can persuade others on their own merit and must admit of a response.[19] Thus Finn concludes that in addition to preserving physical integrity, we must maintain "our identity as political communities founded upon constitutionalism's twin commitments to reason and deliberation in public affairs."[20]

Yet what does it mean to deliberate?

Deliberative Democracy and Legitimacy

Deliberative democracy theory evolved initially as a criticism of liberal and elite democratic theory.[21] The dominant theoretical theme among

American political scientists in the decades following World War II was that of adversary democracy:[22] fundamental conflict is inevitable,[23] there is no common interest and the preferences of one individual are not worth more than those of another.[24] Schumpeter concluded that there is "no such thing as a uniquely determined common good that all people could agree on."[25] Democracy is about electoral competition among potential leaders who scan the "marketplace" to discover voter's preferences: voters function as consumers, and politicians (and political parties) as entrepreneurs.[26] The political act is private, the political process instrumental,[27] and as social choice theory noted, while voting might be a mechanism for aggregating individual preferences, it does not yield a public opinion about a common good.[28]

Critiques of this competitive-pluralist view of politics developed during the 1970s,[29] when among others things, it was emphasized that the task of politics is also "to create justice"[30] and therefore behavior associated with the market is inappropriate in the public arena (or "forum").[31] Political scientists underestimated the role of deliberation and the power of norms and motives, such as fairness.[32]

The evolution of deliberative democracy theory began with Jürgen Habermas, who did not refer to deliberation by name but depicted the core ideas:[33] he expressed in his theory the view that democratic politics is about changing preferences via rational public debate with the aim to reach consensus.[34]

In 1994 Habermas introduced his concept of "discourse theory" as a normative model of democracy.[35] It is a proceduralist view of democracy, which integrates elements of both the liberal and republican view of politics.[36]

According to the liberal view, society is "a market-structured network of interactions among private persons,"[37] and democracy programs the government in the interest of society as political rights, for example the right to vote and free speech, allow citizens to assert their private interests via elections, which aggregate a collective political will.[38] According to the republican view, politics entails more than the mediating function described earlier. Politics is a "form of substantial ethical life," where free and equal citizens shape their relations, and orientation to the common good is a source of social integration.[39] These two views differ on the nature of the political process: while the liberal view sees voters express preferences and license power to rival political parties, and thus "opinion" in the public sphere and in parliament is determined by competition (a market-oriented attitude), the republican view sees the "opinion" occurring in the public sphere and in parliament molded by "public communication oriented to mutual understanding"[40] (a "dialogic" conception).[41]

Habermas claims that although the republican view "preserves the original meaning of democracy"[42] due to the public use of reason, the republican model is too idealistic: conflicting interests drive political goals, and politics is about compromises, not necessarily a "hermeneutical process of self-explication of a shared form of life."[43] Hence the republican view suffers from "ethical overload."[44] He proposes instead a model of "discourse" (or "deliberative politics") where procedures that secure fair bargaining practices and "forms of deliberation" produce democratic outcomes.[45]

This proceduralist view of democracy integrates elements of both the liberal and the republican views: reasonable or fair outcomes are obtained by "weaving together pragmatic considerations, compromises, discourses of self-understanding and justice,"[46] and the success of politics depends neither on the "satisfaction of private preferences" nor on a "collectively acting citizenry" but on the institutionalization of "procedures and conditions of communication."[47]

Consequently, legitimacy is not derived from elections (the liberal view) or a constitutive community (the republican view) but rather from "procedures and communicative presuppositions":[48] public opinion formed in the networks of the public sphere[49] generates "influence," which is transformed into "communicative power" through elections and points the use of "administrative power" in specific directions by means of legislation.[50] (On my criticism on the model of discourse in the "public sphere," see below.)

Drawing on the work of Habermas and others, Joshua Cohen was the first theorist to characterize principles of an ideal deliberative procedure.[51] Cohen maintains that the procedure must capture the principle that "outcomes are democratically legitimate if and only if they could be the object of a free and reasoned agreement among equals."[52] His criteria for an ideal deliberative procedure are: (1) *Freedom* – deliberating participants are not constrained by "prior norms or requirements" but act on the results of their deliberation.[53] (2) *Reason* – parties state reasons for advancing proposals and expect that either supporting or critical reasons will determine the fate of proposals (i.e., collective choices are settled deliberatively).[54] (3) *Equality* – deliberating parties are equal to one another. They are formally equal as everyone has the equal right to introduce proposals, offer support or oppose, that is, actively deliberate, and everyone has an equal voice in the decision; they are substantively equal as the existing distribution of power and resources in society does not have a bearing on their chances to deliberate or on their role in deliberation.[55] (4) *Consensus* – ideal deliberation "aims to arrive at a rationally motivated consensus,"[56] as the procedure involves a free discussion based on reasoning among equals (however, as even under ideal conditions, consensus is not always attainable, deliberation ends with a majority vote).[57]

Cohen further emphasizes that the implications of an ideal deliberative procedure include focus on the common good: while no one is indifferent to their own good, "everyone also seeks to arrive at decisions that are acceptable to all who share the commitment to deliberation."[58] Therefore, one's own preferences are not sufficient reason for advancing a proposal, and reasons that make the proposal acceptable to others are also needed. Thus, the interest, aims and ideals that survive deliberation are those that comprise the common good, those that are legitimate to appeal to in public deliberation. (I view this point crucial to the deliberative process and will refer to it again later.)

Bernard Manin was one of the first theorists to highlight the connection between deliberation and democratic legitimacy:[59] a democratically legitimate decision cannot represent the will of all but should result "from the *deliberation of all*"[60] (emphasis in original).

Manin explains that when individuals make collective decisions, they do not have all the necessary information and a complete set of coherent preferences. In a process of deliberation, of confrontation of various points of view and of exchanging evidence, individuals: (1) discover information they did not previously have (and learn of consequences), (2) may change opinions, and (3) become aware of conflicts in their own desires and as a result modify objectives.[61]

Therefore "the source of legitimacy is not the predetermined will of individuals but rather the process of its formation, that is, deliberation itself"[62] (and as stated earlier, the deliberation of all). In other words, a "legitimate law is the *result of general deliberation* and not the *expression of the general will*"[63] (emphasis in original).

Deliberation is not only a process that enables individuals to ascertain their own preferences; deliberation also makes persuasion possible (through argumentation). Persuasion is different from refutation or demonstration – it is not about discovering the truth; persuasion concerns putting forward arguments, which are more or less convincing, with the aim of producing agreement with the listener.[64]

Of course after deliberation comes a vote. However, Manin argues that the majority principle carries legitimacy, because it comes after a deliberative process in which everyone was able to take part, various points of views were confronted, including that of the minority, but the reasons for deciding on the majority's solution were more convincing.[65] Thus "the procedure preceding the decision is a condition for legitimacy."[66]

Manin also notes, and on this point Cohen joins him, that the concept of deliberation does not justify any action by a majority, including suppression of fundamental liberties that are necessary for deliberation, such as freedom of speech. The ideal of deliberative democracy presupposes freedom of expression.[67]

This is an important point: even if a deliberative process is conducted ideally, its outcome cannot undermine basic tenets of democracy. We would not regard a law that denies, for example, free elections or restricts all kinds of speech as democratically legitimate. Thus, even if participants in an ideal deliberative process arrive at the decision that some votes are not equal to others, or that criticism of a certain government policy is completely forbidden, we would not view these outcomes as legitimate in a democracy.

Seyla Benhabib, writing on deliberation and democratic legitimacy, argues that legitimacy results from free public deliberation of all.[68] In her view, democracy is a form of organizing the public exercise of power on the basis of the principle that decisions are "the outcome of a procedure of free and reasoned deliberation"[69] among equal individuals.

Benhabib claims that Rousseau's political theory incorporates a paradox: legitimacy is based on the "general will," which represents the interests of all, but taking a vote is merely a sum of particular wills and cannot claim legitimacy.[70] Moreover, the aggregation of preferences cannot claim rationality: there are no grounds to conclude that the outcome of such a procedure leads to the best interest.[71] She therefore suggests a deliberative model of democracy, where legitimacy and rationality can be obtained if institutions in a polity are arranged so that the common interest "results from processes of collective deliberation conducted rationally and fairly among free and equal individuals."[72] The deliberative process allows rationality because it: (1) brings forth information, (2) leads to critical reflection and thus to formation of coherent preferences and (3) forces individuals to support their publicly articulated views with good reasons for all involved.[73]

Others have developed Habermas's and Cohen's ideas concerning deliberative democracy and different models were introduced. There has been criticism of the theory, some friendly and others not as much.[74] For instance, claims have been made that deliberative democracy undermines the legitimacy of identity politics,[75] leading contemporary deliberative theorists to expand the classic ideal.[76]

The majority of deliberative theorists think of deliberative democracy in "populist"[77] terms, where equal citizens debate rationally about the common good. However, I disagree with this notion on theoretical, as well as empirical, or practical grounds.

In his discussion of discourse theory, Habermas refers to the public sphere, to public opinion and to "communicative power," stating that "democratically constituted opinion- and will-formation depends on the supply of informal public opinions" that develop in the public sphere.[78] So, on the one hand, as mentioned earlier, Habermas explains that public opinion formed in the networks of the public sphere generates "influence," which is transformed into "communicative power" through elections and points the use of "administrative power" in specific directions by means of legislation.[79] Yet, on the other hand, Habermas states that "within the boundaries of the public sphere...actors can acquire influence, not political power";[80] "political *influence* supported by public opinion is converted into political *power* – into a potential for rendering binding decisions – only when it affects the beliefs and decisions of *authorized* members of the political system"[81] (emphasis in original). This is correct: citizens may discuss policies, but only elected officials have the power to legislate after deliberation. And since this is the case, I argue that the democratic legitimacy of laws does not rest on a "discursively structured public sphere" rather on the level of deliberation by democratically elected assemblies.

I do not dismiss the existence and importance of communicative flows in the public sphere; on the contrary, it is clear that they signal people's preferences, for example, the preference to restrict freedom of speech during war, and by examining them, we have part of the answer to the question why and how such restrictions came about. Yet the only way to examine the degree of democratic legitimacy that these laws carry is to analyze whether the *legislators* have duly deliberated on them, and not by looking at the "discursive level" of opinion- and will-formation in *public spheres*.

Similarly, I dismiss the concept lately advocated by Mansbridge et al. (among others) – "a systemic approach to deliberative democracy"[82] – in regard to the democratic legitimacy of laws. It is not that organizations (e.g., schools, hospitals), the media, elites, experts and so on do not or should not deliberate; it is the fact that only the legislature has the authority to enact laws that bind and force our behavior, and therefore it is the deliberation of its members that we should be concerned about.

In addition to the theoretical argument, I disagree with the ideals put forward by deliberative theorists on empirical, or practical, grounds. First, there is no precise way to observe and measure if in fact communication flows in the public sphere meet discursive criterions. Second, as Conover et al. have pointed out, the citizens of modern liberal states do not deliberate – they have neither a special time nor a special place to do so – and while they do conduct political discussions, using data collected in six communities in the United States and Britain, the researchers concluded that citizen's political discussions fall short of the standards set by theorists for democratic deliberation.[83] Similarly Robert Goodin claims that there is no genuine deliberation in the public sphere – participants do not actively engage with each other – rather opinions are simply voiced in public.[84]

In sum, deliberative democracy as envisioned by political philosophers is incompatible with modern democracy. In practice, we live in large-scale democratic countries, and our democracy is representative. As Robert Dahl writes, in a modern, large-scale democratic nation-state, control over government decisions is vested in officials, who are elected in frequent and fairly conducted elections.[85] One can relatively easily conceive the deliberation of a dozen people in a committee, but how can deliberation work in a country?

John Dryzek calls attention to the "key restraint" of deliberative democracy legitimacy: that of economic scale.[86] Indeed as Michael Walzer observed, "Deliberation is not an activity for the demos...100 million of them, or even 1 million or 100,000 can't plausibly 'reason together'."[87] Goodin writes that the deliberative democratic ideal is not feasible in large-scale societies, adding to the problem of numbers, those of distance and time.[88]

Deliberative Democracy and Representative Government

I maintain that we can reconcile the problem of economy of scale with the fundamental elements of deliberative democracy theory, by viewing deliberative democracy, as some scholars do, as an aspect *of* representative democracy and not as a substitute for it.[89]

Jane Mansbridge argues that "representation is, and is normatively intended to be, something more than a defective substitute for direct democracy."[90] Discussing "forms" of representation, she writes that representation requires good deliberation: between citizens and representatives in periods of communication between elections whenever a representative tries to influence voter's preferences by the time of the next election ("anticipatory representation"), among citizens and between citizens and their representatives at the time the representative is selected ("gyroscopic representation") and to ascertain whether or not representatives have fulfilled their promises or have persuasive reasons for not doing so ("promissory representation").[91] Each form of representation contributes to the quality of deliberation in the legislature: for example, in gyroscopic representation when citizens vote for a representative who is expected to pursue the public interest.[92]

Furthermore, as Nadia Urbinati maintains, representation "plays a key role in forging the discursive democratic character of politics" as it is "a comprehensive filtering, refining, and mediating process of political will formation and expression."[93] Urbinati argues that indirectness ("a constitutive mark of representative democracy") makes room for deliberation and that a deliberative form of politics favors representation as "it fosters a relationship between the assembly and the people that enables the demos to reflect upon itself and judge its laws, institutions, and leaders."[94] Thus representation is more than merely instrumental; it carries a "moral distinctiveness."[95]

John Uhr maintains that deliberative assemblies are the "core institutions in regimes of deliberative democracy."[96] Reviewing requisites of effective representation, he concludes that the fundamental task of a representative legislature is not only to reflect but also to form the views of the public it represents.[97] Therefore in fulfilling its legislative responsibilities, a representative assembly deliberates. As elected legislatures are "multi-minded," deliberation allows the opening up and weighing of merits of options. Duly weighing and considering proposals achieves a "balanced" choice.[98]

Uhr identifies the Australian Parliament as the "centerpiece in the deliberative process" and the "primary deliberative institution."[99] The Australian Constitution framers expected Parliament "to play a prominent part in reflecting, refining and reframing public deliberation."[100] While Parliament is obliged to take note of the views or demands of those it represents, it is also obliged to weigh their contending interests and the community's needs. Thus Parliament does not only reflect public opinion, it also refines it, as competing views of community interests are debated and weighed.[101]

In fact, the idea that democracy is not simply the aggregation of preferences, and that via deliberation, a common interest is attainable, is as old as modern representative democracy itself.[102] Edmund Burke, in his famous speech to the Electors of Bristol in 1774, made the classic early statement on the issue:

> "Parliament is not a *congress* of ambassadors from different and hostile interests; which interests each must maintain, as an agent and advocate, against other agents and advocates, but parliament is a *deliberative* assembly of *one* nation, with *one* interest, that of the whole; where not local purposes, not local prejudices ought to guide, but the general good, resulting from the general reason of the whole."[103]

In the nineteenth century John Stuart Mill advocated "government by discussion"[104] and viewed the representative assembly as a deliberative institution, where the opinions of every section of society are voiced and debated, and decisions are the result of "superior reasons."[105]

Writing in the 1940s, Friedrich distinguished between the dual functions of parliaments in modern democracy: on the one hand, they represent the "will" of the people, and on the other, they deliberate on what to do and how to solve public problems.[106] Parliaments are representative assemblies and deliberative assemblies at the same time. "Speech" in parliament is namely orderly talk and reply, argument and debate.[107] Through argument and discussion, interests are articulated as well as rationalized.[108]

Thus, I've shown that the issue of economy of scale of deliberative democracy theory is reconciled by viewing deliberative democracy as an aspect of representative democracy, in which elected representatives of the people engage in deliberation.

Having established this normative argument, I now consider the following: is the United States a representative deliberative democracy and how so?

Deliberative Democracy and American National Government

In *Federalist* No. 10,[109] James Madison wrote that the efficacy of representative government is "to refine and enlarge the public views by passing them through the medium of a chosen body of citizens, whose wisdom may best discern the true interest of their country,"[110] adding, in *Federalist* No. 49, that only public reason "ought to control and regulate the government" and that passions "ought to be controlled and regulated by government."[111] To ensure that the chosen body will continue to hold the public trust, Madison wrote in *Federalist* No. 57 that the representative's terms of appointment shall be limited.[112]

Cass Sunstein and Joseph Bessette uphold that the framers of the American Constitution sought to establish a deliberative democracy. The first to coin the term "deliberative democracy" and perceive it as an aspect of representative government was Bessette, writing in 1978 on "Deliberation in Congress."[113] Bessette maintains that the framers wanted and designed a deliberative democracy:[114] in this case, one in which the citizenry reasons, or deliberates, through their representatives.[115] Elections ensure that the representatives of the people share citizen's interests, desires and values.[116]

Bessette notes that unlike modern pluralists and social choice theorists, the framers believed that there is a genuine "common good" that is not reducible to the preferences of the states or individuals.[117] Their hope was that by implementing governmental reforms (e.g., limiting state power and expanding the power of national government, restricting legislative authority to legislative matters, having larger assemblies and longer terms), robust deliberation on the national interest could be achieved.[118] During the "critical period" of the 1780s an excessive "local spirit" in both the state legislatures and national Congress had undermined policymaking. While the common interest is not detached from the interests of the parts, it is more than their aggregation. By means of electoral mechanisms and institutional design that would bring into government responsible and experienced men, who together learn and concentrate on national concerns, the framers' expectation was that deliberation on "the common good of society"[119] or "the comprehensive interests of [the] country"[120] could be realized.[121]

In order to promote deliberation on the common good and limit factionalism,[122] the framers proposed elections in large districts and also designed representative bodies that promote informed and reasoned decision making by determining lengthy terms of service:[123] six years for the Senate and two years for the House of Representatives (double the one-year norm for state legislatures). A long term would allow the legislator time to acquire "knowledge of the subjects on which he is to legislate."[124] In addition, lengthy terms would promote farsightedness among legislators. This is true especially in the Senate, where elections were staggered every two years, thus allowing relatively independent judgment as well as consideration on the long-term consequences of legislation.[125]

Sunstein writes that Madison regarded representation as an opportunity for achieving governance by officials dedicated to the public good: representatives "operating above the fray" engage in a collective reasoning process of discussion and debate, in which the legislative outcomes of their deliberation are related to the common good (as opposed to self-regarding outcomes).[126] Separation of powers would not allow a private group's interest to dominate government, thus balancing inclinations to self-interested representation. Structural provisions of the Constitution, such as a bicameral legislature, ensured that some representatives would be closer to local pressures and others more isolated.[127] The result was a "deliberative democracy":[128] the Federalists' understanding was that politics was to be deliberative in the sense that representatives would not "respond mechanically" to private pressure – while they are accountable to the public, their task is first and foremost to deliberate.[129]

Bessette defines the deliberation established by the American constitutional system as "a reasoning process in which the participants seriously consider substantive information and arguments and seek to decide individually and to persuade each other as to what constitutes good public policy."[130] He further elucidates that deliberation is an analytical process: participants identify and investigate problems, evaluate policies, consider proposals and formulate remedies. And in order that a deliberative process be genuine, "participants must be open to the facts, arguments, and proposals that come to their attention and must share a general willingness to learn from their colleagues and others."[131] Similarly, Paul Quirk describes congressional deliberation as "the intellectual process of identifying alternatives, gathering and evaluating information, weighing considerations, and making judgments about the merits of public policies."[132]

Bessette writes that every deliberative process involves three essential elements: information, arguments and persuasion.[133] In Congress, information and arguments are presented and participants are persuaded, not only on the floor of the House and the Senate – clearly floor debates are the most official (and accessible) expression of Congress's deliberative character (bill sponsors explain and defend their proposal, others challenge them and a response is offered) – but actually the deliberative process begins months before, when a policy initiative is born, perhaps outside Congress, afterward continues in congressional committees and their reports and goes on in parallel in informal channels.[134]

As Congress deals with a vast amount of complex legislative issues, the committees of the House and Senate enhance Congress's capacity for deliberation.[135] Committees allow division of labor and development of expertise and make available the thorough examination of information and arguments that deliberation requires, and as such they deliberate for the respective chamber they serve. Oral and written testimonies presented at hearings – by representatives of the administration, other members of Congress, experts and groups – are an important element of committee deliberation as they provide information, put forward views pro and con proposals and clarify the strengths and weaknesses of different positions.[136] At the conclusion of committee deliberation, if the committee decides to report a bill, the committee makes a written report.[137] The committee report is a key mechanism used to persuade members of Congress on the merits of committee decisions regarding a bill.[138]

Over the years, congressmen have acknowledged and case studies have shown that genuine persuasion occurs as a result of floor debate.[139] Persuasion on the floor is not only about changing minds, it also involves "making up minds," that is, "the process whereby the reasoned considerations of information and arguments moves a legislator from broad initial dispositions or preferences to specific decisions."[140] Floor debates usually involve real exchange between opposing sides: a bill's sponsors explain and defend their proposal, others challenge them and a response is accordingly offered.[141]

Hence in the United States a deliberative democracy was created in which deliberative majorities are formed through the operation of governmental institutions as the representatives of the people reason about public policy for their constituents.[142]

Summarizing the theoretical notions discussed earlier, governmental war powers, including the abridgment of rights during war, should be legitimized in law by the national legislature after deliberation. Deliberative democracy theory offers an answer to the question of legitimacy of legislation in democratic political systems: a *democratically* legitimate law is produced in a process of public discussion and debate in which participants reason on the common good. As noted, the theory of deliberative democracy put forward by theorists such as Habermas and Cohen is poorly suited for real world: we live in large-scale democratic countries, and it is impossible for all citizens in a country to participate in an ideal deliberative process. I take the view of those deliberative theorists that regard deliberative democracy as an aspect of representative democracy and not as a substitute for it. The concept of deliberative democracy and American national government acknowledges the importance of deliberation about the common good in the institutions of representative government.

I thus argue that legislation restricting freedom of speech during war can be considered democratically legitimate if members of a national legislature, the representatives of the people, deliberated well; that is, during the process of discussion and debate, they reasoned on the public good, seriously considered information and arguments and sought to decide and to persuade as to the best legislative solution. The higher the extent of deliberation, the more legitimacy is attached to the legislation. I term this "Legislative Deliberative Democracy."

Measuring Legislative Deliberation

Obviously nondeliberative activities or influences, such as bargaining[143] and group and private interests, partly explain lawmaking. However, this is beside the point. My claim is a normative one: that the degree of the democratic legitimacy of a law passed by a national legislature restricting freedom of speech during war lies in the extent of its members' deliberation on the public good.

It is important to note that the question of democratic legitimacy of a law restricting freedom of speech during war is not answered by revealing that procedures were constitutional. Laws restricting freedom of speech during war can be legislated in accordance to constitutional rules, but the degree of their democratic legitimacy depends of the extent of the deliberation made by legislators. Thus, I do not claim that a law is illegitimate (or unconstitutional) if the level of legislative deliberation is low, but rather that the degree of democratic legitimacy attached to a law that restricts freedom of speech during war depends on the extent of legislative deliberation. The higher the extent of deliberation, the more legitimacy is attached to the legislation.

On the basis of fundamental elements of deliberative democracy theory discussed earlier, I contend using the following criteria to measure the extent of legislative deliberation:

1 Committee Hearings. Were there oral testimonies or public hearings? Did external groups, individuals or experts appear before the committee and articulate views concerning the proposed legislation restricting freedom of speech? Did the executive offer written reports?[144] How was the original draft of the law amended as a result of oral or written testimonies at the committee stage?
2 Debate in Both Chambers. Did both houses deliberate on the proposed legislation? For instance, if in the United States, the House of Representatives considered a bill during one session and hastily voted on it, we would view the extent of deliberation on the act as lower as opposed to broad deliberation by both houses.
3 Exchange of Information and Arguments on the Floor. Did the sponsors of proposed legislation explain and defend it? Did others challenge them? Was a response subsequently offered? Did the sponsors answer questions and provide facts?[145] (For example, a review of relevant previous legislation and court rulings or past policies regarding freedom of speech.)
4 Public Good.[146] Were arguments framed in terms of the public good and how so? (For example, arguments in regard to fundamental

questions concerning freedom of speech and the constitutionality of the proposed legislation, or in regard to protecting the welfare of the nation during war.)

5 Persuasion. Did members of the legislature acknowledge that after considering information and arguments, they either reached a position or changed their minds?[147] Were provisions of the draft law amended, and in what way? Was the vote partisan?

Reiterating a point made earlier in this chapter: it is not that debating issues in public is not important. On the contrary, in a democracy, what people, groups and organizations have to say concerning public policies is extremely important. Their opinions matter. But the public at large cannot and does not deliberate. One the other hand, lawmakers in a representative assembly can and should do so. In modern democratic states, the national legislature is the principal deliberative institution. It is there where our elected representatives take opinions and interests into account and after deliberation enact laws that regulate our behavior.[148]

In the remainder of this study, using four acts enacted by the U.S. Congress as case studies, I delve into an empirical analysis and show how deliberations were conducted on them; that is, I assess the extent of congressional deliberations and thus of the degree of the acts' democratic legitimacy.

Notes

1 C. J. Friedrich, *Constitutional Reason of State: The Survival of the Constitutional Order* (Providence: Brown University Press, 1957), 12–13.
2 Clinton L. Rossiter, *Constitutional Dictatorship: Crisis Government in the Modern Democracies* (Princeton: Princeton University Press, 1948), 6.
3 Rossiter, 5.
4 Rossiter, 290.
5 Rossiter, 7.
6 Rossiter, 15; Carl J. Friedrich, *Constitutional Government and Democracy: Theory and Practice in Europe and America* (Boston: Ginn and Company, 1950), 574. Rossiter stating that "nowhere in all history has the belief that a constitutional state can alter its pattern of government temporarily in order to preserve it permanently been more resolutely asserted and successfully proved than it was in the storied Republic of ancient Rome."
7 Friedrich, *Constitutional Government*, 577–578; Rossiter, 8–9. Oren Gross and Fionnuala Ní Aoláin note that "legislative accommodation" is the most common approach of accommodating security needs in times of crisis, that is, modifying existing "ordinary laws" or introducing "emergency legislation." Oren Gross and Fionnuala Ní Aoláin, *Laws in Times of Crisis: Emergency Powers in Theory and Practice* (Cambridge: Cambridge University Press, 2006), 66–67.
8 Rossiter, 296.
9 Rossiter, 300, 302.
10 John E. Finn, *Constitutions in Crisis: Political Violence and the Rule of Law* (Oxford: Oxford University Press, 1991), 44.

11 Finn, 15.
12 Finn, 6.
13 Finn, 7.
14 Finn, 26.
15 Finn, 220.
16 Finn, 30.
17 Finn, 32.
18 Finn, 31–32.
19 Finn, 35.
20 Finn, 219.
21 Fontana Benedetto, Cary J. Nederman, and Gary Remer, "Introduction: Deliberative Democracy and the Rhetorical Turn," In *Talking Democracy: Historical Perspectives on Rhetoric and Democracy* (University Park: The Pennsylvania University Press, 2004), 5.
22 Jane Mansbridge, "Motivating Deliberation in Congress," In *El Pluribus Unum: Constitutional Principles and the Institutions of Government*. Ed. Sarah Baumgartner Thurow (Lanham: University Press of America, 1988), 59.
23 Jane Mansbridge, "A Deliberative Theory of Interest Representation," In *The Politics of Interests: Interest Groups Transformed*. Ed. Mark P. Petracca (Boulder: Westview Press, 1992), 34.
24 Mansbridge, "Motivating Deliberation in Congress," 59–60.
25 Quoted in James Bohman and William Rehg, "Introduction," In *Deliberative Democracy: Essays on Reason and Politics* (Cambridge: The MIT Press, 1997), xi.
26 Bohman and Rehg, xi; Mansbridge, "Motivating Deliberation in Congress," 60–61.
27 Jon Elster, "The Market and the Forum: Three Varieties of Political Theory," In *Deliberative Democracy: Essays on Reason and Politics*. Ed. James Bohman and William Rehg (Cambridge: The MIT Press, 1997), 3.
28 Bohman and Rehg, xi. For a discussion on William Riker's observation that voting is unstable and ambiguous see Jack Knight and James Johnson, "Aggregation and Deliberation: On the Possibility of Democratic Legitimacy." *Political Theory* 22 (1994): 279–281. For a review and critique of social choice theory, see Elster, "The Market and the Forum," 4–11.
29 Bohman and Rehg, xii.
30 Elster, "The Market and the Forum," 11.
31 Elster, 10.
32 James Q. Wilson, "Interests and Deliberation in the American Republic, or Why James Madison Would Never Have Received the James Madison Award," *Political Science and Politics* 23 (1990): 560.
33 Mansbridge, Jane, Hartz-Karp, Janette, Amengual, Matthew and Gastil, John. "Norms of Deliberation: An Inductive Study." *Journal of Public Deliberation* 2 (2006): Article 7: 2.
34 Elster, "The Market and the Forum," 3, 11.
35 Jürgen Habermas, "Three Normative Models of Democracy," *Constellations* 1 (1994): 1–10. See also Jürgen Habermas, *Between Facts and Norms: Contributions to a Discourse Theory of Law and Democracy* trans. William Rehg (Cambridge: The MIT Press, 1996), especially 296–308 (originally published in German in 1992).
36 Habermas, *Models of Democracy*, 1. Bohman and Rehg state that deliberative democratic theory "arises on the terrain staked out by the debates" between liberal theorists and civic republicans regarding conceptions of legitimate government. See Bohman and Rehg, x.
37 Habermas, *Models of Democracy*, 1.

38 Habermas, 1–2.
39 Habermas, 1–2.
40 Habermas, 3.
41 Habermas, 3.
42 Habermas, 3.
43 Habermas, 4.
44 Habermas, 1.
45 Habermas, 4–6.
46 Habermas, 6.
47 Habermas, 7.
48 Habermas, 8–9.
49 Or spheres: "The currents of public communication are channeled by mass media and flow through different publics," Habermas, *Between Facts and Norms*, 307.
50 Habermas, *Models of Democracy*, 8–9; John S. Dryzek, "Legitimacy and Economy in Deliberative Democracy," *Political Theory* 29 (2001): 656.
51 Joshua Cohen, "Deliberation and Democratic Legitimacy," In *The Good Polity: Normative Analysis of the State*, Ed. Alan Hamlin and Philip Pettit (Oxford: Basil Blackwell, 1989), 17–34; Mansbridge, "Norms of Deliberation," 4.
52 Cohen, 22.
53 Cohen, 22.
54 Cohen, 22.
55 Cohen, 22–23.
56 Cohen, 23.
57 Cohen, 23.
58 Cohen, 23.
59 Bernard Manin, "On Legitimacy and Political Deliberation," *Political Theory* 15 (1987): 338–368.
60 Manin, 352.
61 Manin, 349–350.
62 Manin, 351–352. Similarly Habermas notes, "Deliberative politics acquires its legitimating force from the discursive structure of an opinion- and will-formation… Hence the *discursive level* of public debates constitutes the most important variable," Habermas, *Between Facts and Norms*, 304.
63 Manin, 352.
64 Manin, 352–353.
65 Manin, 359–360.
66 Manin, 360.
67 Manin, 362; Cohen, 28–30. Manin adds freedom of conscience, of opinion and of association as fundamental liberties necessary for exercising the right to vote and participate in deliberation. Cass Sunstein writes that rights are regularly preconditions for deliberation, stating freedom of speech as the most obvious example; see Cass R. Sunstein, *The Partial Constitution* (Cambridge: Harvard University Press, 1993), 135, 142.
68 Seyla Benhabib, "Deliberative Rationality and Models of Democratic Legitimacy," *Constellations* 1 (1994): 26.
69 Benhabib, 27.
70 Benhabib, 28–29.
71 Benhabib, 29.
72 Benhabib, 30–31.
73 Benhabib, 32. Note the reiteration of Manin on information (which Benhabib herself recognizes) and of Cohen regarding giving reasons for all those involved.

74 For example see Amy Gutmann and Dennis Thompson, *Democracy and Disagreement* (Cambridge: Harvard University Press, 1996); Stephen Macedo (ed.), *Deliberative Politics: Essays on Democracy and Disagreement* (New York: Oxford University Press, 1999); James Bohman, *Public Deliberation: Pluralism, Complexity, and Democracy* (Cambridge: The MIT Press, 1996); James Bohman and William Rehg (eds.) *Deliberative Democracy: Essays on Reason and Politics* (Cambridge: The MIT Press, 1997); Bruce Ackerman and James S. Fishkin, "Deliberation Day," *The Journal of Political Philosophy* 10 (November 2002): 129–152. Some view John Rawls as a deliberative democrat, and indeed he has contributed to theory, for example, see John Rawls, "The Idea of Public Reason," In *Deliberative Democracy: Essays on Reason and Politics*, Ed. James Bohman and William Rehg (Cambridge: The MIT Press, 1997), 93–141.

75 William H. Simon, "Three Limitations of Deliberative Democracy: Identity Politics, Bad Faith, and Indeterminacy," In *Deliberative Politics: Essays on Democracy and Disagreement*, Ed. Stephen Macedo (New York: Oxford University Press, 1999), 50–53; Iris Marion Young, "Difference as a Resource for Democratic Communication," In *Deliberative Democracy: Essays on Reason and Politics*, Ed. James Bohman and William Rehg (Cambridge: The MIT Press, 1997), 385, and Iris Marion Young, "Communication and the Other: Beyond Deliberative Democracy" In *Democracy and Difference: Contesting the Boundaries of the Political*, Ed. Seyla Benhabib (Princeton: Princeton University Press, 1996), 121.

76 Jane Mansbridge et al., "The Place of Self Interest and the Role of Power in Deliberative Democracy," *The Journal of Political Philosophy* 18 (Nov. 2010): 66. Bächtiger et al. distinguish between "Type I deliberation [which] is rooted in the Habermasian logic of communicative action, and embodies the idea of rational discourse" and type II deliberation, which "incorporates alternative forms of communication" including emotional discourse and storytelling. André Bächtiger et al., "Disentangling Diversity in Deliberative Democracy: Competing Theories, Their Blind Spots and Complementarities," *The Journal of Political Philosophy* 18 (March 2010): 33–34, 36.

77 I borrow the phrase from Ethan J. Leib, "Can Direct Democracy Be Made Deliberative?," *Buffalo Law Review* 54 (2006): 912.

78 Habermas, *Between Facts and Norms*, 308. Habermas describes the public sphere "as a network for communication information and points of view… the streams of communication are, in the process, filtered and synthesized is such a way that they coalesce into bundles of topically specified *public* opinions," Habermas, *Between Facts and Norms*, 360.

79 Habermas, *Models of Democracy*, 8–9. In his book he elaborates at one point that according to the discourse theory of democracy "binding decisions, to be legitimate, must be steered by communication flows that start at the periphery [i.e., professional agencies and associations, charitable organizations, foundations, etc.] and pass through sluices of democratic and constitutional procedures situated at the entrance to the parliamentary complex or the courts," Habermas, *Between Facts and Norms*, 355–356.

80 Habermas, *Between Facts and Norms*, 371.

81 Habermas, *Between Facts and Norms*, 363.

82 Jane Mansbridge, James Bohman, Simone Chambers, Thomas Christiano, Archon Fung, John Parkinson, Dennis F. Thompson and Mark E. Warren, "A Systemic Approach to Deliberative Democracy," In *Deliberative Systems: Deliberative Democracy at the Large Scale*, Ed. John Parkinson and Jane Mansbridge (Cambridge: Cambridge University Press, 2012), 1–2.

83 Pamela Johnston Conover, Donald D. Searing and Ivor M. Crewe, "The Deliberative Potential of Political Discussion," *British Journal of Political Science* 32 (2002): 21, 24, 60–61.

84 Robert E. Goodin, "Democratic Deliberation Within," *Philosophy & Public Affairs* 29 (2000): 90–92.

85 Robert A. Dahl, *On Democracy* (New Haven and London: Yale University Press, 2000), 85.

86 Dryzek, "Legitimacy and Economy in Deliberative Democracy," 651–657. Dryzek's solution – a conception of "discursive democracy that emphasizes the contestation of discourses in the public sphere" (Dryzek, 657) – may solve the issue of economy but is problematic mainly because, as he himself implies, the contestation of discourses can be manipulated by strategy and power, and legitimacy is dependent on the engagement of a "broad variety of competent actors" (Dryzek, 663, 666).

87 Michael Walzer, "Deliberation, and What Else?" In *Deliberative Politics: Essays on Democracy and Disagreement*, Ed. Stephen Macedo (New York: Oxford University Press, 1999), 68. Walzer does not deny the importance of deliberation but observes that "politics has other values in addition to, and often in tension with, reason." For example, democratic politics include compromises that "reflect the balance of forces, not the weight of arguments" (Walzer, 59, 62). I agree but emphasize that deliberation in a legislature is an integral part of democratic politics and, as noted earlier, is a vital link to the democratic legitimacy of laws.

88 Goodin, 82, 98; suggesting to complement "external-collective" deliberation with "internal-reflective" deliberation, that is, making people "imaginatively present" in individual deliberators minds.

89 Interestingly, even Habermas at one point states that while justified decisions about laws demand face-to-face deliberation, not all citizens can join in such a practice and "[a] solution to this problem is provided by the *parliamentary principle* of establishing representative bodies for deliberation and decision making." Habermas, *Between Facts and Norms*, 170.

90 Jane Mansbridge, "Rethinking Representation," *American Political Science Review* 97 (Nov. 2003): 515.

91 Mansbridge, 525.

92 Mansbridge, 525. See also John Parkinson's theoretical discussion on the concept of representation in general, in which he asserts that elected representatives have a *dual* role: not only that of a delegate held accountable to the instructions of voters but also that of a "trustee" that has the authority to decide and act as he sees appropriate. Thus, representation offers influence to those who are not physically present in the deliberative forum while producing an assembly that persuades and reasons together. (In this manner, while decisions by a deliberative body may not necessarily be "representative" of the majority, when those outside it are exposed to the arguments in their own deliberations, they should be convinced.) John Parkinson, "Legitimacy Problems in Deliberative Democracy," *Political Studies* 51 (March 2003): 186–188, 190.

93 Nadia Urbinati, "Representation as Advocacy: A Study of Democratic Deliberation," *Political Theory* 28 (Dec. 2000): 760.

94 Urbinati, 761. Directness, or a direct political presence, does not mean active participation or that all talk. Urbinati, 762.

95 Urbinati, 767–768.

96 John Uhr, *Deliberative Democracy in Australia: The Changing Place of Parliament* (Melbourne: Cambridge University Press, 1998), 3.

97 Uhr, *Deliberative Democracy*, 91.
98 Uhr, *Deliberative Democracy*, 92–94.
99 John Uhr, "Parliament and Public Deliberation: Evaluating the Performance of Parliament," *UNSW Law Journal* 24 (No. 3 2001): 722–723.
100 Uhr, *Parliament and Public Deliberation*, 712.
101 Uhr, *Parliament and Public Deliberation*, 712–713, 723.
102 Jon Elster, "Introduction," In *Deliberative Democracy* (New York: Cambridge University Press, 1998), 1–2; Mansbridge, "Motivating Deliberation in Congress," 60; Joseph M. Bessette, *The Mild Voice of Reason: Deliberative Democracy & American National Government* (Chicago: The University of Chicago Press, 1994), 40.
103 Quoted in Elster, "Introduction," 3.
104 Elster, 4.
105 Bessette, 43.
106 Friedrich, *Constitutional Government*; 324.
107 Friedrich, 325.
108 Friedrich, 259.
109 *The Federalist* is a series of eighty-five essays written by Alexander Hamilton, James Madison and John Jay, during 1787–1788, promoting the ratification of the U.S. Constitution.
110 Jay, Hamilton, James, Madison and John, Jay. *The Federalist Papers*, edited by Clinton Rossiter with an introduction and notes by Charles R. Kesler (New York: Signet Classic, 2003), 76. All references to *The Federalist* are to the Rossiter edition.
111 *Federalist* No. 49, 314.
112 *Federalist* No. 57, 348.
113 Both Bohman and Rehg, as well as Mansbridge et al. concur that Bessette first coined the term. See Bohman and Rehg, xii, and Mansbridge, "Norms of Deliberation," 4. In 1978 Bessette completed his dissertation on deliberation in Congress, in 1979 he delivered a paper at the annual meeting of the American Political Science Association on deliberation in Congress and in 1980 he published an article on deliberative democracy. See Bessette, xi; Mansbridge, "Motivating Deliberation in Congress," 62; and Bohman and Rehg, xii and xxviii ft. 10. Bessette's detailed perceptions on deliberative democracy in America were elaborated in his 1994 book on deliberative democracy and American national government: Joseph M. Bessette, *The Mild Voice of Reason: Deliberative Democracy & American National Government* (Chicago: The University of Chicago Press, 1994).
114 Bessette, 1, 6, 40.
115 Bessette, 1.
116 Bessette, 2, 36, 46. Bessette argues that "the theory of deliberative democracy that undergirds the American constitutional order rests on the central proposition that there are two kinds of public voice in a democracy – one more immediate or spontaneous, uninformed, and unreflective; the other more deliberative, taking longer to develop and resting on a fuller consideration of information and arguments – and that only the latter if fit to rule" (Bessette, 35).
117 Bessette, 256–257, ft. 97.
118 See also Charles Kessler's reading of the Federalist authors' argument for separation of powers, which leads to the conclusion that the "Constitution conduces to a deliberative legislature," in *The Federalist Papers*, pp. xxvii.
119 *Federalist* No. 57, quoted in Bessette, 27.
120 *Federalist* No. 62, quoted in Bessette, 27.

121 Bessette, 26–28.
122 Defined by Madison as "a number of citizens, whether accounting to a majority or minority of the whole, who are united and actuated by some common impulse or passion, or of interest, adverse to the rights of other citizens, or to the permanent and aggregate interests of the community." *Federalist* No. 10, 72.
123 Cass R. Sunstein, "Beyond the Republican Revival," *The Yale Law Journal* 97 (1987–1988): 1560; Bessette, 14–16, 23–26.
124 Madison in *Federalist* No. 53, quoted in Bessette, 23.
125 Bessettee, 24–25. Bessette observes that the executive branch would also contribute to deliberation, among other measures, in its "Information on the State of the Union Address," in formally giving reasons for a veto and in persuading Congress to ratify international treaties; but its unique contribution to "effective and competent governance" is through "energy" – concentrating authority in one person who can act quickly, decisively and often secretly. See Bessette, 28–31.
126 Cass R. Sunstein, "Interest Groups in American Public Law," *Stanford Law Review* 38 (1985–1986): 41–42.
127 Sunstein, *Interest Groups*, 43–44.
128 Sunstein, *Interest Groups*, 45.
129 And not to bargain, Sunstein, *Interest Groups*, 45–47. In *The Partial Constitution*, Sunstein writes that "above all, the American constitution was designed to create a deliberative democracy." In such a system, representatives, on the one hand, are accountable to the people, but on the other, they deliberate free from the influence of the self-interest of private groups, reasoning collectively on the common good. Therefore in American public law, outcomes should not be a reflection of private or self interests yet are to be formed via deliberation. Sunstein, *The Partial Constitution*, 19–23, 134.
130 Bessette, 46.
131 Bessette, 46.
132 Paul J. Quirk, "Deliberation and Decision Making," In *The Legislative Branch*, Eds. Paul J. Quirk and Sarah A. Binder (New York: Oxford University Press, 2005), 316.
133 Bessette, 49–54. Concerning persuasion, Bessette suggests, as does Manin, that legislators often have no initial preferences on an issue, but after considering information and arguments on an issue – or reasoning on its merits – they reach a position. This constitutes to persuasion (of course, in some instances, participants may actually change their minds). Bessette, 52–54. In similar fashion, Quirk maintains that members of Congress make their own respective "judgements" about legislation, by obtaining information and arguments, and assessing the information, Quirk, 316, 317.
134 Bessette, 151–176, 51–52; Quirk, 316–317.
135 Friedrich, *Constitutional Government*, 333.
136 Bessette, 156–157, 51; Malcolm E. Jewell and Samuel C. Paterson, *The Legislative Process in the United States* 3rd ed. (New York: Random House, 1977), 177, 417.
137 Jewell and Paterson, 424.
138 Bessette, 159–160.
139 Bessette, 166.
140 Bessette, 167.
141 Bessette, 168–169. Low attendance on the floor does not necessarily mean that there isn't any deliberation: members of the House and Senate are informed and influenced on what is said on the floor through staff, the *Congressional Record* and informal word of mouth.

142 Bessette, 213–215, 36. Sunstein, *The Partial Constitution*, 19–20.
143 Including legislators trading support, rewards and punishment, compromise and coalition building – see Bessette, 58–62, Steiner et al., *Deliberative Politics in Action*, 4, 23–24, and Quirk, 316.
144 See Bessette's discussion on deliberating within U.S. Congressional committees, 156–165, 51; and Edward L. Lascher, "Assessing Legislative Deliberation: A Preface to Empirical Analysis," *Legislative Studies Quarterly* 21 (1996): 508–509.
145 Bessette, 151–152, 49–51; Lascher, 509; Quirk, 335.
146 As mentioned earlier, reasoning on the common good is an essential principle of deliberation. See also the claim that deliberation on "public ideas" is the core responsibility of elected officials when formulating policy, and that indeed in practice many times it is so, in Robert B. Reich, "Introduction," The Power of Public Ideas, Ed. Robert B. Reich (Cambridge: Ballinger Publishing Company, 1988), 3–4, 6, 11 and Garry R. Oren, "Beyond Self-Interest," 13–14, 27–28 and Steven Kelman, "Why Public Ideas Matter," 31, 39–53 in the same edited volume.
147 Bessette, 51–55, 166–169; Manin, 353.
148 Furthermore, since we deliberate through our representatives, the aftermath of legislature deliberation is in certain respects consequential to it: we would expect the executive to enforce and the courts to rule on the basis of legislature underpinnings. For example, if the extent of legislative deliberation on a law restricting freedom of speech during war was high – hence the law had a high level of democratic legitimacy – we would expect that the law be enforced and adjudicated according to its legislative understandings.

References

Ackerman, Bruce and Fishkin, James S. "Deliberation Day." *The Journal of Political Philosophy* 10 (November 2002): 129–152.

Bächtiger, André, Niemeyer, Simon, Neblo, Michael, Steenbergen, Marco R. and Steiner, Jürg. "Disentangling Diversity in Deliberative Democracy: Competing Theories, Their Blind Spots and Complementarities." *The Journal of Political Philosophy* 18 (March 2010): 32–63.

Benedetto, Fontana, Nederman, Cary J., and Remer, Gary. "Introduction: Deliberative Democracy and the Rhetorical Turn." *Talking Democracy: Historical Perspectives on Rhetoric and Democracy*, 1–25. University Park: The Pennsylvania University Press, 2004.

Benhabib, Seyla. "Deliberative Rationality and Models of Democratic Legitimacy." *Constellations* 1 (1994): 26–52.

Bessette, Joseph M. *The Mild Voice of Reason: Deliberative Democracy & American National Government*. Chicago: The University of Chicago Press, 1994.

Bohman, James. *Public Deliberation: Pluralism, Complexity, and Democracy*. Cambridge: The MIT Press, 1996.

Bohman, James and Rehg, William. "Introduction." *Deliberative Democracy: Essays on Reason and Politics*, ix–xxx. Cambridge: The MIT Press, 1997.

Bohman, James and Rehg, William (Eds.) *Deliberative Democracy: Essays on Reason and Politics*. Cambridge: The MIT Press, 1997.

Cohen, Joshua. "Deliberation and Democratic Legitimacy." *The Good Polity: Normative Analysis of the State*. Ed. Alan Hamlin and Philip Pettit, 17–34. Oxford: Basil Blackwell, 1989.

Conover, Pamela Johnston, Searing, Donald D. and Crewe, Ivor M. "The Deliberative Potential of Political Discussion." *British Journal of Political Science* 32 (2002): 21–62.

Dahl, Robert A. *On Democracy*. New Haven and London: Yale University Press, 2000.

Dryzek, John S. "Legitimacy and Economy in Deliberative Democracy." *Political Theory* 29 (2001): 651–669.

Elster, Jon. "The Market and the Forum: Three Varieties of Political Theory." *Deliberative Democracy: Essays on Reason and Politics*. Ed. James Bohman and William Rehg, 3–33. Cambridge: The MIT Press, 1997.

Elster, Jon. "Introduction." *Deliberative Democracy*, 1–18. New York: Cambridge University Press, 1998.

Finn, John E. *Constitutions in Crisis: Political Violence and the Rule of Law*. Oxford: Oxford University Press, 1991.

Friedrich, Carl J. *Constitutional Government and Democracy: Theory and Practice in Europe and America*. Boston: Ginn and Company, 1950.

Friedrich, C. J. *Constitutional Reason of State: The Survival of the Constitutional Order*. Providence: Brown University Press, 1957.

Goodin, Robert E. "Democratic Deliberation Within." *Philosophy & Public Affairs* 29 (2000): 81–109.

Gross, Oren and Ní Aoláin, Fionnuala. *Laws in Times of Crisis: Emergency Powers in Theory and Practice*. Cambridge: Cambridge University Press, 2006.

Gutmann, Amy and Thompson, Dennis. *Democracy and Disagreement*. Cambridge: Harvard University Press, 1996.

Habermas, Jürgen. "Three Normative Models of Democracy." *Constellations* 1 (1994): 1–10.

Habermas, Jürgen. *Between Facts and Norms: Contributions to a Discourse Theory of Law and Democracy*. trans. William Rehg. Cambridge: The MIT Press, 1996.

Hamilton, Jay, Madison, James and Jay, John. *The Federalist Papers*. Ed. Clinton Rossiter with an introduction and notes by Charles R. Kesler. New York: Signet Classic, 2003.

Jewell, Malcolm E. and Paterson, Samuel C. *The Legislative Process in the United States*, 3rd ed. New York: Random House, 1977.

Kelman, Steven. "Why Public Ideas Matter." *The Power of Public Ideas*. Ed. Robert B. Reich, 31–53. Cambridge: Ballinger Publishing Company, 1988.

Knight, Jack and Johnson, James. "Aggregation and Deliberation: On the Possibility of Democratic Legitimacy." *Political Theory* 22 (1994): 277–296.

Lascher, Edward L. "Assessing Legislative Deliberation: A Preface to Empirical Analysis." *Legislative Studies Quarterly* 21 (1996): 501–519.

Leib, Ethan J. "Can Direct Democracy be Made Deliberative?" *Buffalo Law Review* 54 (2006): 903–925.

Macedo, Stephen. "Introduction." *Deliberative Politics: Essays on Democracy and Disagreement*, 3–14. New York: Oxford University Press, 1999.

Manin, Bernard. "On Legitimacy and Political Deliberation." *Political Theory* 15 (1987): 338–368.

Mansbridge, Jane. "Motivating Deliberation in Congress." *El Pluribus Unum: Constitutional Principles and the Institutions of Government*. Ed. Sarah Baumgartner Thurow, 59–86. Lanham: University Press of America, 1988.

Mansbridge, Jane J. "A Deliberative Theory of Interest Representation." *The Politics of Interests: Interest Groups Transformed.* Ed. Mark P. Petracca, 32–57. Boulder: Westview Press, 1992.

Mansbridge, Jane. "Rethinking Representation." *American Political Science Review* 97 (Nov. 2003): 515–528.

Mansbridge, Jane, Hartz-Karp, Janette, Amengual, Matthew and Gastil, John. "Norms of Deliberation: An Inductive Study." *Journal of Public Deliberation* 2 (2006): Article 7, 1–47.

Mansbridge, Jane with Bohman, James, Chambers, Simone, Estlund, David, Føllesdal, Andreas, Fung, Archon, Lafont, Critina, Manin, Bernard and Martí, José Luis. "The Place of Self Interest and the Role of Power in Deliberative Democracy." *The Journal of Political Philosophy* 18 (Nov. 2010): 66–100.

Mansbridge, Jane, Bohman, James, Chambers, Simone, Christiano, Thomas, Fung, Archon, Parkinson, John, Thompson, Dennis F. and Warren, Mark E. "A Systemic Approach to Deliberative Democracy." *Deliberative Systems: Deliberative Democracy at the Large Scale.* Ed. John Parkinson and Jane Mansbridge, 1–26. Cambridge: Cambridge University Press, 2012.

Oren, Garry R. "Beyond Self-Interest." *The Power of Public Ideas.* Ed. Robert B. Reich, 13–29. Cambridge: Ballinger Publishing Company, 1988.

Parkinson, John. "Legitimacy Problems in Deliberative Democracy." *Political Studies* 51 (March 2003): 180–196.

Quirk, Paul J. "Deliberation and Decision Making." *The Legislative Branch.* Eds. Paul J. Quirk and Sarah A. Binder, 314–348. New York: Oxford University Press, 2005.

Rawls, John. "The Idea of Public Reason." *Deliberative Democracy: Essays on Reason and Politics.* Ed. James Bohman and William Rehg, 93–141. Cambridge: The MIT Press, 1997.

Reich, Robert B. "Introduction." *The Power of Public Ideas*, 1–12. Cambridge: Ballinger Publishing Company, 1988.

Rossiter, Clinton L. *Constitutional Dictatorship: Crisis Government in the Modern Democracies.* Princeton: Princeton University Press, 1948.

Simon, William H. "Three Limitations of Deliberative Democracy: Identity Politics, Bad Faith, and Indeterminacy." *Deliberative Politics: Essays on Democracy and Disagreement*, Ed. Stephen Macedo, 49–57. New York: Oxford University Press, 1999.

Steiner, Jürg, Bächtiger, André, Spörndli, Markus, and Steenbergen, Marco R. *Deliberative Politics in Action: Analysing Parliamentary Discourse.* Cambridge: Cambridge University Press, 2004.

Sunstein, Cass R. "Interest Groups in American Public Law." *Stanford Law Review* 38 (1985–1986): 29–87.

Sunstein, Cass R. "Beyond the Republican Revival." *The Yale Law Journal* 97 (1987–1988): 1539–1590.

Sunstein, Cass R. *The Partial Constitution.* Cambridge: Harvard University Press, 1993.

Uhr, John. *Deliberative Democracy in Australia: The Changing Place of Parliament.* Melbourne: Cambridge University Press, 1998.

Uhr, John. "Parliament and Public Deliberation: Evaluating the Performance of Parliament." *UNSW Law Journal* 24 (No. 3 2001): 708–723.

Urbinati, Nadia. "Representation as Advocacy: A Study of Democratic Deliberation." *Political Theory* 28 (Dec. 2000): 758–786.

Walzer, Michael. "Deliberation, and What Else?" *Deliberative Politics: Essays on Democracy and Disagreement*. Ed. Stephen Macedo, 58–69. New York: Oxford University Press, 1999.

Wilson, James Q. "Interests and Deliberation in the American Republic, or Why James Madison Would Never Have Received the James Madison Award." *Political Science and Politics* 23 (1990): 558–562.

Young, Iris Marion. "Communication and the Other: Beyond Deliberative Democracy." *Democracy and Difference: Contesting the Boundaries of the Political*. Ed. Seyla Benhabib, 120–135. Princeton: Princeton University Press, 1996.

Young, Iris Marion. "Difference as a Resource for Democratic Communication." *Deliberative Democracy: Essays on Reason and Politics*. Ed. James Bohman and William Rehg, 383–406. Cambridge: The MIT Press, 1997.

Part II

World War I and the Espionage and Sedition Acts

During World War I, Congress passed the Espionage Act, which prohibits when the United States is at war, inciting disloyalty in the armed forces and obstructing enlistment (and declares nonmailable items in violation of the act), and the Sedition Act of 1918, which prohibited during war language provoking resistance to the United States.

In Part II, I first analyze the political system in order to explain how these laws came about; subsequently, I answer the question regarding the degree of their democratic legitimacy by examining the extent of deliberation in Congress.

2 The Espionage Act and the Sedition Act

Enactment, Enforcement and Judgment

Political Socialization Processes: Uniting the Nation to the War Effort

The end product of political socialization processes is a set of attitudes – cognitions, values and feelings – toward the political system.[1] Manifest political socialization appears as explicit transmission of information, values or feelings in relation to the roles, inputs and outputs of the political system. All political socialization involves affection – emotions such as respect, love, loyalty and pride in the political system. In a modern political system, the love felt by a citizen is a civic love, but it may be strong even up to death, "when the chips are down."[2] These affective elements are combined with instrumental components, such as rationally calculated strategies of influence.[3] This was evident in empirical events during World War I in the United States.

In 1914, after the outbreak of war in Europe, President Wilson proclaimed a policy of American neutrality. Many Americans did not view the war as a threat to the United States and therefore favorably accepted President Wilson's proclamation. However, despite this proclamation of neutrality, the United States permitted American manufacturers to ship materials and American banks to make loans to Britain and France. In early 1917 Germany responded with a naval blockade and submarine warfare, which included the sinking of three American vessels. These sinkings, the drop of American trade and the publication of a secret German plot against the United States in Mexico led Wilson on April 2, 1917, to ask Congress to declare war on Germany to make the world "safe for democracy." Congress declared war on April 6, 1917.[4]

As president Wilson won reelection in the fall of 1916 on the slogan that "He Kept Us Out of War," he was concerned about the way the public felt in relation to declaring war, and worried that opposition to the war could be demoralizing, thus making it difficult to execute the war successfully.[5] Citizens would be reluctant to serve in the armed forces, commit financial resources and support the war politically. Wilson also recognized that war is not simply a battle of armies but also a contest of wills: defeat could come from a breakdown in the home front as well as from a failure in the trenches in Europe. Resilience of the nation to fight was important to winning the war no less than equipping and training the army.[6] Wilson recognized that in a conflict such as World War I, where millions of soldiers backed by the civilians of their nations fought one another, literally trying to bleed each other to surrender, unity was vital, and internal antagonism or even indifference might be of disastrous consequences.[7] Therefore, the government responded with both persuasion and coercion: on the one hand, the Wilson administration used a massive propaganda campaign to fire up public enthusiasm, supplying information to the American public along with psychic and material rewards for service; and on the other hand, the government prosecuted and imprisoned those who tried to hinder the war effort using tools such as the Espionage and Sedition Acts.[8]

Although millions of Americans enlisted in the armed service and volunteered for civilian service, many were critical of the reasons for fighting and preferred not to take part. Among them were farmers in the South and Midwest, Scandinavian and Russian immigrants who had left the Old World to avoid war, Irish-Americans who were torn between their new American home and their hatred of England, German and Austrian Americans who feared to face relatives on the battlefield, socialists who considered the war an imperialist struggle, pacifists and even progressives – supporters of Wilson – who were worried about the unraveling of domestic reforms. The White House received several reports of apathy and dissent, and a week after Congress declared war, the president issued on April 13, 1917 an executive order establishing a Committee on Public Information (CPI) to conduct American propaganda and on April 30, 1917 Congress began floor debate on the Espionage Act.[9]

Wilson appointed George Creel, a Progressive journalist, as director of the CPI, who remarked that his aim was to weld Americans into "one white-hot mass...with fraternity, devotion, courage, and deathless determination."[10] Indeed a unity motif was one of three major themes that appeared in CPI's messages, the other two being the image of a despicable enemy and the idea of a crusade for peace and freedom.[11]

The CPI used sophisticated methods from the world of commercial advertising to reach every segment of society and try to manage public thinking about the war. It issued press releases, placed ads in newspapers and magazines, attached posters to walls and billboards and produced cartoons and even war movies; it sent "Four-Minute Men" to motion-picture theaters to lead the audience in patriotic songs during the four minutes it took to change reels; it organized with other organizations conferences, exhibitions, essay contests and parades; and it prepared special messages for immigrants, farmers and workers.[12]

With a budget of several million dollars of executive funds,[13] CPI films being distributed to a third of the nation's theaters, ads in newspapers and magazines (one ad of a female Red Cross nurse cradling in her arms a tiny wounded soldier appeared over fifty million times), rallies and so on, this was an enormous governmental effort to persuade the American public and mobilize feelings about the war.[14]

Interest Articulation and Aggregation Regarding Disloyalty and Obstructing Enlistment

Interests, claims and demands are articulated and aggregated in political systems. In effect, the aggregative function may be performed within subsystems of the political system, including structures that are involved in interest articulation, such as political executives, bureaucracies and parties.[15] During World War I, in the United States the functions of interest articulation and aggregation overlapped[16] as regards restricting freedom of speech:

The 1916 Democratic Party platform condemned the undermining of national unity by any group or individual.[17] In the same year, when Wilson was questioned about "tolerance" at a Flag Day event, he proclaimed that there shouldn't be any tolerance for disloyal persons.[18]

As the chances of American participation in the war increased, lawyers in the Department of Justice became concerned that existing federal law would be insufficient to deal with disloyal speech, particularly that which threatened the formation and maintenance of the armed forces.[19] This was mainly because there was doubt whether the treason statute could be successfully used to punish disloyal acts, such as speech that promotes the success of the enemy or obstructs the enlistment service. Consequently the department drafted the Espionage bill, its chief author being the Assistant Attorney General Charles Warren.[20]

In Wilson's joint address to Congress leading to a declaration of war, he said that most of the "millions of men and women of German birth and sympathy" who live in the United States are "loyal Americans" but "if there should be disloyalty, it will be dealt with a firm hand of stern repression."[21]

Bar associations expressed patriotism and supported the war effort. Lawyers who criticized the war or defended war critics were isolated and occasionally subjected to formal discipline. The Illinois Bar Association, for example, adopted a resolution proclaiming it unpatriotic and unprofessional for a lawyer to defend a draft evader.[22]

The American Association of University Professors declared that professors could legitimately be fired for knowingly speaking words that could arouse resistance to the draft.[23] In addition, the association declared that professors of Teutonic origin should refrain from public discussion of the war,[24] and if they made offensive statements about the United States or its government they should be let go.[25]

Legislating, Applying and Ruling on the Espionage and Sedition Acts

Legislating the Espionage Act and the Sedition Act

As mentioned earlier, three weeks after Congress declared war, it began debating the Espionage Act on the floor (of the House). After five weeks of deliberation (at intervals), which included the removal of a provision that would have allowed the president to censor the press (see Chapter 3), it became law.[26]

The Espionage Act is concerned with espionage matters and the protection of military secrets, but two parts have to do with free speech during war (see Appendix A for full text of relevant sections of the act):

- Title I section 3 prohibits, when the United States is at war, to "willfully make or convey false reports or false statements with intent to interfere with the operation or success of the military or naval forces of the United States or to promote the success of its enemies"; and "willfully cause or attempt to cause insubordination, disloyalty, mutiny, or refusal of duty, in the military or naval forces of the United States," or "willfully obstruct the recruiting or enlistment service of the United States."[27]
- Title XII deals with the use of mail and declares nonmailable every letter, writing, circular, postal card, picture, print, engraving, photograph, newspaper, pamphlet, book or other publication, matter, or thing, of any kind, in violation of any of the provisions of the Act or containing any matter advocating or urging treason, insurrection, or forcible resistance to any law of the United States.[28]

The Sedition Act, which amended the Espionage Act, was legislated one year later. In the spring of 1918, the Department of Justice sought to amend the Espionage Act following the acquittal of a man in Montana who was charged with violating the Espionage Act (*United States v. Hall*),[29] despite his using language that was harsher than that used by convicted speakers.[30] The indictment charged Ves Hall that at "divers times in the presence of sundry persons," he declared, among other things, that "he would flee to avoid going to war; that Germany would whip the United States, and he hoped so; that the President was a Wall Street tool...and the crookedest ________ ever President" and "that Germany had right to sink ships and kill Americans without warning."[31]

Judge George Bourquin directed a verdict of acquittal mainly on two major grounds:[32] (1) Hall could not have *intended* to interfere with the operation and success of the armed forces since "the declarations were made at a Montana village of some 60 people, 60 miles from the railway, and none of the armies or Navy within hundreds of miles," in a hotel kitchen, at a picnic and in saloon arguments.[33] Therefore they failed "of the required proximity to constitute attempts."[34] (2) Hall's speech did not obstruct the recruiting and enlistment service of the United States as no "injury" was caused to the service: "The espionage act does not create the crime of attempting to obstruct, but only the crime of actual obstruction, and when causing injury to the service."[35]

Judge Bourquin also noted that Hall's "beliefs, opinions, and hopes are not within the statute." He added that the Espionage Act is not intended to suppress "loose talk" and concluded that the "impression that for any slanderous or disloyal remarks the utterer can be prosecuted by the United States is a mistake."[36]

Bourquin's decision in *Hall* disturbed lawyers at the Department of Justice since they realized that the law was not effective in relation to individual disloyal utterances that were occurring throughout the country, utterances that also irritated the members of the communities in which they occurred, thereby causing, sometimes, acts of violence, and they sought an amendment of the Espionage Act.[37] The Attorney General requested Congress to amend the act to clarify that the act prohibited attempts to obstruct recruiting and enlistment, as well as actual obstruction (and to prohibit any person from interfering with the government's efforts to borrow funds for the war).[38] In an address to the executive committee of the American Bar Association in April 1918 (parallel to Congress's debate on the amendment), he referred to the *Hall* case as an example of the "ineffectiveness" of the Espionage Act "when applied by a judge not in accord with its purposes."[39]

Members of the Senate, among them the Senators from Montana, asked to make the proposed amendments more extreme. Senator Thomas Walsh of Montana (D) argued that because dissenters would be "emboldened" by decisions like *Hall* to make "disloyal and seditious utterances," Congress had to ensure that "no possible means of escape would prevent themselves" to such persons.[40] Senator Henry Myers of Montana (D) demanded that the bill punish disloyalty and treason in the proper way "and making the bill good and strong, all powerful and far-reaching, without throwing any unnecessary obstacles in the way of its enforcement…Loyalty to our country demands [such a law]."[41] Senator Kenneth McKellar of Tennessee (D) announced that "if we cannot reason with men to be loyal, it is high time we forced them to be loyal."[42]

The Senators from Montana took such positions because feelings of loyalty ran high in Montana – per capita, more Montanans served (and more Montanans volunteered) in the armed forces during World War I than from any other state, and Montana ranked among the highest states in purchase of Liberty bonds;[43] but, on the other hand, Montana was the site of action by fierce opponents of the war – the radical labor organization named the Industrial Workers of the World (IWW).[44] IWW organizers achieved major strength in the Butte, Montana copper mines,[45] which were essential for producing war materials.[46] At one point, when strikes in June and July 1917 curtailed copper production,[47] an IWW activist, Frank Little, who not only encouraged workers to strike but also made antiwar remarks at a rally, was dragged from his room in Butte, Montana, into the streets and hanged.[48] The Montana press, many owned by the mining companies that were in favor of the war effort,[49] viewed the lynching as patriotic.[50] Six months later, after the acquittal in *Hall*, editors of Montana newspapers, as well as the Governor of Montana, criticized Judge Bourquin's decision, called for the enactment of a law to stop sedition and wrote Senator Myers.[51] In addition, the Department of Justice received letters from Montana citizens and members of Congress criticizing Judge Bourquin.[52]

The Sedition Act was approved in the Senate by a vote of 48 to 26, in the House by a vote of 293 to 1 (see Chapter 3 as regards the congressional debate) and on May 16, 1918, President Wilson signed it into law.[53] It indeed prohibited "disloyal" language. The Sedition Act forbade, when the United States is in war, among other things (see appendix A for full text of relevant sections of the act):

- to "willfully utter, print, write, or publish": any disloyal, profane, scurrilous, or abusive language about the form of government, or the Constitution, or the military or naval forces, or the flag of the United States; or any language intended to bring the government, the Constitution, the military or naval forces, or the flag of the United States into contempt, scorn, contumely, or disrepute;
- to "willfully utter, print, write, or publish any language intended to incite, provoke or encourage resistance to the United States";
- to urge, incite, or advocate any curtailment of production of products necessary or essential to the prosecution of war; and
- in addition, the act prohibited making false reports or false statements, or saying or doing anything except by way of bona fide and not disloyal advice to an investor or investors, with intent to obstruct the sale or making of loans by or to the United States.[54]

Application

The Post Office: The nonmailability section of the Espionage Act was immediately enforced. The day after the Espionage Act was signed, the Postmaster General Albert S. Burleson directed all local postmasters to forward to Washington "unsealed matter, newspapers, etc." that might violate the act (including causing disloyalty, refusal of duty or obstruction of the draft) or otherwise "embarrass or hamper the Government in conducting the war."[55] By mid July 1917, the Post Office had denied the mailing of the *Masses*, the *International Socialist Review*, the *Appeal to Reason*, the *American Socialist*, the *Milwaukee Leader* and other publications. While some of these journals were critical of the war, Burleson also excluded the *Public* from the mails for advocating raising money by taxes rather than by loans.[56]

When asked about the standards for suppressing mail, Burleson at first refused to comment, but eventually declared that no publication could

> "say that this Government got in the war wrong, that it is in it for wrong purposes, or anything that will impugn the motives of the Government for going into the war. [A publication] can not say that this Government is the tool of Wall Street or the munitions-makers."[57]

Burleson said that these ideas made "for insubordination in the Army and Navy and breeds a spirit of disloyalty through the country. It is a false statement, a lie, and it will not be permitted."[58]

The Justice Department: The Head of the War Emergency Division of the Justice Department reported after the war that the department's view was not to confuse expression of opinion relating to government policy with attempts to interfere with the conduct of the war, though "immense pressure" was put on the department for "indiscriminate prosecution" and "wholesale repression" of public opinion.[59] President Wilson for his part did not direct the Justice Department to limit prosecutions.[60] In effect, during the war, the Department of Justice instituted 2,168 prosecutions and secured 1,055 convictions.[61]

Attorney General Thomas W. Gregory asked loyal Americans on the onset of the war to act as voluntary officials and report suspicions to the Department of Justice. As a result, thousands of accusations of disloyalty turned up in the department. The Justice Department was assisted by voluntary associations, the largest of them being the American Protection League (APL) with over 200,000 members.[62] In APL's effort to recruit members, Gregory authorized it to state on its letterhead "Organized with the Approval, and Operating under the Direction of the United States Department of Justice, Bureau of Investigation."[63] APL members not only reported disloyal remarks of individuals, they opened mail, wiretapped telephones, broke into offices, conducted searches and delivered material they discovered to the Bureau of Investigation in the Department of Justice.[64] Gregory reported in April 1918 that with the help of the APL and other voluntary associations, the Department of Justice was able to investigate hundreds of thousands of complaints and keep thousands of people under observation.[65]

Adjudication

Most lower federal courts interpreted the Espionage Act relying on the "bad tendency" test of language:[66] people were found guilty of violating the law if they made statements that had the tendency to cause insubordination or the tendency to obstruct the recruiting and enlistment service (title I, section 3 of the act).[67] Thus judges observed, for example, that the relationship between language and the statutory prohibitions need not be direct, or that speech need not be made in the presence of soldiers, or that statements need not be necessarily false.[68] Following are some examples:[69]

- A movie producer, who made a film on the Revolutionary War that included a scene on the Wyoming Valley Massacre showing British soldiers bayoneting women and children, was sentenced to ten years in prison for attempting to cause insubordination in the armed forces. The judge commented that "fact is fact" but "this is no time" for "those things that may have the tendency or effect of sowing… animosity or want of confidence between us and our allies."[70]
- The son of the chief justice of the Supreme Court of New Hampshire was convicted for mailing a chain letter stating that Germany did not break a promise to end submarine warfare (the Sussex Pledge). The government argued that this "would have a direct tendency to obstruct the recruiting and enlistment service"[71] and he was sentenced to eighteen months in prison.
- A reverend was found guilty of an attempt to cause insubordination for distributing a pamphlet teaching that Christians should not kill in wars. He was sentenced to fifteen years in prison.
- Twenty-seven farmers in South Dakota were charged for willfully obstructing the recruitment and enlistment service for petitioning the governor regarding reforms in the Selective Service procedure.
- The socialist Rose Pastor Stokes made a speech that was subsequently published in the *Kansas City Star*, in which she said that she didn't believe every citizen should give the government unqualified support and that "No government which is for the profiteers can also be for the people, and I am for the people while the government is for the profiteers."[72] The judge sentenced her to ten years in prison for language that might cause insubordination and tended to chill enthusiasm among relatives of servicemen.[73]

All cases that reached the Supreme Court upheld the Espionage Act: in interpreting the First Amendment ("Congress shall make no law… abridging the freedom of speech, or of the press"), the Supreme Court decided that speech by those convicted was not protected by the First Amendment and was in violation of the Espionage Act.[74]

In March 1919, the Supreme Court made its first decision in *Schenck v. United States*. In this case the defendants had been charged with conspiring to cause insubordination in the military forces and to obstruct the recruiting and enlistment service, by distributing leaflets to men who had been called for military service in which they advocated opposition to the draft.[75] The leaflets argued that the draft was unconstitutional and was designed to further the interests of Wall Street, urged not to "submit to intimidation," called readers to "assert and support your rights" and encouraged to write Congress to protest the draft.[76] They were convicted because the "natural and probable tendency" of the leaflet was to weaken motivation to serve in the armed forces.[77] The Supreme Court unanimously upheld the conviction. Justice Oliver Wendell Holmes wrote that

> "the documents would not have been sent unless it had been intended to have some effect, and we do not see what effect it could be expected to have upon persons subject to the draft except to influence them to obstruct the carrying of it out."[78]

Justice Holmes then addressed the question of whether the leaflet was protected by the First Amendment and wrote the following passage, which has since become famous and, in the context of the current analysis of the American political system, fits very well to the structural functionalist approach:

> We admit that in many places and in ordinary times the defendants in saying all that was said in the circular would have been within their constitutional rights. But the character of every act depends upon the circumstances in which it is done. The most stringent protection of free speech would not protect a man in falsely shouting fire in a theater, and causing a panic.
>
> The question in every case is whether the words used are used in such circumstances and are of such a nature as to create a clear and present danger that they will bring about the substantive evils that Congress has a right to prevent. It is a question of proximity and degree. When a nation is at war many things that might be said in time of peace are such a hindrance to its effort that their utterance will not be endured so long as men fight and no Court could regard them as protected by any constitutional right.[79]

That is to say, war matters. According to the Supreme Court of the Unites States, the circumstances of war create an extraordinary "clear and present danger" and therefore Congress has a right to prevent certain speech.[80]

The Supreme Court also upheld the conviction of Eugene V. Debs, leader of the Socialist Party of America, the third-largest political party, who received almost a million votes as candidate for president in 1912. He opposed both the draft and the war. In June 1918 he visited three socialists who were imprisoned for violating the Espionage Act and spoke to a crowd nearby the prison about socialism while condemning the war:[81]

> I have just returned from a visit over yonder where three of our most loyal comrades are paying the penalty for their devotion to the cause

> of the working class. They have come to realize, as many of us have, that it is extremely dangerous to exercise the constitutional right of free speech. ... I realize that, in speaking to you this afternoon, there are certain limitations placed upon the right of free speech. I must be exceedingly careful, prudent, as to what I say. ...I may not be able to say all I think. ...[Our three comrades] are simply paying the penalty, that all men have paid in all the ages of history for standing erect, and for seeking to pave the way to better conditions for mankind.
>
> Wars throughout history have been waged for conquest and plunder. ...The feudal barons of the Middle Ages, the economic predecessors of the capitalists of our day, declared all wars. And their miserable serfs fought all the battles. ...And that is war in a nutshell. The Master class has always declared the wars; the subject class has always fought the battles. The Master Class has had all to gain and nothing to lose, while the subject class has had nothing to gain and all to lose – especially their lives.[82]

Debs was tried for obstructing the recruitment and enlistment service of the United States and was sentenced to ten years in prison. The Supreme Court unanimously upheld the conviction (*Debs v. United States*). Justice Holmes agreed that Deb's speech was mainly about socialism and that is not a violation of the Espionage Act. However, he concluded that the speech contained sufficient evidence "to warrant the jury in finding that one purpose of the speech...was to oppose not only war in general but this war, and that opposition was so expressed that its natural and intended effect would be to obstruct recruiting."[83]

The Supreme Court affirmed judgment on the Sedition Act as well. Since the amendment to the Espionage Act was legislated late in the war, relatively few were prosecuted on its violation; however, one case reached the Supreme Court in October 1919: *Abrams v. Unites States*. This case involved a group of Russian immigrants who claimed themselves as socialists and anarchists. Following the Bolshevik revolution of 1917, Russia and Germany signed a peace agreement (the Treaty of Brest-Litovsk), and the following summer, the United States sent a contingent of Marines to Vladivostok and Murmansk (presumably to protect stranded allied soldiers). In protest, Abrams and his colleagues printed and threw from a building in New York City two leaflets: one signed "REVOLUTIONISTS," which denounced the sending of troops to Russia and stated that it would be criminal for the workers of America to fight the workers of Russia; the other, written in Yiddish, warned that money being loaned to the government via buying Liberty bonds is being used to "make bullets not only for Germans but also for the Workers of Soviet Russia,"[84] cautioned munitions workers that they are producing weapons to "murder not only the Germans" but also those in Russia and called for a general strike.[85] They were charged and convicted under the Sedition Act for conspiracy to incite, provoke and encourage resistance to the United States during the war and for conspiracy to urge the curtailment of production of war materials with intent to cripple and hinder the prosecution of the war and were sentenced to prison terms ranging from three to twenty years.[86] The Supreme Court ruled 7-2 that the Sedition Act did not violate freedom of speech protected by the First Amendment.[87] Justice John H. Clark admitted that the primary purpose of the defendants might have been to aid the cause of the Russian revolution, but the "obvious effect" of their language was to defeat "the war program of the United States"[88] and to this they must be held accountable.

Except for a handful of judges who narrowly interpreted the Espionage Act, most judges imposed severe sentences on those charged with its violation, including those on the circuit courts reviewing appeals.[89] A case in point was the declaring in summer 1917 of *The Masses* nonmailable by the New York Postmaster for certain cartoons and text that, according to the Postmaster, tended to violate the Espionage Act. District Judge Learned Hand granted the editor's request for an injunction, but his decision was reversed by the court of appeals.[90]

Political Communication

The media enabled manifest feedback from the enactment, enforcement and judgment on the Espionage and Sedition Acts. For example, the media expressed criticism on the few judges who did acquit defendants from violating the Espionage Act. In Montana, for instance, the *Helena Independent* called for the removal from the state of Judge George Bourquin, who ruled in *United States v. Hall.* Judge Charles Fremont Amidon of North Dakota was also condemned by the press for his decisions.[91]

In general, the press agreed with the government. In the summer of 1917, for example, the *New York Times* published an editorial stating, "It is the duty of every good citizen to communicate to proper authorities any evidence of sedition that comes to his notice."[92] In an editorial in April 1918, the *New York Times* printed: "While we are at war with Germany utterances in support of the enemy...can not be tolerated" and added its hope the Sedition Act be "speedily enacted" and "rigorously enforced."[93]

Using a structural functionalist approach, I have explained how laws restricting freedom of speech were established during World War I in the United States: in order to unite the nation during the war, certain restrictions on speech were required as part of the war effort – inputs in the system demanded them (the bureaucracy, the president), Congress produced the Espionage and Sedition Acts, they were enforced and judges upheld them.

The epilogue of the Espionage and Sedition Acts may be analyzed in the same way: after the war came to an end, the need to restrict freedom of speech diminished; and further to inputs from Congress, the bureaucracy and different associations, as well as feedback from the press, the Sedition Act was repealed and all prisoners were released. In March 1921 Congress repealed the Sedition Act (the Espionage Act is still in force). The matter of amnesty for those convicted under the Espionage and Sedition Acts arose as well. The *Washington Times* wrote in an editorial that those in jail "did nothing against the war except talk" and in March 1919, Attorney General Gregory recommended to President Wilson the release or reduction in sentence of two hundred prisoners (the government also abandoned most of the pending prosecutions under the Espionage and Sedition Acts). Wilson accepted the recommendations with the exception of that pertaining to Debs. Then in December 1921 President Warren G. Harding pardoned Debs and twenty-four other prisoners, and in December 1923 President Calvin Coolidge ordered the release of those who remained behind bars.[94]

But, to what degree were the Espionage and Sedition Acts democratically legitimate laws? Did the representatives of the people of the United States duly deliberate before enacting the Espionage and Sedition Acts? This is the focus of the next chapter. Using the criteria mentioned above to measure legislative deliberation – committee hearings, debate in both chambers, exchange of information and arguments on the floor, framing arguments in terms of the public good and persuasion – I will evaluate the extent of congressional deliberation and thus the degree of the acts' democratic legitimacy.

Notes

1 Gabriel A. Almond, "Introduction: A Functional Approach to Comparative Politics," In *The Politics of Developing Areas*, Eds. Gabriel A. Almond and James S. Coleman (Princeton: Princeton University Press, 1960), 27–28.
2 Almond, 30.
3 Almond, 30.
4 Ronald Schaffer, *America in the Great War: The Rise of the War Welfare State* (New York: Oxford University Press, 1991), xvi–xvii; Geoffrey R. Stone, *Perilous Times: Free Speech in Wartime from the Sedition Act of 1798 to the War on Terrorism* (New York: W.W. Norton & Company, 2004), 136–137. Already in May 1915, a German submarine sank a British liner, the *Lusitania*, killing 128 Americans, but after that Germany refrained submarine attacks.
5 Schaffer, 3; Stone, 137–138.
6 Stone, 138.
7 Schaffer, 3, xi.
8 Schaffer, xi–xii, 4–5.
9 Schaffer, 3–4; 65th Congress, 1st Session, *Congressional Record - House*, Vol. 55, 1590, April 30, 1917.
10 Quoted in Schaffer, 5.
11 Schaffer, 6.
12 Schaffer, 6–12.
13 Schaffer, 4.
14 Schaffer, 11–12.

15 Almond, 33, 38–40.
16 Almond writes that the functions of articulation and aggregation may overlap and that the distinction between interest articulation and aggregation is fluid. Almond, 38.
17 Stone, 145.
18 Stone, 145. Citing Paul L. Murphy, Stone writes that in 1916, Wilson also mentioned the need for new legislation to suppress disloyal activities. See Stone, 145.
19 David M. Rabban, *Free Speech in Its Forgotten Years* (New York: Cambridge University Press, 1997), 249.
20 Rabban, 249–250; Zechariah Chafee, *Free Speech in the United States* (Cambridge: Harvard University Press, 1967, 37. The Department of Justice also proposed an amendment to the Espionage Act, which became the Sedition Act.
21 Woodrow Wilson, "Transcript of Joint Address to Congress Leading to a Declaration of War Against Germany (1917)," http://www.ourdocuments.gov/doc.php?doc=61&page=transcript [accessed: January 4, 2020].
22 Stone, 159.
23 Schaffer, 146; Stone, 202–203.
24 Stone, 202–203.
25 Schaffer, 146.
26 Stone, 146–152; Rabban, 249–255.
27 Act of June 15, 1917, Espionage, *Statutes at Large of the United States of America*, Vol. 40, 219.
28 Act of June 15, 1917, Espionage, *Statutes at Large of the United States of America*, Vol. 40, 230.
29 Rabban, 266–267; Stone, 184.
30 Rabban, 266.
31 Court decision in *United States v. Hall* printed in the Congressional Record: 65th Congress, 2nd Session, *Congressional Record – Senate*, Vol. 56, 4560, April 4, 1918.
32 This is my reading of Bourquin's ruling. See also discussions in Rabban, 266–267, and Stone, 161–162, 174–177. See also the entire opinion of the court in 65th Congress, 2nd Session, *Congressional Record – Senate*, Vol. 56, 4560, April 4, 1918.
33 Court decision in *United States v. Hall* printed in the Congressional Record: 65th Congress, 2nd Session, *Congressional Record - Senate*, Vol. 56, 4560, April 4, 1918.
34 "It was as if A shot with a .22 pistol with intent to kill B two or three miles away...A could not be convicted of attempted murder." Court decision in *United States v. Hall* printed in the Congressional Record: 65th Congress, 2nd Session, *Congressional Record – Senate*, Vol. 56, 4560, April 4, 1918.
35 Court decision in *United States v. Hall* printed in the Congressional Record: 65th Congress, 2nd Session, *Congressional Record – Senate*, Vol. 56, 4560, April 4, 1918.
36 Court decision in *United States v. Hall* printed in the Congressional Record: 65th Congress, 2nd Session, *Congressional Record – Senate*, Vol. 56, 4560, April 4, 1918.
37 Rabban, 267; Chafee, 39–40.
38 Stone, 184; Statements of Senator Thomas Hardwick of Georgia (D.), 65th Congress, 2nd Session, *Congressional Record – Senate*, Vol. 56, 4639–4640, April 5, 1918; Chafee, 40.
39 Attorney-General Gregory, "Suggestions of Attorney-General Gregory to Executive Committee in Relation to the Department of Justice," *The American Bar Association Journal* 4 (1918): 306; Quoted also in Rabban, 267.

40 Quoted in Stone, 186. See 65th Congress, 2nd Session, *Congressional Record – Senate*, Vol. 56, 4560, April 4, 1918.

41 65th Congress, 2nd Session, *Congressional Record – Senate*, Vol. 56, 4715, April 6, 1918.

42 Quoted in Stone, 187. See 65th Congress, 2nd Session, *Congressional Record – Senate*, Vol. 56, 4718, April 6, 1918.

43 Arnon Gutfeld. "The Ves Hall Case, Judge Bourquin, and the Sedition Act of 1918," *Pacific Historical Review* 37 (May 1968): 163–164.

44 Gutfeld, 164. The Industrial Workers of the World (IWW, frequently called "Wobblies") is a workers' union that was founded in 1905, and unlike the American Federation of Labor (AFL), it advocated the revolutionary overthrow of capitalism and undertook spontaneous strikes and slowdowns, picketing, parades and public speaking that provoked free speech fights. See Rabban, 79.

45 Robert Justin Goldstein, *Political Repression in Modern America: From 1870 to 1976*. 2nd ed. (Urbana and Chicago: University of Illinois Press, [1978] 2001), 115.

46 Schaffer, 15, 33.

47 Melvyn Dubofsky, *We Shall Be All: A History of the Industrial Workers of the World* (Chicago: Quadrangle Books, 1969), 368, 391; Goldstein, 115.

48 Schaffer, 24–25; Dubofsky, 391–392.

49 Gutfeld, 163.

50 Schaffer, 25.

51 Gutfeld, 170–171.

52 Gutfeld, 174.

53 65th Congress, 2nd Session, *Congressional Record – Senate*, Vol. 56, 6057, May 4, 1918; 65th Congress, 2nd Session, *Congressional Record – House*, Vol. 56, 6186–6187, May 7, 1918; Stone, 191; 65th Congress, 2nd Session, *Congressional Record – House*, Vol. 56, 7042–7043, May 24, 1918.

54 Act of May 16, 1918, *Statutes at Large of the United States of America*, Vol. 40, 553.

55 Donald Johnson, "Wilson, Burleson and Censorship in the First World War," *The Journal of Southern History* 28.1 (Feb. 1962): 48; Schaffer, 14.

56 Schaffer, 14.

57 Quoted in Johnson, 51. See also Johnson, 49–52 and Schaffer, 14–15.

58 Quoted in Johnson, 51–52; See also Schaffer 15. While many magazines, newspapers and books were excluded from the mails, Stone claims that the number of publications excluded significantly understates the amount of expression suppressed, because many publications autonomously controlled their texts so as not to lose their mailing rights. He gives one example – the Yiddish *Daily Forward*. See Stone, 180–181.

59 Quoted in Stone, 212–213.

60 Clinton L. Rossiter, *Constitutional Dictatorship: Crisis Government in the Modern Democracies* (Princeton: Princeton University Press, 1948), 252–253.

61 Stone, 593, ft. 136; Schaffer, 15. (There were relatively few prosecutions under the Sedition Act since it was enacted so late in the war; Stone, 191.)

62 Stone, 156; Schaffer, 17.

63 Stone, 590, ft. 85.

64 Schaffer, 17.

65 Attorney-General Gregory, "Suggestions of Attorney-General Gregory to Executive Committee in Relation to the Department of Justice," *The American Bar Association Journal* 4 (1918): 309; quoted also in Stone, 156. There were also numerous instances of violence. Stone writes that to President Wilson's credit, he was uneasy about this effort and told Gregory in June 1917 that "it seems to me it would be very dangerous to have such an organization

operating in the United States." Toward the end of the war, he even publicly condemned those who took "punishment into their own hands." See Stone 156–157. During the war, states set up "councils of defense" that dealt with a range of activities in support of the war effort, and there were many violent events. See Schaffer, 18–28 and Stone, 181–182.

66 Rabban, 256; Stone, 171; Chafee, 50.

67 Rabban, 256–261; Stone, 171–173; Chafee, 52. Rabban writes that the majority of Espionage Act prosecutions were secured under title I, section 3. Chafee determines that almost all convictions "were for expressions of opinion about the merits and conduct of the war" and only a few people were convicted for actually obstructing enlistment; Chafee, 51. In 1921 the Supreme Court also upheld the Postmaster General's order from 1917 denying mailing of the *Milwaukee Leader*; Chafee, 299 (for a critique of this decision, see Chafee, 298–305).

68 Rabban, 257–258.

69 Examples taken from Schaffer, 15–17; Stone, 171–173; Rabban, 256–260.

70 Quoted in Stone, 173.

71 Quoted in Stone, 172 and in Chafee, 54–55.

72 Quoted in Schaffer, 16, and in Chafee, 52. See also "Mrs. Rose P. Stokes Convicted of Disloyalty; Illegal to Impair National Morale, Says Judge," *The New York Times*, May 24, 1918.

73 Stone, 172; Chafee, 52–53. See also "Mrs. Rose P. Stokes Convicted of Disloyalty; Illegal to Impair National Morale, Says Judge," *The New York Times*, May 24, 1918.

74 Rabban, 279–285; Stone, 192.

75 *Schenck v. United States*. 249 U.S. 47. Supreme Court of the United States (1919).

76 Quoted in Stone, 192.

77 Quoted in Stone, 192.

78 *Schenck v. United States*. No. 249. Supreme Court of the United States. March 3, 1919, quoted in Stone, 192.

79 *Schenck v. United States*. No. 249. Supreme Court of the United States. March 3, 1919, quoted in Stone, 193.

80 Rabban, 282; Stone, 193. Indeed, reviewing crisis government and "abnormal legislative and administrative measures" in the United Stated during the World War I, Rossiter concluded that "in no case did the Court intimate that the tremendous wartime delegations of power had been unconstitutional. *Inter arma silet curia suprema*" Rossiter, *Constitutional Dictatorship*, 254.

81 Stone, 142, 196.

82 Quoted in Stone, 142, 196–197.

83 Rabban, 284. Some scholars view Deb's conviction and imprisonment, indeed the entire issue of restriction of freedom of speech during World War I (i.e., the Espionage and Sedition Acts), as part of a broader struggle – that of class conflict. The claim goes as follows: World War I itself was the outcome of class conflict. At the turn of the twentieth century, there was a poor, oppressed and angry working class in the United States, which began to organize itself in unions and parties, expressed itself against capitalism and went on strikes, therefore posing a threat to the capitalist class. In response to workers' attempts to change the unequal social order, capitalists came up with war and sent the working class to die in the battlefields of Europe (in addition, the business community had an economic interest in war – government procurement and the opening up of foreign markets to American goods). The purpose of the Espionage and Sedition Acts was to silence the socialists at home and assure the continuation of capitalists' control. See, for

example, Howard Zinn, *A People's History of the United States: From 1492 to the Present*. 2nd ed. (London: Longman, 1966).
84 Quoted in Stone, 205.
85 Quoted in Stone, 205.
86 Stone, 206.
87 Surprisingly, Justice Holmes dissented (along with Justice Louis D. Brandeis). On Holmes' transformation and his main dissenting arguments, see Stone, 198–203, 206–210; Rabban, 343–355; and Paul Starr, *The Creation of the Media: Political Origins of Modern Communications* (New York: Basic Books, 2004), 282–284.
88 Quoted in Rabban, 345.
89 Stone, 160, 170; Rabban, 261.
90 Rabban, 261–266; Stone, 164–170; Starr, 281.
91 Stone, 169.
92 Quoted in Zinn, 360.
93 Editorial of *The New York Times* "Punishment for the Disloyal" dated April 3, 1918, printed in 65th Congress, 2nd Session, *Congressional Record – Senate*, Vol. 56, 4709, April 6, 1918. Rossitter adds that the press voluntarily self-censored itself as a result of its cooperation with the CPI; Rossiter, *Constitutional Dictatorship*, 253.
94 Stone, 230–232.

References

Almond, Gabriel A. "Introduction: A Functional Approach to Comparative Politics." *The Politics of Developing Areas*. Eds. Gabriel A. Almond and James S. Coleman, 3–64. Princeton: Princeton University Press, 1960.

Chafee, Zechariah. *Free Speech in the United States*. Cambridge: Harvard University Press, 1967.

Congressional Record: Containing the Proceedings and Debates of the First Session of the Sixty-Fifth Congress of the United States of America, Vol. LV, Parts 1–3. Washington: Government Printing Office, 1917.

Congressional Record: Containing the Proceedings and Debates of the Second Session of the Sixty-Fifth Congress of the United States of America, Vol. LVI, Parts 5–7. Washington: Government Printing Office, 1918.

Dubofsky, Melvyn. *We Shall Be All: A History of the Industrial Workers of the World*. Chicago: Quadrangle Books, 1969.

Goldstein, Robert Justin. *Political Repression in Modern America: From 1870 to 1976*. 2nd ed. Urbana and Chicago: University of Illinois Press, [1978] 2001.

Gregory. "Suggestions of Attorney-General Gregory to Executive Committee in Relation to the Department of Justice." *The American Bar Association Journal* 4 (1918): 305–316.

Gutfeld, Arnon. "The Ves Hall Case, Judge Bourquin, and the Sedition Act of 1918." *Pacific Historical Review* 37 (May 1968): 163–178.

Johnson, Donald. "Wilson, Burleson and Censorship in the First World War." *The Journal of Southern History* 28 (Feb. 1962): 46–58.

"Mrs. Rose P. Stokes Convicted of Disloyalty; Illegal to Impair National Morale, Says Judge." *New York Times*, 24 May 1918.

Rabban, David. *Free Speech in Its Forgotten Years*. Cambridge: Cambridge University Press, 1997.

Rossiter, Clinton L. *Constitutional Dictatorship: Crisis Government in the Modern Democracies.* Princeton: Princeton University Press, 1948.
Schaffer, Ronald. *America in the Great War: The Rise of the War Welfare State.* New York: Oxford University Press, 1991.
Schenck v. United States. 249 U.S. 47. Supreme Court of the United States. 1919.
Starr, Paul. *The Creation of the Media: Political Origins of Modern Communications.* New York: Basic Books, 2004.
Statutes at Large of the United States of America, Vol. 40, Part 1. Washington: Government Printing Office, 1919.
Stone, Geoffrey R. *Perilous Times: Free Speech in Wartime from the Sedition Act of 1798 to the War on Terrorism.* New York: W.W. Norton & Company, 2004.
Zinn, Howard. *A People's History of the United States: From 1492 to the Present.* 2nd ed. London: Longman, 1996.

3 Congressional Deliberation on the Espionage and Sedition Acts

We all have our heart and soul in this war, but because we have our heart in it is no reason why we should lose our head. It is our patriotic duty to remain calm, cool, and deliberate.

Representative Fiorello Henry LaGuardia, May 2, 1917

Senators, in times of war people grow hysterical...even legislative bodies, are not exempt from the contagion of hysteria. It is better to move along slowly; it is better to deliberate.

Senator Thomas Hardwick, April 5, 1918

The Espionage Act

As mentioned earlier, the Espionage Act does in fact deal mostly with issues of espionage and the protection of military secrets, while two parts – one concerning making statements to cause insubordination or obstruct recruiting (title I, section 3), and the other on nonmailability (Title XII) – restrict freedom of speech when the United States is at war. The original bill included an additional provision, relating to censorship of the press; however, after deliberating the bill, with extensive debate on the censorship provision, Congress made various amendments and also stroke out the censorship provision.

In what follows, I analyze the House Judiciary Committee hearings on the Espionage Act, and the deliberation on the floor, that is, the exchange of information and arguments, including framing arguments in terms of the public good and persuasion.[1]

House Judiciary Committee Hearings and Deliberation

In the case of the Espionage bill, the House Judiciary Committee conducted public hearings and heard oral testimonies. External individuals and groups appeared before the committee and articulated views concerning the proposed legislation restricting freedom of speech, and the executive offered written review. As a result, the original draft of the law was amended.

On April 2, 1917, the same day President Wilson asked Congress to declare war on Germany, the Espionage bill was introduced to Congress by the chairman of the House Committee of the Judiciary, Representative Edwin Webb of North Carolina (D), and referred to that committee.[2]

The Committee on the Judiciary held public hearings on April 9 and 12, 1917,[3] and also held an executive session on April 10, 1917, in which Assistant Attorney General Charles Warren – who "drafted the principal portions of the bill"[4] – gave an oral statement explaining provisions of the bill and answered questions posed to him by committee members (in addition, one day earlier he prepared and sent the committee members a letter, in which he reviewed the bill).[5]

Many lawyers, professors and political activists testified before the committee, speaking for themselves or on behalf of organizations such as the Women's Peace Party of America, the Free Speech League and the American Federation of Labor.[6] Indeed Representative Webb pointed out on the first day of the hearings that "The doors of this committee are always open to…who may want to be heard in criticism or support of any measure."[7]

There were a few statements objecting the bill in general, since the "underlining principles behind some of the specifications" of the bill strike at freedom of speech,[8] but the majority of speakers addressed concerns and argued specifically con Title I section 3, which wording at that stage made it unlawful in time of war to willfully make or convey false statements with intent to interfere with the operation or success of the military and willfully cause or attempt to cause disaffection in the military.[9]

On account of Title I section 3, there was concern that the right of suffragists to free speech would be denied,[10] that people who do not believe in conscription would not have the right to express their opinion,[11] that the bill will not give liberty to say things in regard to an international solution to world disputes[12] or in regard to wrongdoings in ordnance factories, rolling mills, munition factories and in the shipyards,[13] and it was argued that the bill will end the "spirit of free discussion."[14]

Gilbert E. Roe, Esq., representing the Free Speech League, argued that Title I section 3 made the bill unconstitutional: the Constitution did not provide that freedom of speech and of the press could be abridged in time of war, and there is no suggestion that speech is to be less free in war than in peace.[15] Moreover, voters need full discussion of every phase of the war, its origin, its manner of prosecution and its manner of termination, to form an intelligent opinion and vote for a senator and representative in either opposition or in accord with the war;[16] soldiers who are at the front giving their lives to the service of their country are entitled to know the truth;[17] and if people and the press are denied the right to freely discuss the war, the antiwar sentiment will increase and become aggressive.[18]

Assistant Attorney General Charles Warren and certain members of the committee did not subscribe with the above-mentioned concerns and arguments on the section: Representative Thaddeus Horatius Caraway of Arkansas (D) asserted that the section does not deny freedom of speech to suffragists, as it outlaws *false* statements with intent to due injury to the country;[19] Representative Leonidas Carstarphen Dyer of Missouri (R) noted that it did not limit the right to complain to the government concerning wrongdoings in the factories;[20] and according to Assistant Attorney General Warren, the section did not make the discussion of conscription by peace societies illegal if it is not their intention to cause disaffection.[21]

In addition, Assistant Attorney General Warren argued that the right of free speech should "yield to the supreme right of the nation." Conveying the position of the Army and Navy, which was that no man should have the right of free speech to the extent that it should interfere with the success of his country in time of war, he explained: "Of course, we cannot pass a statute that will infringe a man's constitutional right, but if he has any other loose right, the right of free speech you see in the newspaper editorials, that right should yield to the supreme right of the nation."[22]

There were many who argued against the term "disaffection" in the section. Originally drawn, the section prohibited anyone in time of war to willfully "cause or attempt to cause *disaffection* in the military or naval forces of the United States"[23] (emphasis added). The term was deemed "vague,"[24] "elastic,"[25] "too broad" and "ambiguous."[26] The representative of the American Federation of Labor observed that by encouragement of disaffection, Americans "have grown to be free people"[27] and a war correspondent asserted that disaffection is the only way anything is done in a democracy because "People have got to be dissatisfied before they will change anything."[28] Gilbert Roe argued that the language in effect provided that whoever by "any means whatsoever" will cause disaffection shall be punished – that is, it is not limited – and that "Disaffection means dissatisfaction, discontent, disgust, dislike"; therefore any speech that causes discontent or disgust, even it may be the truth, violates the bill.[29] Professor Emily Balch, replying to a remark by Representative Caraway, noted that the question of intent to cause disaffection is "a very delicate one."[30] She hoped the committee would decide to recommend striking out the entire clause, but if retained, she asked to make an amendment and insert "by attempting to induce desertion, insubordination, or any failure of duty," thereby making the law more specific and removing the danger in the "very wide phrasing."[31]

Members of the committee engaged with the speakers on the language of the bill, including the term "disaffection." For example, the chairman, Representative Webb, asked Professor William I. Hull what would "disaffection" cover, what it means; Representative Dick Thompson Morgan of Oklahoma (R) asked what would he substitute for the word "disaffection"; and Webb concluded that the Committee will "certainly consider very carefully" Hull's suggestions for amendments.[32]

At the end of the public hearings, the chairman declared that he hoped that anyone who felt that their rights may be infringed by some provision in the bill had their say "before an open-minded body of men who want to do the right thing" adding that the committee "will draft a bill to present to Congress which we think will do justice to our Government in time of war and at the same time protect and preserve the rights of the American people."[33]

On April 25, 1917, an amended bill was reported to the House of Representatives, accompanied by a written report (No. 30).[34] As a result of the public hearings, the provision concerning making statements to cause disaffection in the military was significantly amended by the committee.

Taking into account the concerns articulated at the hearings, the Judiciary Committee decided that the term "disaffection" was "too broad and too elastic and too indefinite."[35] To clarify the provision, the term "disaffection" was replaced so that instead of the phrase to "cause or attempt to cause disaffection" in the armed forces, the bill read "to cause or attempt to cause insubordination, disloyalty, mutiny, or refusal of duty."[36] The chairman of the committee, Representative Webb, explained

> that to make it a crime to create disaffection...might ofttimes subject a perfectly innocent person to punishment. A mother might write to a boy and tell him the sad conditions back home. That would create disaffection...[but not] create disloyalty...insubordination...or refusal to perform duty, and so we have made that section so that it will protect an honest man, and...get the dishonest fellow who deliberately undertakes to spread disloyalty, insubordination, or refusal to perform duty in our armed forces.[37]

Floor Debate: Information and Arguments

Members of Congress took their duty to deliberate on the Espionage bill quite seriously. Not only did they in fact engage alternately in debate over a period of five weeks, they also stated that it is their duty to reason and deliberate on the common good (befitting deliberative democracy norms).[38] Aptly on the first day of debate, Representative Martin Madden of Illinois (R) stated:

> There ought to be considerable discussion of this bill. It is one of the most important bills that has ever come before the Congress of the United States...there ought to be wide discussion on it, and everybody in the House ought to have an opportunity to express his opinion about it.[39]

Representative Fiorello Henry LaGuardia of New York (R) avowed that he could not "rubber stamp" every proposal and properly do his duty to his country, and that it is members' of Congress "patriotic duty to remain calm, cool and deliberate."[40] Representative Issac Siegel also of New York (R) said that his concern is the "best interests of the Nation."[41] With respect to the censorship provision, Senator Oscar Underwood of Alabama (D) stated that "in matters of this kind we should act slowly, deliberately, and with careful, matured judgment."[42] Concerning the nonmailability provision, Senator Thomas Sterling of South Dakota (R) talked about the "public interest."[43]

The floor debate on the Espionage bill involved real exchange between opposing sides: the bill's sponsors explained and defended their proposal, others challenged them and a response was offered. Members of Congress engaged in a reasoning process in which they seriously considered information and arguments and sought to decide individually and to persuade each other as to the best law, as illustrated below.

Deliberation on the Censorship Provision

Much of the debate was on the censorship provision, with extensive discussion on the meaning and history of the First Amendment. The provision authorized the president by proclamation to declare the existence of a national emergency and prohibit the publishing of "any information relating to the national defense which, in his judgment, is of such character that it is or might be useful to the enemy." Although the provision added that "nothing in this section shall be construed to limit or restrict any discussion, comment or criticism of the acts or policies of the Government,"[44] it was fiercely opposed.

When presenting the bill to the House, Representative Webb defended the Judiciary Committee's proposal and argued that the newspapers should

> remember that in time of war, while men are giving up their sons and while people are giving up their money, they should at least be willing to give up their right...to publish broadcast those things which the President of the United States thinks would be hurtful to the United States.[45]

He further elaborated that

> we are in just one of those situations where we have to trust somebody. The President is the Commander in Chief of the Army and Navy of the United States, and he has in his hands the military control of the boys and mothers of the country, and I take it that it as sacred a trust as it is for him to prescribe what in his opinion is information which would be useful to the enemy.[46]

Challenges to the provision were raised on three major accounts:[47] (1) that it would allow prior restraints while the First Amendment precludes a system of prior restraints, (2) that it proposed unconstitutional legislative power to the president and (3) that it lacked any intent requirement. (Underlying these arguments lay a fundamental claim that in effect the provision is tantamount to an unconstitutional abridgment of the freedom of the press. See below.)

1. Prior restraints: In relation to the argument on prior restraints, Representative Horace Towner of Iowa (R) said that "it is not an order upon that which has been done; it is an order prohibiting that which may be done" and that it is wrong to prohibit in advance the publishing of any fact or truth.[48] Senator Henry Ashurst of Arizona (D) quoted William Blackstone and said that freedom of the press

    > means freedom from the restraints of a censor, means the absolute liberty and right to publish whatever you wish; but you take your chances of punishment in the courts of your country for the violation of the laws of libel, slander, and treason.[49]

    Therefore he concluded that the provision is unconstitutional. He also added that it is bad public policy as a "censorship of the press results in the diffusion and spread of misinformation and idle tales."[50] Senator William Borah of Idaho (R) said that

    > to control a publication previous to its publication is in violation of...the Constitution, and that is precisely what we are proceeding to do by this proposed law. We are boldly, brazenly, indifferently disregarding a plain, vital provision of our fundamental law.[51]

2. Unconstitutional legislative power to the president: The argument concerning awarding unconstitutional legislative power to the president was taken up among other ways, by way of contesting the reasoning of the Judiciary Committee, like when Representative Charles Dillon of South Dakota (R) asked if a committee member "thinks that Congress can delegate to the Executive the power to say what shall constitute a crime."[52] Representative William Graham of Illinois (R) thought it "not advisable" for Congress to "deputize powers that ought to be exercised by it" to the president.[53] Representative Walter Chandler of New York (Progressive) opposed the provision because it was "unconstitutional" as it "[confers] upon the President of the United States legislative power; that is, we have conferred upon him the right to define a crime" (i.e., the publishing of information).[54] Representative Harold Knutson of Minnesota (R) said, "I do not think that simply because we are at war it shall be necessary that Congress should abrogate its powers and turn them over to the President."[55] Representative Joseph Walsh of Massachusetts (R), a member of the committee, stated that he was in favor of the bill

but "unalterably opposed" to the censorship provision because "it is placing a wide authority in the hands of the President" and "no matter how well intentioned he may be," it will "work great hardship" as the press will suffer "unjustly."[56]

3. Intent requirement: Senator Charles Thomas of Colorado (D) objected the provision "largely because it enables the President to establish regulations the violation of which, without regard to the question of intent, is made a very serious crime."[57] Representative George Graham of Pennsylvania (R) argued:

> Where a man does a thing with intent to hurt his country, then he ought to be punished; but when an individual or a newspaper criticizes the act of the Government with the hope of bettering conditions for his Government...that man, I say, in the interest of liberty and the welfare of the country ought not to be prosecuted or convicted.[58]

Notwithstanding these arguments, the provision had its supporters. They disagreed to the argument regarding the provision's unconstitutionality:

- Representative William Venable of Mississippi (D) disagreed that the censorship provision was unconstitutional saying that "freedom of speech and freedom of the press never included protection for a speech or a publication which would do harm" adding that "there is no such thing as an inherent, inalienable right to say anything that a citizen wants to say, whether by word of mouth or in the newspapers...without regard to the public interest."[59]
- Representative Andrew Volstead of Minnesota (R), answering a question on the floor, said that the provision does not conflict with the First Amendment and further argued that

> in preparing for and carrying on this war many things will be done and many things will happen that can not be anticipated. ... Somebody should determine what may be published. It seems to me that the President, who is in touch with every department, had better, by proclamation, regulate these matters.[60]

- Representative Dick Morgan of Oklahoma (R), a member of the Judiciary Committee said in its defense: "the very object and intention of this section is to protect the interests of the people" and that "freedom of the press under the Constitution does not mean that one is entitled to absolute freedom to publish what he pleases" when doing so "he injures the public at large."[61]
- Senator Miles Poindexter of Washington (R) said that freedom of the press does not mean that "newspapers must be allowed...to publish anything that they choose to publish, whether it is detrimental to the vital interests of the country or not."[62]

Others highlighted the security of the nation and of the armed forces and how times of war make a difference:

- Representative William Igoe of Missouri (D) pointed out that "the safety of the country comes first."[63]
- Representative Dick Morgan of Oklahoma (R) said that "the object of the bill is not to restrict an American citizen in any right he has under the Constitution" rather "to guard and protect those rights"; it is a war measure and that in time of war "it is necessary sometimes that individual citizens shall be willing to surrender some of the privileges which they have for the sake of the greater good."[64]
- Representative Thaddeus Caraway of Arkansas (D), a committee member, defended the committee and the provision:

> If you are going to compel the young men of this country to offer their lives as a sacrifice and bare their breasts to death in the forefront of battle, if you are going to expose them to all the perils incident of war, why, in the name of God, are you not willing to give them what protection that may come to them by preventing newspapers or anyone else from advising the enemy and giving him information that will make our boys' position more perilous and our country less safe and secure?[65]

- Senator William Stone of Missouri (D) said:

> we may reach a point in times of national peril when, for the protection of the public interests and to safeguard the national welfare, some restraint must be imposed upon what ordinarily we hold to be the freedom of speech and the freedom of the press. We have reached that point now. ...We are at war with some of the most stupendous and puissant powers of the world. When, in the opinion of the Government, it would be unwise, hurtful, perhaps dangerous, to have the secret plans of the Government published to the world it should not be permitted.[66]

- Representative William Rucker of Missouri (D):

> Gentlemen draw finespun theories about the Constitution. ...I say to you that when it comes to protecting those boys who will be dragged from the homes of the patriotic people of this country I would muzzle the press until doomsday, if necessary, rather than sacrifice the blood of one of those boys.[67]

But the provision was defeated. Even an amendment agreed by conferees of both chambers,[68] which narrowed the section to meet particular objections, was stricken out of the bill (defeated in the House and then a second conference returned the bill devoid of the censorship provision). Members' of Congress major argument was that the provision was an abridgement of freedom of speech and the press and therefore unconstitutional:

- Representative Albert Johnson of Washington (R) on the first day the bill was presented said, "The truth of the thing is, that we are going to make an effort to abridge free press and free speech under the guise that it is a war necessity."[69]
- Representative LaGuardia of New York (R) declared:

  > there can be no mistake about the intent and effect of this law. It is absolutely a limitation on the freedom of the press and speech. It is a flagrant and daring violation of the spirit of Article I of the first amendment to the Constitution.[70]

- Representative Issac Siegel of New York (R) proclaimed that the "press-muzzler section, is unconstitutional beyond any doubt."[71]
- Representative James Clark of Missouri (D) said that the First Amendment is the most important part of the constitution, that the principle which underlies the government of the United States is free speech and that the press censorship section "is in flat violation of the Constitution of the United States."[72]
- Senator Hiram Johnson of California (R) claimed that he does "not speak for the metropolitan press" but for the "man who reads and who is entitled to read the truth" and that the Senate should not follow the president into "autocracy" and the "destruction of the very fundamentals of democracy, the very pillars upon which this government of ours rests."[73]
- Representative John McKenzie of Illinois (R) opposed the censorship provision primarily because "the Constitution of our country specifically says in Article I that 'Congress shall make no law... abridging the freedom of speech or of the press'."[74]

Additional arguments were made in opposition to the provision on instrumental lines:

- Representative Melvin Kelly of Pennsylvania (Progressive) argued that "if we desire a united and invincible public opinion in America, we must make sure that we do not prevent knowledge being given to the people who must make up the public opinion."[75]
- Representative James Mann of Illinois (R) argued that "the best way for us to conduct this war is to let people know what is going on. ... If we are defeated on the front, we ought to know it. If we win at the front, we ought to know it."[76]
- Representative William Wood of Indiana (R) asked to consider "that the American people are an independent people, boasting of their

freedom of speech and freedom of the press since this Government was founded, and they will not easily submit to being kept in the dark." He added that Americans "feel that if they are furnishing the money to carry on this war they are entitled to know something of its conduct."[77]

- Representative Martin Madden of Illinois (R) explained that

> what we need is to know every movement of the troops, whether they are being fed properly, whether they are being clothed properly, whether they are being given the accommodations they ought to have in the camp or in the field, and whether the war is being conducted as it should be conducted; whether the men in command are qualified to command, and whether they are conducting their commands with wisdom or with unwisdom. Such information as this ought to be in the possession of the people who fight this war and who pay the bills...the widest latitude should be given to the press to criticize grafts, crooked contracts, extravagance in the conduct of the war, bad management of the Government, excessive expenditures in all lines.

- He also said that

> if we expect the confidence of the people and their enthusiastic support in the conduct of the war, we must take them into the confidence of the Government. ...The Government is made by the people and for the people. ...Censorship to the extent provided for in this section is unjust. It is un-American; it is against freedom; and it is against the liberty for which we are fighting. While we are fighting to establish the democracy of the world, we ought not to do the thing that will establish autocracy in America.[78]

- Senator William Borah of Idaho (R) stated that in the war public opinion must be carried along day to day, month to month and year to year, that the people's confidence must be secured and that there is no "possible way to do it other than to permit the free interchange of opinion upon all questions that concern the interest of the people and the Government." (He added: "Besides, we have no constitutional right to establish a censorship.")[79]

A last-minute personal appeal for the censorship provision was made by President Wilson.[80] On May 31, 1917, Representative Webb, chairman of the House Committee of the Judiciary, read a letter from President Wilson on the House floor, in which Wilson explained that "censorship is absolutely necessary to the public safety" and "for the protection of the Nation."[81] Nevertheless, the provision was defeated in the House by a vote of 184 to 144, with thirty-six Democrats joining the Republicans[82] – an indication that representatives in the House deliberated seriously and did not act according to partisan dictates. A second conference[83] returned the bill devoid of the censorship provision, and it was approved.[84]

Deliberation on the Nonmailability Provision

The nonmailability provision was also seriously debated. Arguments were raised against it, and after undergoing deliberation, the provision was amended.

The provision that was presented on April 30, 1917, to the House by the chairman of the Judiciary Committee, Representative Webb, stated that letters, newspapers and so on "in violation of this act or of treasonable or anarchistic character" are nonmailable.[85] He and Representative Andrew Volstead of Minnesota (R), a member of the committee, gave details on the committee's reasoning process: the original provision that was submitted to the committee would have given "wide power" to the Postmaster General by granting him the authority to deny the use of mails to anyone who might publish a treasonable article. The committee refused to this "for fear that it might work an injustice" and instead gave the postmasters the right to "exclude" treasonable matter, that is, "exclude that particular edition, that particular article."[86] Representative Webb told the House that at first only the adjective "treasonable" was in the bill, but after receiving from the Post Office Department "some mail matter that was so horrible...so anarchistic – that it absolutely compelled the committee...to insert the word 'anarchistic' in the bill."[87] Representative Volstead defended the committee's decision regarding the nonmailability provision:

> We have [these] sort of statute[s] all over this country. There is nothing drastic about that; every State has statutes to protect assaults upon the character of its citizens. Why should we not pass like statutes to protect the Nation and its defenders. When our boys are out in the trenches fighting...it seems to me we ought not to hesitate to pass laws to protect them against any insidious foe at home.[88]

There was considerable attention to the meaning of the words "anarchistic" and "treasonable". Representative Webb quoted the definition of "anarchism" from the dictionary, and a discussion developed that referred also to nihilism and the views of Tolstoy and Ralph Waldo Emerson.[89] Representative Henry Cooper of Wisconsin (R) said that enacting the word "anarchism" into the law "without some qualifying adjective" would be "absolutely opposed to all our theory of free discussion."[90] Representative James Mann of Illinois (R) voiced concern in relation to the term "treasonable" saying that

> a whole lot of people here and elsewhere seem to think that if a man does not agree with you he is a traitor and is guilty of treasonable utterances. ...The very principles of our Government, the basis upon which we founded our liberty, is the right of people to differ with them in opinion. Then the majority is supposed to have control of the Government, but not to oppress those who differ with them in opinion.[91]

A central argument against the nonmailability provision concerned concentrating power with the Postmaster General. Representative William Stafford of Wisconsin (R) told the members of the House

> that in the stress of war we should not confer upon any executive authority such absolute power that he may exercise it to the detriment of the people in the use of the mails or in the exercise of the privilege of the press. There is no occasion for us to confer upon the Postmaster General this authority that would enable him to exercise such power. We have never heretofore...conferred such autocratic power upon the Postmaster General.[92]

Representative Meyer London of New York (Socialist) said that "there is nothing more oppressive in the world than a democracy gone mad than a democracy which has surrendered its rights to an individual [the postmaster]."[93] He added another argument: that the provision is "an attack on the liberties of the little fellow, of the helpless man, of the defenseless man," therefore while he was "entirely willing to vote for every measure that will guard the military and naval secrets of the country," he was not willing to "surrender any of the liberties of the humblest citizen of the United States."[94]

Other arguments in opposition to nonmailability involved the broad authority in exclusion of mails and distinguishing between legitimate and illegitimate publications: Senator Albert Cummins of Iowa (R) opposed broadening "judgment or discretion of the Post Office Department so as to take in practically everything that relates to our political, social and industrial life."[95] Senator Charles Thomas of Colorado (D) agreed that certain matters should not got through the mails, but the provision might

> inflict a far greater injury upon a hundred million people by giving power to the Post Office Department that...will be utilized, is such a way as to produce a far greater evil than the evil which is sought to be prevented.[96]

Senator William Borah of Idaho (R) also agreed that "certain kinds of material...ought not to go through the mails" but cautioned that

> it is perfectly useless to talk about stopping the dissemination and interchange of thought and views upon these questions among the people of the United States, and the more you dam up the stream the more liable you are to have a flood when it breaks over.[97]

Arguments were made in support of a non-mailabililty provision. Senator Thomas Sterling of South Dakota (R) focused his reasoning on the common good and asked rhetorically: "Is it proper or reasonable that Congress having, in the public interest, and for the national safety...declared certain acts to be crimes against the United States should at the same time proceed to declare that the mails over which it has control shall not be used to aid in the commission of such crimes?" And "why should [the Government] not exercise its power in the interests of national safety and deny the use of the mails to the furtherance of any treacherous scheme which in any way imperils that safety?"[98]

Senator Paul Husting of Wisconsin (D) addressed the argument that war makes a difference:

> It has been said here that these are extraordinary measures. They are extraordinary measures, and I would not support them as peace measures, but we are now in extraordinary times. This is an extraordinary period...and it would seem that some extraordinary remedies are necessary if we want to maintain the integrity and the safety of this Nation.[99]

Although motions to strike out the provision were defeated,[100] as a result of the congressional deliberation, the provision was meaningfully amended. First, as noted earlier, the House Judiciary Committee narrowed the Postmaster General's authority from "denying" the use of mails to people, to "excluding" anarchistic and treasonable matter. More importantly, Congress eventually adopted an amendment offered by Senator Thomas Hardwick of Georgia (D) that substituted the phrase "treasonable or anarchistic" with "matter advocating or urging treason, insurrection or forcible resistance to any law of the United States."[101] Therefore, statements of treasonable or anarchistic character would not be unlawful; only statements expressing advocacy of treason would be illegal.[102] In offering the amendment, Senator Hardwick explained that

> in conferring upon executive officers arbitrary power it is most important...that the power should be as sharply limited and as clearly defined as human language can limit and define it. The words...anarchistic or treasonable...are words in which there is large room for construction. Something that would not be accounted treason under the principles of law applicable to this question might be said

> to be, with some show of plausibility and reason, of a treasonable character.[103]

Throughout the congressional deliberations on the Espionage bill, congressmen produced information and sought out to discover information, so that they could examine and use it for reasoning on the merits of the bill. In addition to the examples given above in relation to the arguments presented pro and con the different provisions, it is worthy to point out the following deliberative moments as well:

- When introducing the bill to the House, Representative Webb not only set about giving information, for example, concerning the Judiciary Committee's work, he also gave information by answering questions of several representatives. Representative Horace Towner of Iowa (R), for instance, asked what legislation already exists regarding the first section of the bill and Webb presented a pamphlet (prepared by the Department of Justice) to the House.[104] Representative Richard Austin of Tennessee (R) asked Webb to name newspapers that endorsed the bill, saying specifically, "I am seeking information."[105]
- During the debate on the nonmailability provision, Senator Thomas Walsh of Montana (D) reviewed existing postal laws and regulations.[106]
- While discussing the censorship provision, Senator John Shields of Tennessee (D) quoted legal scholars such as Thomas M. Cooley, and over thirty relevant State constitutional provisions.[107]

Even though the official floor proceedings and debates are the formal form of deliberation, congressmen confessed to informally deliberating when not taking the floor. Representative William Graham of Illinois (R) stated that he had "conversations" with members of the House[108] and Senator Lawrence Sherman of Illinois (R) declared that when absent from the floor, he read the *Congressional Record*, and what he did not hear, he learned from his colleagues who gave him "fairly accurate reports" of what he did not hear.[109]

Floor Debate: Persuasion

As before-mentioned, persuasion involves considering information and arguments on an issue (or reasoning on its merits) and reaching a position. Sometimes, participants may actually change their minds. In the course of reasoning on the merits of the Espionage bill, members of Congress were persuaded.

During the first days of debate on the bill, with respect to the censorship provision, Representative George Graham of Pennsylvania (R) acknowledged that after listening to information and arguments made on the floor and considering the issue, his "own mind has reached the conclusion with respect to this section...to move to strike [it] out."[110] A couple of days later he recommended that a member in voting should "confine his thought and attention" to the question "has the discussion that has taken place on the floor and my own thought convinced me."[111] Another member of the House, Representative Clarence Miller of Minnesota (R) also admitted to being persuaded:

> "Mr. Speaker, I frankly confess that for some days after I began the study of the bill I was in some doubt as to whether or not I should vote for this fourth section. However, after I had indulged in a somewhat more mature investigation and thought upon the matter, all doubt was removed" (Miller concluded that it was "dangerous" to "pass a law of this kind").[112]

Senators also confessed to being persuaded. Thus, Senator Oscar Underwood of Alabama (D) admitted to have initially "made a mistake" and after obtaining "information in reference to the bill", after having "full information on the subject", he opposed the bill, and more specifically, the censorship provision (this was on May 11, 1917, approximately three weeks before the House voted down the provision).[113] The following day, Senator Albert Cummins of Iowa (R) let known his change of mind,[114] and Senator Hoke Smith of Georgia (D) did the same, saying that after giving his "most earnest consideration to the question" he will vote against the censorship provision.[115] Two days later Senator Henry Lodge of Massachusetts (R) also took the floor to explain his change of mind.[116]

In sum the Espionage bill was indeed seriously deliberated by members of Congress, the representatives of the people of the United States. Information and arguments were put forward in a collective reasoning process on the merits of the bill and on the greater good, and persuasion took place. Hence the Espionage Act is a democratically legitimate law.

The fact that debate and vote on the Espionage bill were not a partisan matter is a manifestation of the serious deliberation that was conducted on the bill: Democrats as well as Republicans challenged different parts the bill, and Republicans in addition to Democrats argued in its favor.

While the provision that was later used the most to prosecute individuals during the war (Title I section 3) received relatively less attention than others, as indicated the original bill had far more reaching implications vis-à-vis free speech. But, congressmen took the bill under serious consideration, displayed sensitivity to the issue of free speech and narrowed the bill, drafting its provisions as to impair free speech – during war – to a minimum they thought was necessary for the safety of nation.

The Sedition Act

The Sedition Act further restricted freedom of speech during war. The Sedition Act was deliberated by Congress in 1918 since on the floor, arguments were made pro and con, information was presented and amendments were put in the bill; but, the *extent* and *quality* of the deliberation on the bill were not the same as in 1917, when Congress deliberated the Espionage Act: public hearings were not held at a congressional committee, the House scantily deliberated the pending bill, arguments on the floor were only occasionally framed in terms of the common good and sporadically focused on issues of constitutionality and the right of free speech and there is not much evidence of informal deliberation and of persuasion.

Initiative of Sedition Act and Senate Judiciary Committee Defense

As mentioned in Chapter 2, in early spring of 1918, following the verdict of acquittal in *United States v. Hall*, the Department of Justice sought to amend the Espionage Act to clarify that the act prohibited attempts to obstruct recruiting and enlistment, as well as actual obstruction; and speech with intent to obstruct the government's efforts to borrow funds for the war.[117] In March 1918 the House adopted the Justice Department's proposal with little debate, but then the Senate Committee on the Judiciary amended it with significant additions,[118] without hearing oral testimonies.[119] In the words of Senator Thomas Hardwick of Georgia (D):

> [This bill] contains seven substantive propositions, three of which came from the House in the form of a bill that passed there practically without contest, ...[The] amendments that make the bill particularly obnoxious...come from the Senate committee...; the Department of Justice, that framed this bill is not committed...to any such monstrous proposition as those now embodied in [it].[120]

The additions included the prohibition to utter, print, write or publish any disloyal, profane, scurrilous, contemptuous or abusive language about the form of government, or the Constitution, or the soldiers or sailors, or the flag, or the uniform of the Army or Navy of the United States; or any language calculated to bring the government, the Constitution, the soldiers or sailors, or the flag, or the uniform of the Army or Navy of the United States into contempt, scorn, contumely or disrepute; or any language calculated to incite or inflame resistance to any duly constituted Federal or State authority in connection with the prosecution of the war. It also prohibited to advocate, favor, teach, defend or suggest the doing of any of the acts or things enumerated; or by word or act oppose the cause of the United States.[121]

On April 2, 1918, Senator Lee Overman of North Carolina (D), representing the Senate Judiciary Committee, orally reported the bill to the Senate,[122] and in the next couple of days, he and another committee member, Senator Thomas Walsh of Montana (D) gave two explanations in the committee's defense:

1. The legislation was necessary "because of the strange construction which has been given to the espionage act by some Federal courts, ...the most startling of these, and possibly the most notorious, was rendered by the district court for the district of Montana"[123] (*United States v. Hall* – see discussion in Chapter 2). Therefore the proposed bill amended the law "as that no possible means of escape would present themselves to those who might be disposed to assist the cause of our enemies in this war by disloyal and seditious utterances" (and specifically made it a crime to attempt to obstruct, as well as actually obstruct, the recruiting and enlistment service).[124]
2. The Espionage Act did not include a provision "for the punishment of those who through disloyalty or some kindred sentiment might be moved to discountenance investments on the liberty bonds and other securities of the United States."[125] Senator Overman noted that "criminals" who interfered with the sale of liberty loans were put on trial, but some judges have held that they could not be convicted for their anti-liberty bond speeches.[126] As a bond sale was about to begin on April 6, the attorney general and Department of Justice were "very anxious" to have the bill passed by Congress.[127]

It is worthy to note that the Senate Judiciary Committee members who were present voted unanimously for the bill,[128] and unlike in the case of the Espionage Act, those committee members who voted for the bill did not disagree or oppose it at a later stage.

Extent and Quality of Deliberation on the Floor

The extent and quality of deliberation on the Sedition Act by Congress on the floor wasn't as high as the extent and quality of deliberation conducted by Congress a year earlier when it considered the Espionage bill. The deliberation on the Sedition Act differed in numerous ways.

To start with, as opposed to several calls by both members of the House and Senate during the debate on the Espionage Act to reason and deliberate on the common good, only three congressmen made such statements in relation to the Sedition Act, and they were all senators. Two days after the amendment on the bill was reported to the Senate, Senator James Reed of Missouri (D) asserted:

> Mr. President, this bill was only brought to my notice yesterday...I should like to have an opportunity to consider it a little more carefully. With the House bill...no one can, of course, find any fault; but

> the long amendment introduced by the Judiciary Committee...seems to me...rather sweepingly and loosely drawn...Before debating it I should like to examine it further.[129]

Senator Charles Thomas of Colorado (D) agreed:

> I have had no opportunity whatever to examine this bill;...in view of the fact that this is a matter which concerns the liberties...of many of our fellow citizens...we should consider this bill carefully and exhaustively before coming to vote upon it.[130]

The following day Senator Thomas Hardwick of Georgia (D) also appealed for deliberation saying that "in times of war people grow hysterical...even legislative bodies, are not exempt from the contagion of hysteria. It is better to move along slowly; it is better to deliberate about these things."[131] At a later stage in the debate, Senator Hardwick eloquently explained the duty of a congressman:

> [Until policies crystallize into law, it is] the undoubted duty of every Senator and Representative to give the country the best that is in his heart and head and to give the country his independent judgment, based on the best information that he can obtain and the most careful consideration of which he is capable.[132]

No such appeals for deliberation were made by members of the House. In fact, the House only considered the amended bill once, on May 7, 1918, before voting on it. As mentioned earlier, in *Federalist* No. 49 Madison wrote that only public reason "ought to control and regulate the government" and that passions "ought to be controlled and regulated by government."[133] In the case of the House, it seems that in 1918, passions, as opposed to reason, had the upper hand. With the sole exception of the only Socialist member of the 65th Congress, Representative Meyer London of New York, all members of the House who took the floor that day, argued in favor of the bill using emotional and jingoistic expressions. For example, Representative Patrick Norton of North Dakota (R) declared, "In these times, when the blood of our country is being freely given to preserve the glorious institutions of free government handed down to us by the forefathers of the Republic, these selfish, lying demagogues should not be tolerated."[134] Representative Thaddeus Caraway of Arkansas (D) asked, "Shall we be more tender of the civil rights of the disloyal few whom this law will strangle than of the lifeblood of this gallant band of patriotic boys who are dying beyond the seas? I answer, No."[135] He also expressed dismay at opposition to the legislation: "Every time a measure is brought upon this floor that seeks to curb the soap-box orators and throttle the damnable German propaganda in this country they discover that some one's civil rights are violated."[136] Representative Warren Gard of Ohio (D) said that "loose speech should be obliterated" and "there should be a tightening of action toward one thing, and that is...the purpose of obtaining victory for American arms."[137]

All in all, the Senate deliberated the Sedition Act for ten days: six after the amended bill was reported (April 4–April 10) and four more after it returned from a conference of both chambers (April 24–May 4). Taking a closer look at the actual deliberations that the Senate had on the Sedition Act, three reservations can be made as to the extent and quality of the Senate deliberations in the first round:

1. Instead of reasoning on the merits of the proposed legislation, the Senate spent most of its time, literally dozens of hours, debating the meaning of an assortment of words: "calculated," "favor," "resist," "inflame," "incite" and "scurrilous."[138] In a charged and somewhat humorous finale, Senator John Williams of Mississippi (D) stated:

   > The Senate spent 48 hours...trying to make up its mind whether it wanted to put the past participle "calculated" or the past participle "intended" into the bill. The Senate has stood here as part of the national legislative body...tweedledeeing and tweedleduming – camouflaging – and trying to fool one another...you have had [unrestricted debate] about nothing; whether you should say "intended" or whether you should say "calculated,""...Any man in the world might have gone to Bouvier's Law Dictionary and found out the difference between "intended" and "calculated,""...Who cares a cent which one of the two words you put into the statute? I voted to leave "calculated" in because it happened to be in the bill, but would have voted to leave "intended" if "intended" had been in the bill.[139]

   Indeed, one would expect that on such a bill such as the Sedition Act, senators would have been spending more time debating the fundamental questions at stake in regard to the common good, such as free speech and constitutional issues.
2. In Edward Lascher's discussion on standards for assessing the quality of deliberation,[140] he suggests to evaluate arguments in terms of commonly recognized fallacies, such as the ad hominem fallacy, explaining that legislative deliberation could be judged to be of higher quality in instances where debate is absent of attacks on the character of people making arguments. During the first round of Senate debate, there were personal attacks and partisanship snaps, thus indicating to a lower quality of deliberation. For example, a Democratic senator called the Republican press "miserable" and "reptile,"[141] and in another instance, a Republican senator accused a Democrat of making an "insulting imitation" and using "insolent

and opprobrious epithets" directed at him.[142] These sorts of attacks didn't occur during the congressional deliberation on the Espionage Act.

3. Although Bessette correctly points out that low attendance on the floor does not necessarily mean that there isn't any deliberation (as members of Congress are informed and influenced by what is said on the floor by other means),[143] unlike the case of the Espionage Act, there was one occasion, on April 5, 1918, when there wasn't even a quorum present. The secretary called the roll and only thirty-six senators answered.[144] After calling the names of the absent senators, no more than forty-one senators answered the roll call, and the Sergeant at Arms was directed to request the attendance of absent members. Only after the Sergeant at Arms executed the order of the Senate was there a quorum present and the proceedings continued.[145]

Information and Arguments

Having examined to this point the shortcomings of deliberation on the floor, it deserves to balance the assessment of deliberation (in effect, Senate deliberation) with a review of three essential elements of deliberation – information, arguments and persuasion.

One major argument for those who supported the bill concerned containing law and order at a period when mobs took to lynching people who opposed the war. (That is to say, these senators supported abridging free speech, in fact punishing those who spoke freely, in order to prevent violence). While reporting the amended bill to the Senate, Senator Lee Overman of North Carolina (D) said:

> The people of this country are taking the law in their own hand on the ground that Congress is not doing its duty. In numerous cases it is said that men are being mobbed all over the country because Congress does not pass laws under which the guilty ones can be adequately punished.[146]

In the following days several senators reiterated this theme. For example: Senator William Borah of Idaho (R) said, "If we do not do our duty here, the impulses of loyal men and women will seek justice in rougher ways... already...citizens are taking the law into their own hands...";[147] Senator Henry Myers of Montana (D) contained that one of the principle objects of the bill was "to prevent mob law" and that "There is going to be more of mob law and lawlessness and lynching in this country unless we speedily enact a measure of this kind";[148] and Senator Knute Nelson of Minnesota (R) agreed that the legislation's object is to

> prevent men from making utterances of a kind that will breed riot, breach of the peace, and disorder, and lead to violence....It is needed

> for the good of the American people, for our own good, in order to preserve law and order.[149]

A supporting argument was that legislation was needed to attack and punish disloyalty. Senator Henry Myers of Montana (D) came "to the rescue...of the language of the committee amendment to the pending bill," explaining that he "[favors] hitting deviltry and disloyalty and mischief in this critical crisis just as hard as we can hit them. I believe in making this bill just as comprehensive and drastic as it may legitimately be made."[150] He added that the object of the bill was to remove all doubt that there is sufficient law for the punishment of utterances of disloyal and traitorous people in the country and "administer proper punishment, drastic punishment, to that class of creatures who are carrying on their insidious, loathsome, poisonous, disloyal, and traitorous work in this country."[151] Senator John Shields of Tennessee (D) agreed that the object of the bill "is to punish these men who are now lurking in every city and infesting every rural community of this country...and sowing the seeds of murder, sedition, and treason."[152] His colleague from Tennessee, Senator Kenneth McKellar (D) concurred that the object and purpose of the bill is to punish the disloyal, that it is "high time" to take steps to "stamp out" disloyalty.[153]

Some senators disagreed that the bill was needed or intended to prevent violence or punish disloyalty. Senator James Reed of Missouri (D) told his companions:

> I do not feel that this country is rotten and reeking with German sympathizers. I do not believe that condition is general. ...I believe, on the contrary, that all the history of this world does not furnish an example of such loyalty, such deathless love of country, as that which animates the hearts of the American people. ...Mothers have given up their sons with a sacrifice unexampled in history. ...There has been no general slacking.[154]

Senator Henry Lodge of Massachusetts (R) commented that the "bill will not touch a single spy or a single German agent" since "The spies or agents do not go around uttering, publishing, and writing."[155] Senator Warren Harding of Ohio (R) argued "that the real – in fact, practically the only – object of this section is to get some men call I.W.W.'s, who are operating in a few of the Northwestern States"[156] and added that he "[disliked] to be confronted by a situation in which in the name of patriotism we are asked to jeopardize the fundamental rights and liberties of 100,000,000 American people in order to meet a situation in a few Northwestern States."[157]

To these arguments against the Sedition Act a few senators added an additional utilitarian claim: that the Sedition Act will bring about disunity in the nation while unity is needed to win the war. Senator Hiram Johnson of California (R) explained:

> The purpose of those of us who oppose this legislation is to prevent... disunion among our people, discontent among those behind the lines, to unite...all our people in a homogeneous entity for the success of the war. ...Measures such as this do not unite a people; they breed discontent; they cause suspicion to stalk through the land.[158]

Senator Joseph France of Maryland (R) corrected the senators' "fallacy":

> This proposed legislation arises from a total misconception of the very nature of modern war. ...War is no longer a matter of armies, it is a matter of whole nations, and we can not win this war with one, two, three, or four million men in France. We can only win it by calling into the combat all the great resources of the American people. We can only win it by a great organized and united nation. I am opposed to this legislation, because I believe it makes not for unity but for disorganization and for disintegration. ...I do not think that the voice of the people, of the sovereign people of the Republic, should be silenced at this time when the winning of the war depends...upon the masses of the sovereign people all over the Republic.[159]

However, the underlying line of reasoning in the Senate against the Sedition Act was that it was a wrong, unnecessary abridgement of free speech, as well as unconstitutional. Following are some examples of arguments made in opposition to the bill on these grounds:

- Senator Hiram Johnson of California (R) declared:

  > that this is not a bill for the punishment of disloyalty or treason, but it is a bill to suppress the freedom of the press in the United States of America, and to prevent any man, no matter who he is, from indulging in fair and decent expression, or voicing legitimate criticism concerning the present Government, the present administration, or any department in respect to the war.[160]

- Senator Thomas Hardwick of Georgia (D) said:

  > [C]ertain provisions in this law may quite probably be construed to deny a great many of the fundamental rights of free speech to people...who have a right to differ with anybody on earth they please about what policy this Government shall adopt, or what plan it shall pursue, or what methods it may take, either in prosecution of this war or in the conclusion of a peace.[161]

- He added:

> We are in this war. We ought to prosecute it vigorously, effectively, with every power of mind and body and heart and soul. ... But it is by no means necessary...in the proper execution of the war to either sacrifice or abridge American rights or American liberties. ...If we are fighting freedom's battles, let us fight in a cause worthy of freedom. Let us preserve the ancient and immemorial rights of freemen.[162]

- He opposed the bill "as wholly unnecessary and as utterly violative of the constitutional guaranty of freedom of speech and freedom of press."[163]
- Senator Jacob Gallinger of New Hampshire (R) and Senator Lawrence Sherman of Illinois (R) asked rhetorically how will criticism of the form of government be made with the committee's amendment prohibiting contemptuous, or abusive language about the form of government;[164] Senator Sherman added that "Congress has no power to regulate freedom of speech."[165]

There was also concern that it was too broad. Senator Gilbert Hitchcock of Nebraska (D), for instance, asked if advocates of women suffrage, who utter, print, write and publish language calculated "to bring the form of government or Constitution of the United States into disrepute" would be in violation of the law.[166] Others questioned the legality of remarks made in the past in opposition to the war.[167]

The bill's supporters disagreed and explained that the bill was not in fact an abridgement of free speech; it allows for criticism of the government and it is constitutional. Senator Albert Fall of New Mexico (R) explained that the wording of the bill would not prevent criticism,

> But the law proposed is plain, that anyone using language...to incite resistance to the enforcement of a law...in the prosecution of this war, should be guilty. ...That is what liberty of the press and of free speech means. The liberty of speech and liberty of the press guaranteed under the Constitution of the United States does not mean the license of the bolsheviki or of the Mexican bandit character to resist the operation of a law.[168]

Senator William Borah of Idaho (R) in exchanges with other senators made clear that the bill allows to demand changes to the Constitution (as long as they are not advocated in "disloyal, profane, scurrilous, or abusive language"); allows the advocacy of women suffrage (as "it does not affect the form of government in any way, shape or form; if anything, it accentuates and strengthens the form of government from the standpoint of a wider basis for the electorate"); even allows discussion on different forms of government for the United States ("a presentation of a man's view in a proper way, as to his difference of opinion as to the worth of different forms of government, or as to a change in the Constitution... would not come within the purview of the law at all."); and allows criticism of the administration ("[the law does not all touch] the proposition of discussing the competency or the incompetency of an administration, the policy or the wisdom or the unwisdom of an administration, ...the inefficiency of an administration", or the incompetency or corruption of an officer).[169]

Advocates of the bill strengthened their case by arguing that it is a unique war measure. Senator Borah asserted, "We would not pass this law in peace, but I believe it is demanded now."[170] Senator Miles Poindexter of Washington (R) justified the legislation as "a product of the times. Many of the things that are proposed to be punished...are of trivial public importance in times of peace; but the bill ought to be judged by its application to the emergency that confronts this country."[171] Representative Warren Gard of Ohio (D), a member of the House Committee on the Judiciary and a member of the conference committee, explained that the bill is "a necessary extension in time of war, and time of war only, to punish speech and act which have for their purpose the giving of aid to the enemy."[172]

Throughout the debate, champions and opponents of the bill supported their arguments with information: court rulings acquitting defendants in violation of the Espionage Act,[173] petitions and memorials from state legislatures,[174] newspaper articles and editorials,[175] letters from the Department of Justice,[176] works of legal scholars,[177] past Supreme Court rulings[178] and even dictionary and encyclopedia definitions of words.[179]

One issue that caused some serious debate concerned an amendment to the bill offered by Senator Joseph France of Maryland (R): "That nothing in this act shall be construed as limiting the liberty or impairing the right of any individual to publish or speak what is true, with good motives and for justifiable ends."[180] Senator Lee Overman of North Carolina (D) immediately objected, arguing that if it were adopted "it would be difficult for any jury in the world to convict. ...The question under this bill is not whether a man has spoken words which are true or false; but the whole basis of the bill is disloyalty; it is all founded on that."[181] The amendment was rejected.[182] The following day Senator France offered it again and it was adopted,[183] but then the conference committee decided to strike it out.[184] Senator Hiram Johnson of California (R) retorted:

> You may assert that this particular bill...is absolutely essential for this crisis;...but...it is equally essential for the preservation of free speech in this Nation...that we preserve...the right of any man to speak truth with good motives and for justifiable ends...what a travesty...today is presented when the Congress of the United States refuses to permit the people of the Union to speak what is true, with good motives and for justifiable ends.[185]

Senator Overman replied that that is not the case, and he explained the reasons for the conferees striking out the amendment by means of a letter from Special Assistant Attorney General John Lord O'Brian, which stated that "dangerous propaganda...on its face shows a motive entirely legitimate...motives prompting propaganda are irrelevant" and therefore the proposed amendment "would very seriously interfere with the successful prosecution of cases" arising under the Act.[186] Though the amendment was debated some more, it was not adopted and stayed out of the Act.[187]

Persuasion

Evidence on persuasion during deliberations on the Sedition Act is less noticeable than that on the Espionage Act, although as far as persuasion is defined as considering information and arguments on an issue and reaching a position, and not only as changing minds, there are some instances demonstrating the former. On April 9, 1918, Senator Hiram Johnson of California (R) declared, "last week...I called attention to the specific language embraced within the committee amendment," and after collecting and considering information "upon reflection, I am confirmed in the views I then expressed" (in opposition to the bill).[188] Senator Thomas Hardwick of Georgia (D) also stated that some amendments the Senate has made improved the bill and he "considered very carefully the question as to whether the improvements were so great as to authorize a man...to support the bill" yet he regretted to say that in his "judgment" that was not the case.[189]

To sum, the Sedition Act was deliberated by Congress, but because the extent and quality of congressional deliberations were intermediate, it was only a moderately democratic legitimate law. Comparing congressional deliberations on both acts illustrates how deliberations were different and accordingly how the Sedition Act was not as democratically legitimate as the Espionage Act: in the case of the Sedition Act, public hearings were not held at a congressional committee, the House scantily deliberated the pending bill, arguments in both chambers were only occasionally framed in terms of the common good while an underlying current in the arguments that were advanced was that of an unreflective and war-frenzied public voice and there were instances of personal attacks on those who took the floor. With regard to the issue of partisanship, as opposed to deliberation on the Espionage Act, the total effect of deliberation is mixed: on the one hand, as illustrated above, for the most part only two Democrats argued against the bill, Senators Hardwick and Reed, and on May 4, 1917, they voted nay, along with twenty-four Republicans. Not much in favor of serious deliberation devoid of party influence. On the other hand, numerous Republican senators supported the bill and out of the forty-eight Senators who voted yea, ten were Republicans.[190]

The Sedition Act was repealed in March 1921 with the passage of a House Joint Resolution declaring that certain acts of Congress, joint resolutions and proclamations shall be construed as if the war had ended.[191] This House Joint Resolution itself was also deliberated by Congress (and has its own legislative history).[192] A congressional committee deliberated on it, and congressmen presented information and made arguments regarding its merits in relation to the public good (e.g., "it is a most extraordinary situation that here, two years after actual war has ceased...we have remaining in full force and effect all of the war laws, with their vey onerous and oppressive provisions"[193]). A few congressmen inquired specifically into the effect it would have on the Espionage Act and one congressman, Representative Thomas McKeown of Oklahoma (D), took the floor to voice opposition saying he does not want to "repeal anything" that would permit "using language that would tend to cause insurrection against our government" and bring the government "into contempt...as was done before the war by these soap-box orators."[194] Representative Warren Gard of Ohio (D), a member of the House Judiciary Committee answered:

> I am decidedly in favor of all elements of free speech and that of free press, and I do not consider that the so-called soap-box orator in this country has been injurious...it is far more injurious to the body politic to attempt to muzzle or prevent speech.[195]

Representative Andrew Volstead of Minnesota (R), chairman of the House Judiciary Committee, made clear that "the amendment to the espionage act, with reference to seditious language" would be repealed.[196] On March 1, 1921, Representative Volstead laid the House Joint Resolution before the House, with Senate amendments, one of them being a provision specifically providing that the Sedition Act be repealed and the language of Title 1 section 3 of the Espionage Act be revived,[197] and it was agreed to.[198]

Notes

1 The forthcoming analysis of congressional deliberation, as well those in Chapters 5 and 7, is based predominantly on primary sources, specifically official documents – hearings before the House and Senate committees and subcommittees, and the *Congressional Record*, which is a word-for-word account of the floor proceedings and debates of the House of Representatives and Senate.

2 65th Congress, 1st Session, *Congressional Record – House*, Vol. 55, 128, April 2, 1917.

3 Espionage and Interference with Neutrality, *Hearings Before the Committee on the Judiciary, House of Representatives, 65th Congress 1st Session on H.R. 291: April 9 and 12, 1917* (Washington: Government Printing Office, 1917). (Hereafter cited April 1917 Public House Hearings.)

4 Representative Webb, Revision and Strengthening of Espionage, Neutrality, Passport and Shipping Regulations, *Hearings Before the Committee on the*

Judiciary, House of Representatives: April 10, 1917 (unpublished hearings) reprinted in *Civil Liberties in Wartime: Legislative Histories of the Espionage Act of 1917 and the Sedition Act of 1918*, Ed. William H. Manz (Buffalo: William S. Hein & Co., 2007). (Hereafter cited April 1917 Closed House Hearings.)

5 April 1917 Closed House Hearings.

6 April 1917 Public House Hearings; David M. Rabban, *Free Speech in Its Forgotten Years* (New York: Cambridge University Press, 1997), 255.

7 April 1917 Public House Hearings, 6.

8 Rev. R.W. Houge of Baltimore, April 1917 Public House Hearings, 68.

9 April 1917 Closed House Hearings.

10 Ida M. Waters, April 1917 Public House Hearings, 4–5.

11 Mrs. Glendower Evans of Boston and Rev. R.W. Houge of Baltimore, April 1917 Public House Hearings, 25–29 and 74–75.

12 Jane Adams of Chicago, president of the Women's Peace Party of America, April 1917 Public House Hearings, 50–51.

13 Arthur Holder, legislative representative of the American Federation of Labor, April 1917 Public House Hearings, 55–56.

14 Charles T. Hallinan, representing the American Union Against Militarism, April 1917 Public House Hearings, 44.

15 April 1917 Public House Hearings, 37, 43.

16 April 1917 Public House Hearings, 39–41.

17 April 1917 Public House Hearings, 39.

18 April 1917 Public House Hearings, 41–42.

19 April 1917 Public House Hearings, 4.

20 April 1917 Public House Hearings, 56.

21 Only if that is their intent, and it causes disaffection, then they would come under the provision, April 1917 Closed House Hearings.

22 April 1917 Closed House Hearings.

23 April 1917 Closed House Hearings. Quoted also in Geoffrey R. Stone, *Perilous Times: Free Speech in Wartime from the Sedition Act of 1798 to the War on Terrorism* (New York: W.W. Norton & Company, 2004), 147.

24 Professor Horace A. Eaton, April 1917 Public House Hearings, 11.

25 Professor William I. Hull, April 1917 Public House Hearings, 77.

26 Arthur Holder, legislative representative of the American Federation of Labor, April 1917 Public House Hearings, 53, 56.

27 April 1917 Public House Hearings, 53–54.

28 John Reed of the Metropolitan Magazine, April 1917 Public House Hearings, 65.

29 April 1917 Public House Hearings, 38–39.

30 April 1917 Public House Hearings, 12.

31 April 1917 Public House Hearings, 71–72.

32 April 1917 Public House Hearings, 80–81.

33 April 1917 Public House Hearings, 81.

34 65th Congress, 1st Session, *Congressional Record – House*, Vol. 55, 1149, April 25, 1917.

35 65th Congress, 1st Session, *Congressional Record – House*, Vol. 55, 1594, April 30, 1917.

36 65th Congress, 1st Session, *Congressional Record – House*, Vol. 55, 1594, April 30, 1917.

37 65th Congress, 1st Session, *Congressional Record – House*, Vol. 55, 1594–1595, April 30, 1917.

38 The House deliberated on the bill on April 30, 1917, on May 2–4, 1917 and on May 30–31, 1917; the Senate deliberated on May 5, 1917, on May 9–12, 1917, and on May 14, 1917. The measure passed on June 5, 1917.

39 65th Congress, 1st Session, *Congressional Record – House*, Vol. 55, 1590, April 30, 1917.
40 65th Congress, 1st Session, *Congressional Record – House*, Vol. 55, 1700, May 2, 1917.
41 65th Congress, 1st Session, *Congressional Record – House*, Vol. 55, 1706, May 2, 1917.
42 65th Congress, 1st Session, *Congressional Record – Senate*, Vol. 55, 2116, May 11, 1917.
43 65th Congress, 1st Session, *Congressional Record – Senate*, Vol. 55, 2063, May 10, 1917.
44 65th Congress, 1st Session, *Congressional Record – House*, Vol. 55, 1599, April 30, 1917.
45 65th Congress, 1st Session, *Congressional Record – House*, Vol. 55, 1590–1591, April 30, 1917.
46 65th Congress, 1st Session, *Congressional Record – House*, Vol. 55, 1592, April 30, 1917.
47 See also Harold Edgar and Benno C. Schmidt, "The Espionage Statutes and Publication of Defense Information," *Columbia Law Review* 73 (May 1973): 959; Thomas F. Carroll, "Freedom of Speech and of the Press in War Time: The Espionage Act," *Michigan Law Review* 17 (June, 1919): 624–625; and Rabban, 250–251.
48 65th Congress, 1st Session, *Congressional Record – House*, Vol. 55, 1750–1751, May 3, 1917.
49 65th Congress, 1st Session, *Congressional Record – Senate*, Vol. 55, 2005, May 9, 1917.
50 65th Congress, 1st Session, *Congressional Record – Senate*, Vol. 55, 2004, May 9, 1917
51 65th Congress, 1st Session, *Congressional Record – Senate*, Vol. 55, 2118–2119, May 11, 1917.
52 65th Congress, 1st Session, *Congressional Record – House*, Vol. 55, 1712, May 2, 1917.
53 65th Congress, 1st Session, *Congressional Record – House*, Vol. 55, 1715, May 2, 1917.
54 65th Congress, 1st Session, *Congressional Record – House*, Vol. 55, 1751, May 3, 1917.
55 65th Congress, 1st Session, *Congressional Record – House*, Vol. 55, 1704, May 2, 1917.
56 65th Congress, 1st Session, *Congressional Record – House*, Vol. 55, 1601, April 30, 1917.
57 65th Congress, 1st Session, *Congressional Record – Senate*, Vol. 55, 2072, May 10, 1917.
58 65th Congress, 1st Session, *Congressional Record – House*, Vol. 55, 1818, May 4, 1917.
59 65th Congress, 1st Session, *Congressional Record – House*, Vol. 55, 1701–1702, May 2, 1917.
60 65th Congress, 1st Session, *Congressional Record – House*, Vol. 55, 1605, April 30, 1917.
61 65th Congress, 1st Session, *Congressional Record – House*, Vol. 55, 1808–1809, May 4, 1917.
62 65th Congress, 1st Session, *Congressional Record – Senate*, Vol. 55, 2118, May 11, 1917.
63 65th Congress, 1st Session, *Congressional Record – House*, Vol. 55, 1602, April 30, 1917.
64 65th Congress, 1st Session, *Congressional Record – House*, Vol. 55, 1695, May 2, 1917.

65 65th Congress, 1st Session, *Congressional Record – House*, Vol. 55, 1770, May 3, 1917.
66 65th Congress, 1st Session, *Congressional Record – Senate*, Vol. 55, 2102, May 11, 1917.
67 65th Congress, 1st Session, *Congressional Record – House*, Vol. 55, 3139, May 30, 1917.
68 In the U.S. Congress, reconciliation of differences between the House of Representatives and the Senate regarding an important bill is conducted by a temporary working group –a "conference committee" –consisting of members from both chambers. See Malcom E. Jewell and Samuel C. Paterson, *The Legislative Process in the United States*. 3rd ed. (New York: Random House, 1977), 435.
69 65th Congress, 1st Session, *Congressional Record – House*, Vol. 55, 1604, April 30, 1917.
70 65th Congress, 1st Session, *Congressional Record – House*, Vol. 55, 1700, May 2, 1917.
71 65th Congress, 1st Session, *Congressional Record – House*, Vol. 55, 1705, May 2, 1917.
72 65th Congress, 1st Session, *Congressional Record – House*, Vol. 55, 1764, May 3, 1917.
73 65th Congress, 1st Session, *Congressional Record – Senate*, Vol. 55, 2097, May 11, 1917.
74 65th Congress, 1st Session, *Congressional Record – House*, Vol. 55, 3133, May 31, 1917.
75 65th Congress, 1st Session, *Congressional Record – House*, Vol. 55, 1769, May 3, 1917.
76 65th Congress, 1st Session, *Congressional Record – House*, Vol. 55, 1766, May 3, 1917.
77 65th Congress, 1st Session, *Congressional Record – House*, Vol. 55, 1773, May 3, 1917.
78 65th Congress, 1st Session, *Congressional Record – House*, Vol. 55, 1773, May 3, 1917.
79 65th Congress, 1st Session, *Congressional Record – Senate*, Vol. 55, 2120, May 11, 1917.
80 Bessette acknowledged the contribution presidents have made to congressional deliberations, including "direct deliberative methods," such as formal messages to Congress. Joseph M. Bessette, *The Mild Voice of Reason: Deliberative Democracy & American National Government* (Chicago: The University of Chicago Press, 1994), 193–194, 182.
81 65th Congress, 1st Session, *Congressional Record – House*, Vol. 55, 3144, May 31, 1917.
82 65th Congress, 1st Session, *Congressional Record – House*, Vol. 55, 3144–3145, May 31, 1917.
83 As mentioned in ft. 68, in the U.S. Congress, reconciliation of differences between the House of Representatives and the Senate regarding an important bill is conducted by a temporary working group –a "conference committee" –consisting of members from both chambers.
84 65th Congress, 1st Session, *Congressional Record – Senate*, Vol. 55, 3259–3264, June 5, 1917; Edgar and Schmidt, 965
85 65th Congress, 1st Session, *Congressional Record – House*, Vol. 55, 1595, April 30, 1917.
86 65th Congress, 1st Session, *Congressional Record – House*, Vol. 55, 1607, April 30, 1917.
87 65th Congress, 1st Session, *Congressional Record – House*, Vol. 55, 1595, April 30, 1917. "Anarchistic" mail matter was read to the House, but

members agreed to keep it out of the *Congressional Record* so that it would not "go over the country."

88 65th Congress, 1st Session, *Congressional Record – House*, Vol. 55, 1607, April 30, 1917.

89 65th Congress, 1st Session, *Congressional Record – House*, Vol. 55, 1595–1596, April 30, 1917. See also 65th Congress, 1st Session, *Congressional Record – House*, Vol. 55, 1779–1780, May 3, 1917, and 1820–1824, May 4, 1917.

90 65th Congress, 1st Session, *Congressional Record – House*, Vol. 55, 1596, April 30, 1917.

91 65th Congress, 1st Session, *Congressional Record – House*, Vol. 55, 1822, May 4, 1917.

92 65th Congress, 1st Session, *Congressional Record – House*, Vol. 55, 1836, May 4, 1917.

93 65th Congress, 1st Session, *Congressional Record – House*, Vol. 55, 1779, May 3, 1917.

94 65th Congress, 1st Session, *Congressional Record – House*, Vol. 55, 1780, May 3, 1917.

95 65th Congress, 1st Session, *Congressional Record – Senate*, Vol. 55, 1871, May 5, 1917.

96 65th Congress, 1st Session, *Congressional Record – Senate*, Vol. 55, 2062, May 10, 1917.

97 65th Congress, 1st Session, *Congressional Record – Senate*, Vol. 55, 2062, May 10, 1917; see also 1869, May 5, 1917.

98 65th Congress, 1st Session, *Congressional Record – Senate*, Vol. 55, 2063, May 10, 1917.

99 65th Congress, 1st Session, *Congressional Record – Senate*, Vol. 55, 2087, May 11, 1917.

100 For example see, 65th Congress, 1st Session, *Congressional Record – Senate*, Vol. 55, 2072, May 10, 1917.

101 65th Congress, 1st Session, *Congressional Record – Senate*, Vol. 55, 2056, May 10, 1917; Conference Report, 65th Congress, 1st Session, *Congressional Record – House*, Vol. 55, 3129, May 31, 1917, and 65th Congress, 1st Session, *Congressional Record – Senate*, Vol. 55, 3263, June 5, 1917.

102 Stone, 150.

103 65th Congress, 1st Session, *Congressional Record – Senate*, Vol. 55, 2056, May 10, 1917.

104 65th Congress, 1st Session, *Congressional Record – House*, Vol. 55, 1591, April 30, 1917. See also the rest of the discussion on April 30, 1917, especially 1591–1596.

105 65th Congress, 1st Session, *Congressional Record – House*, Vol. 55, 1714, May 2, 1917.

106 65th Congress, 1st Session, *Congressional Record – Senate*, Vol. 55, 2069, May 10, 1917.

107 65th Congress, 1st Session, *Congressional Record – Senate*, Vol. 55, 2262–2264, May 14, 1917.

108 65th Congress, 1st Session, *Congressional Record – House*, Vol. 55, 1705, May 2, 1917.

109 65th Congress, 1st Session, *Congressional Record – Senate*, Vol. 55, 2067, May 10, 1917.

110 65th Congress, 1st Session, *Congressional Record – House*, Vol. 55, 1719, May 2, 1917.

111 65th Congress, 1st Session, *Congressional Record – House*, Vol. 55, 1808, May 4, 1917.

112 65th Congress, 1st Session, *Congressional Record – House*, Vol. 55, 1778, May 3, 1917.

113 65th Congress, 1st Session, *Congressional Record – Senate*, Vol. 55, 2116, May 11, 1917.

114 65th Congress, 1st Session, *Congressional Record – Senate*, Vol. 55, 2164–2165, May 12, 1917.

115 65th Congress, 1st Session, *Congressional Record – Senate*, Vol. 55, 2165, May 12, 1917.

116 65th Congress, 1st Session, *Congressional Record – Senate*, Vol. 55, 2262, May 14, 1917.

117 Stone, 184; Statements of Senator Thomas Hardwick, 65th Congress, 2nd Session, *Congressional Record – Senate*, Vol. 56, 4639–4640, April 5, 1918.

118 Stone, 185; Statements of Senator Thomas Hardwick of Georgia (D), 65th Congress, 2nd Session, *Congressional Record – Senate*, Vol. 56, 4639–4640, April 5, 1918. See also statements of Senator James Reed of Missouri (D) 65th Congress, 2nd Session, *Congressional Record – Senate*, Vol. 56, 4838, April 9, 1918.

119 There is no evidence to support that testimony was heard – neither in the *Congressional Record* nor in scholarly works.

120 65th Congress, 2nd Session, *Congressional Record – Senate*, Vol. 56, 4639–4640, April 5, 1918. Earlier in the debate, Senator Hardwick said that "as this legislation passed the House it did not contain anything that was seriously offensive or that could be used to either mistreat or abuse some of our people if they happened to have honest differences of opinion." See 65th Congress, 2nd Session, *Congressional Record – Senate*, Vol. 56, 4637, April 5, 1918. On April 9th, Senator James Reed of Missouri (D) stated that the Attorney General's office, after discovering certain legal difficulties in the Espionage Act, prepared a bill that was passed by the House, but amendments were made by the Senate committee that "are outside the purpose of the Attorney General." See 65th Congress, 2nd Session, *Congressional Record – Senate*, Vol. 56, 4838, April 9, 1918.

121 65th Congress, 2nd Session, *Congressional Record – Senate*, Vol. 56, 4426, April 2, 1918.

122 There isn't any information in the Congressional Record on a written report submitted by the Senate Committee on the Judiciary (earlier the bill was reported to the House by the House Committee on the Judiciary, accompanied by a written report –H. Rept. 250). See 65th Congress, 2nd Session, *Congressional Record – Appendix and Index*, Vol. 56, "H.R. 8753."

123 65th Congress, 2nd Session, *Congressional Record – Senate*, Vol. 56, 4559, April 4, 1918.

124 65th Congress, 2nd Session, *Congressional Record – Senate*, Vol. 56, 4560, April 4, 1918. Part of the bill was in fact a copy of an act of the Legislature of Montana passed after the decision in *United States v. Hall*. See 65th Congress, 2nd Session, *Congressional Record – Senate*, Vol. 56, 4632, and 4646 April 5, 1918.

125 65th Congress, 2nd Session, *Congressional Record – Senate*, Vol. 56, 4559, April 4, 1918.

126 65th Congress, 2nd Session, *Congressional Record – Senate*, Vol. 56, 4526, April 3, 1918.

127 65th Congress, 2nd Session, *Congressional Record – Senate*, Vol. 56, 4526, April 3, 1918.

128 65th Congress, 2nd Session, *Congressional Record – Senate*, Vol. 56, 4715, April 6, 1918. And there was no minority report; see statement of Senator

Albert Cummins of Iowa (R) in 65th Congress, 2nd Session, *Congressional Record – Senate*, Vol. 56, 4781, April 8, 1918.
129 65th Congress, 2nd Session, *Congressional Record – Senate*, Vol. 56, 4561, April 4, 1918.
130 65th Congress, 2nd Session, *Congressional Record – Senate*, Vol. 56, 4562, April 4, 1918.
131 65th Congress, 2nd Session, *Congressional Record – Senate*, Vol. 56, 4637, April 5, 1918.
132 65th Congress, 2nd Session, *Congressional Record – Senate*, Vol. 56, 5942, May 2, 1918.
133 Jay, Hamilton, James, Madison and John, Jay. *The Federalist Papers*. Ed. Clinton Rossiter with an introduction and notes by Charles R. Kesler (New York: Signet Classic, 2003), 314.
134 65th Congress, 2nd Session, *Congressional Record – House*, Vol. 56, 6183, May 7, 1918.
135 65th Congress, 2nd Session, *Congressional Record – House*, Vol. 56, 6182, May 7, 1918.
136 65th Congress, 2nd Session, *Congressional Record – House*, Vol. 56, 6181, May 7, 1918.
137 65th Congress, 2nd Session, *Congressional Record – House*, Vol. 56, 6180, May 7, 1918.
138 65th Congress, 2nd Session, *Congressional Record – Senate*, Vol. 56, 4561, 4564, 4570, 4631, 4640–4641, 4646–4647, 4649, 4651, 4719, 4780–4783, 4829, 4833–4843, April 4–9, 1918. See also Stone's remarks at Stone, 187.
139 65th Congress, 2nd Session, *Congressional Record – Senate*, Vol. 56, 4850, April 9, 1918.
140 Edward L. Lascher, "Assessing Legislative Deliberation: A Preface to Empirical Analysis," *Legislative Studies Quarterly* 21, No. 4 (November 1996): 511.
141 65th Congress, 2nd Session, *Congressional Record – Senate*, Vol. 56, 4851, April 9, 1918.
142 65th Congress, 2nd Session, *Congressional Record – Senate*, Vol. 56, 4778, April 6, 1918.
143 Bessette, 168–169.
144 The Constitution requires a majority of senators (i.e., 51) to be present so as to constitute a quorum to do business. The Senate presumes that a quorum is present unless the contrary is shown by a roll call.
145 65th Congress, 2nd Session, *Congressional Record – Senate*, Vol. 56, 4653, April 5, 1918.
146 65th Congress, 2nd Session, *Congressional Record – Senate*, Vol. 56, 4562, April 4, 1918.
147 65th Congress, 2nd Session, *Congressional Record – Senate*, Vol. 56, 4633, April 5, 1918.
148 65th Congress, 2nd Session, *Congressional Record – Senate*, Vol. 56, 4714, April 6, 1918.
149 65th Congress, 2nd Session, *Congressional Record – Senate*, Vol. 56, 4764, 4767, April 8, 1918. Concerning the argument described in this paragraph, see also Stone, 184–185, 187 and Zechariah Chafee, *Free Speech in the United States* (Cambridge: Harvard University Press, 1967, 41.
150 65th Congress, 2nd Session, *Congressional Record – Senate*, Vol. 56, 4712, April 6, 1918.
151 65th Congress, 2nd Session, *Congressional Record – Senate*, Vol. 56, 4714, April 6, 1918.

152 65th Congress, 2nd Session, *Congressional Record – Senate*, Vol. 56, 4715, April 6, 1918.
153 65th Congress, 2nd Session, *Congressional Record – Senate*, Vol. 56, 4718, April 6, 1918.
154 65th Congress, 2nd Session, *Congressional Record – Senate*, Vol. 56, 4839, April 9, 1918.
155 65th Congress, 2nd Session, *Congressional Record – Senate*, Vol. 56, 4562, April 4, 1918.
156 65th Congress, 2nd Session, *Congressional Record – Senate*, Vol. 56, 4639, April 5, 1918. The Industrial Workers of the World (IWW, frequently called "Wobblies") is a workers' union that was founded in 1905 and, unlike the American Federation of Labor (AFL), it advocated the revolutionary overthrow of capitalism and undertook spontaneous strikes and slowdowns, picketing, parades and public speaking that provoked free speech fights. See Rabban, 79.
157 65th Congress, 2nd Session, *Congressional Record – Senate*, Vol. 56, 4639, April 5, 1918.
158 65th Congress, 2nd Session, *Congressional Record – Senate*, Vol. 56, 6036, May 4, 1918.
159 65th Congress, 2nd Session, *Congressional Record – Senate*, Vol. 56, 6049, May 4, 1918.
160 65th Congress, 2nd Session, *Congressional Record – Senate*, Vol. 56, 4566, April 4, 1918.
161 65th Congress, 2nd Session, *Congressional Record – Senate*, Vol. 56, 4636, April 5, 1918.
162 65th Congress, 2nd Session, *Congressional Record – Senate*, Vol. 56, 4637, April 5, 1918.
163 65th Congress, 2nd Session, *Congressional Record – Senate*, Vol. 56, 5941, May 2, 1918.
164 65th Congress, 2nd Session, *Congressional Record – Senate*, Vol. 56, 4762, 4765, 4768, April 8, 1918.
165 65th Congress, 2nd Session, *Congressional Record – Senate*, Vol. 56, 4772, April 8, 1918.
166 65th Congress, 2nd Session, *Congressional Record – Senate*, Vol. 56, 4564, April 4, 1918. See also Senator Thomas Hardwick's (D) remarks at 4640 and Senator George Norris's (R) at 4630, April 5, 1917.

A note: As noted in Chapter 1, Sunstein and Bessette uphold that the Framers sought to establish a deliberative democracy where the citizenry deliberates through their representatives. According to Bessette, elections ensure that the representatives of the people share citizen's interests, desires and values. In 1917, not all women had the right to vote. However, even though the Nineteenth Amendment, which extended the right to vote to women throughout the United States, did not become effective until August 1920, the female population was enfranchised at intervals before then. By 1914, Wyoming, Colorado, Utah, Idaho, Washington, California, Kansas, Oregon, Arizona, Montana and Nevada had enfranchised women. In 1917, the state of New York did so as well (Walter S.G., Kohn, *Women in National Legislatures: A Comparative Study of Six Countries* (New York: Praeger Publishers, 1980), 26–27; Alexander Keyssar, *The Right to Vote: The Contested History of Democracy in the United States* (New York: Basic Books, 2000), 368. (See Keyssar, 172–222 for a historical analysis of women's suffrage). In fact a woman, Jeannette Rankin (R), of Montana served as a member in the House of Representatives from 1917 to 1919 (Kohn, 25). In addition, voting patterns and partisan alignments were not much affected after women were enfranchised and few issues distinctly divided men and women (Keyssar, 218–219). Thus, there is no reason to suppose that Congressional deliberations on the Espionage Act and Sedition Act would have been any different than they were, if the entire female population did have a right to vote prior to the 65th Congress.

167 65th Congress, 2nd Session, *Congressional Record – Senate*, Vol. 56, 4565 & 4778, April 4 & 8 1918.

168 65th Congress, 2nd Session, *Congressional Record – Senate*, Vol. 56, 4572, April 4, 1918

169 65th Congress, 2nd Session, *Congressional Record – Senate*, Vol. 56, 4629, April 5, 1918, 4762, April 8, 1918.

170 65th Congress, 2nd Session, *Congressional Record – Senate*, Vol. 56, 4633, April 5, 1918

171 65th Congress, 2nd Session, *Congressional Record – Senate*, Vol. 56, 4631, April 5, 1918.

172 65th Congress, 2nd Session, *Congressional Record – House*, Vol. 56, 6180, May 7, 1918.

173 65th Congress, 2nd Session, *Congressional Record – Senate*, Vol. 56, 4560, 4569–4570, April 4, 1918.

174 65th Congress, 2nd Session, *Congressional Record – Senate*, Vol. 56, 4623, April 5, 1918; 4823, April 9, 1918.

175 65th Congress, 2nd Session, *Congressional Record – Senate*, Vol. 56, 4694, 4709–4711, 4714, April 6, 1918; 4772–4773, April 8, 1918.

176 65th Congress, 2nd Session, *Congressional Record – Senate*, Vol. 56, 4824, April 9, 1918; 5542, April 24, 1918; 6051–6052, May 4, 1918.

177 65th Congress, 2nd Session, *Congressional Record – Senate*, Vol. 56, 4836, April 9, 1918.

178 65th Congress, 2nd Session, *Congressional Record – Senate*, Vol. 56, 6039, May 4, 1918; 65th Congress, 2nd Session, *Congressional Record – House*, Vol. 56, 6178, May 7, 1918.

179 65th Congress, 2nd Session, *Congressional Record – Senate*, Vol. 56, 4567, April 4, 1918; 4713, April 6, 1918; 4776, April 8, 1918.

180 65th Congress, 2nd Session, *Congressional Record – Senate*, Vol. 56, 4826, April 9, 1918.

181 65th Congress, 2nd Session, *Congressional Record – Senate*, Vol. 56, 4826, April 9, 1918.

182 65th Congress, 2nd Session, *Congressional Record – Senate*, Vol. 56, 4826, April 9, 1918.

183 65th Congress, 2nd Session, *Congressional Record – Senate*, Vol. 56, 4897, April 10, 1918.

184 65th Congress, 2nd Session, *Congressional Record – Senate*, Vol. 56, 5541, April 24, 1918.

185 65th Congress, 2nd Session, *Congressional Record – Senate*, Vol. 56, 5542, April 24, 1918.

186 65th Congress, 2nd Session, *Congressional Record – Senate*, Vol. 56, 5542, April 24, 1918.

187 65th Congress, 2nd Session, *Congressional Record – Senate*, Vol. 56, 5543–5545, April 24, 1918; 5580, 5990–5992, May 3, 1918; 6039–6040, 6044–6045, 6051–6052, May 4, 1918; 65th Congress, 2nd Session, *Congressional Record – House*, Vol. 56, 6172–6173, May 7, 1918.

188 65th Congress, 2nd Session, *Congressional Record – Senate*, Vol. 56, 4831, April 9, 1918.

189 65th Congress, 2nd Session, *Congressional Record – Senate*, Vol. 56, 4898, April 10, 1918
190 65th Congress, 2nd Session, *Congressional Record – Senate*, Vol. 56, 6057, May 4, 1918.
191 Joint Resolution of March 3, 1921, chap. 136, *Statutes at Large of the United States of America*, Vol 41, 1359–1360 (Washington: Government Printing Office, 1921); 66th Congress, 3rd Session, *Congressional Record – House*, Vol. 60, 4206–4210, March 1, 1921; 66th Congress, 3rd Session, *Congressional Record – House*, Vol. 60, 288, 290, 293, 303–304, December 13, 1920.
192 66th Congress, 3rd Session, *Congressional Record – House*, Vol. 60, 289–302, December 13, 1920.
193 Representative George Huddleston of Alabama (D), 66th Congress, 3rd Session, *Congressional Record – House*, Vol. 60, 289, December 13, 1920.
194 66th Congress, 3rd Session, *Congressional Record – House*, Vol. 60, 293–294, December 13, 1920.
195 66th Congress, 3rd Session, *Congressional Record – House*, Vol. 60, 294, December 13, 1920.
196 66th Congress, 3rd Session, *Congressional Record – House*, Vol. 60, 293, December 13, 1920.
197 66th Congress, 3rd Session, *Congressional Record – House*, Vol. 60, 4206–4208, March 1, 1921.
198 66th Congress, 3rd Session, *Congressional Record – House*, Vol. 60, 4209–4210, March 1, 1921. And approved by the president, Congress, 3rd Session, *Congressional Record – House*, Vol. 60, 4521, March 3, 1921.

References

Bessette, Joseph M. *The Mild Voice of Reason: Deliberative Democracy & American National Government*. Chicago: The University of Chicago Press, 1994.

Carroll, Thomas F. "Freedom of Speech and of the Press in War Time: The Espionage Act." *Michigan Law Review* 17 (June 1919): 621–665.

Chafee, Zechariah. *Free Speech in the United States*. Cambridge: Harvard University Press, 1967.

Congressional Record: Containing the Proceedings and Debates of the First Session of the Sixty-Fifth Congress of the United States of America, Vol. LV, Parts 1–3. Washington: Government Printing Office, 1917.

Congressional Record: Containing the Proceedings and Debates of the Second Session of the Sixty-Fifth Congress of the United States of America, Vol. LVI, Parts 5–7. Washington: Government Printing Office, 1918.

Congressional Record: Containing the Proceedings and Debates of the Third Session of the Sixty-Sixth Congress of the United States of America, Vol. LX, Part 1. Washington: Government Printing Office, 1921.

Edgar, Harold and Schmidt, Benno C. "The Espionage Statutes and Publication of Defense Information." *Columbia Law Review* 73 (May 1973): 929–1087.

Espionage and Interference with Neutrality, *Hearings before the Committee on the Judiciary, House of Representatives, 65th Congress 1st Session on H.R. 291: April 9 and 12, 1917.* Washington: Government Printing Office, 1917.

Hamilton, Jay, Madison, James and Jay, John. *The Federalist Papers*. Ed. Clinton Rossiter with an introduction and notes by Charles R. Kesler. New York: Signet Classic, 2003.

Jewell, Malcolm E. and Paterson, Samuel C. *The Legislative Process in the United States*. 3rd ed. New York: Random House, 1977.

Keyssar, Alexander. *The Right to Vote: The Contested History of Democracy in the United States*. New York: Basic Books, 2000.

Kohn, Walter S.G. *Women in National Legislatures: A Comparative Study of Six Countries*. New York: Praeger Publishers, 1980.

Lascher, Edward L. "Assessing Legislative Deliberation: A Preface to Empirical Analysis." *Legislative Studies Quarterly* 21 (1996): 501–519.

Manz, William H. (Ed.) *Civil Liberties in Wartime: Legislative Histories of the Espionage Act of 1917 and the Sedition Act of 1918*. Buffalo: William S. Hein & Co., 2007.

Rabban, David. *Free Speech in Its Forgotten Years*. Cambridge: Cambridge University Press, 1997.

Statutes at Large of the United States of America, Vol. 41. Washington: Government Printing Office, 1921.

Stone, Geoffrey R. *Perilous Times: Free Speech in Wartime from the Sedition Act of 1798 to the War on Terrorism*. New York: W.W. Norton & Company, 2004.

Part III

World War II – Fascism, Communism and the Smith Act

In Part III, I will look into the phenomenon of restricting the freedom to advocate the necessity of overthrowing the government by force, embodied in the Smith Act, which Congress legislated in response to the threats of fascism and communism (introduced in Congress on the eve of World War II and passed one week after Germany conquered Paris).

4 Antifascism, Anticommunism, the Demand to Prohibit Subversive Expression, and Legislation, Enforcement and Judgment on the Smith Act

Antifascist and Anticommunist Political Culture

In order to understand the fact that in June 1940 Congress legislated a law to prohibit "subversive activities" that made it unlawful for any person to (1) advise insubordination by any member of the armed forces of the United States and (2) advocate the necessity of overthrowing the government by force, that this law was enforced and that convictions were upheld by the Supreme Court, it is necessary to examine and take account of the acute American antifascist and anticommunist political culture.[1]

The First Red Scare

Communism (as opposed to socialism) was never popular in the United States and anticommunism is a phenomenon with deep historical roots in the United States.[2] Prominent American values – individualism, political democracy and the right to own property – were contradictory to communism, which sought to abolish private property and form a collectivistic society based on one party. In addition, the vast majority of Americans are religious, believe in God and support the right to worship as one pleases. Conversely, communism promoted atheism and the new Soviet state suppressed Christian worship.[3] Americans were shocked by Soviet condemnation of religion and private property.[4]

After the Bolsheviks seized control in Russia, a "Red Scare" spread in the United States. Extensive labor unrest in 1919, including a strike by the Boston police, a general strike in Seattle that paralyzed the city, and that of half a million steel workers, along with a terrorist bombing campaign, led to a fear – reflected in the press – that a communist revolution that would change American life was imminent.[5] In June 1919 bombs exploded simultaneously in eight cities and numerous business leaders, legislators, judges, politicians and public officials were targeted with letter bombs, including Attorney General A. Mitchell Palmer and members of President Wilson's cabinet.[6]

Several politicians and associations demanded action. For example, business organizations such as the National Association of Manufacturers, the National Metal Trades Association and the National Founders

Association stirred up public opinion against labor unions; and conservative patriotic groups, such as the National Security League, the American Defense Society, the American Protective League and the National Civic Federation, promoted "Americanism."[7]

As a result, federal and local authorities set out to crush radical activity. In late 1919 and early 1920 Attorney General Palmer ran raids (later to become known as the "Palmer Raids"), aimed at aliens, confiscating radical literature and arresting over 5,000 people. Non-U.S. citizens were retained for deportation, and many U.S. citizens were prosecuted under anti-subversive laws (over thirty states passed criminal syndicalism, criminal anarchy, as well as laws prohibiting displaying the Red flag).[8]

By 1921 the Red Scare subsided. The strikes were over, bombings ceased and short-lived communist regimes in Eastern Europe were overthrown. The immediate fear faded away, although a legacy of antiradical legislation and popular anticommunist perceptions remained.[9] Indeed, America's historical antiradicalism became increasingly identified with anticommunism.[10]

The Fascist Threat

During the Great Depression, Americans became even more concerned with fascism than with communism. The left was horrified with Hitler and Mussolini, and Americans overall saw the regimes they headed as a threat to their way of life. Fascism was viewed as an evil movement, rooted in national chauvinism and anti-Semitic hatred, and as a challenge to American values.[11]

In 1933 William Dudley Pelley founded the Silver Legion of America ("Silver Shirts") with the open goal of bringing fascism to America and having him becoming America's dictator. The Silver Shirts were his version of Hitler's SS. In his weekly newsletter he blamed the Depression on the Jews, and travelling throughout the nation, he promoted a fascist and anti-Semitic doctrine. By 1934 there were 15,000 Silver Shirts, making it the largest fascist organization in the United States.[12]

Sympathetic to the Nazi regime and an admirer of Hitler, Gerald Winrod was a fundamentalist Protestant preacher who blamed the Great Depression and the New Deal on repudiation of God's will and on the Jews. In 1925 he established the Defenders of the Christian Faith to counter modernism, and in 1926, a monthly magazine, which reached a national circulation of 110,000 in 1938.[13]

In the mid-1930s the Roman Catholic priest Charles Coughlin rose to national prominence with a radio audience numbering millions and a journal with a circulation of over one million. He denounced communism as well as President Franklin D. Roosevelt. In 1936 he backed the Union Party's candidate for president, who failed, and later, his popularity declined as he became anti-Semitic and praised the Third Reich.[14]

The most visible fascist organization was the German-American Bund, whose members wore Nazi-style uniforms and used the Hitler salute. The Bund held rallies parading in uniform and made violent anti-Semitic speeches. At its peak it drew 32,000 supporters to a rally held on February 1939 in Madison Square Garden, New York, where swastikas stood beside a portrait of George Washington on the speaker's platform.[15]

Concerned with the threat of fascism, Roosevelt asked the Federal Bureau of Investigation (FBI) in 1934 to investigate the Nazi movement in the United States.[16]

The House Committee on Un-American Activities

Even though the times of the Great Depression were favorable for American communists, the majority of Americans continued to disapprove of communism, and anticommunist congressmen were increasingly active during the 1930s.[17] Public concern of communism, together with the rise of Hitler and pro-Nazi groups, enabled Representative Samuel Dickstein of New York (D) to convince the House in 1934 to establish a Special Committee on Un-American Activity. Representative John McCormack of Massachusetts (D) was named chairman and Dickstein vice-chairman. Dickstein conducted an intense campaign, exaggerating the fascist threat, harassing witnesses and openly naming persons as Nazi spies. The McCormack-Dickstein committee helped to develop a popular antifascist constituency. While the McCormack-Dickstein committee focused on fascism, including the German-American Bund and the Silver Shirts, it also reported on the danger of the Communist Party to the United States. The committee submitted to Congress a list of subversive organizations[18] and, in 1935, recommended that Congress legislate it unlawful to advocate overthrow of the government by force and unlawful to advise members of the armed forces to disobey their regulations – a prelude to sections 1 and 2 of the Smith Act (see below).[19]

In 1937 Dickstein proposed that the House in effect continue the temporary McCormack-Dickstein committee and establish a new committee to investigate un-American propaganda of subversive political prejudices. This proposal was defeated. However, in early 1938, with the annexation of Austria by Germany, the emergence of the Sudeten crisis (Czechoslovakia) and the escalating activities of communist and pro-Nazi groups, Dickstein, a liberal Democrat unpopular with the House, allied himself with Representative Martin Dies of Texas (D), a conservative and popular Democrat, and with the backing of the Speaker, the majority leader and the vice president, a resolution to create a House committee to investigate subversive and un-American propaganda passed by a vote of 191 to 45. Except Dickstein was excluded from the committee, Martin Dies was named chairman, and the House Un-American Activities Committee became popularly known as the Dies Committee.[20]

Dies initially investigated fascist groups and Nazis, such as the German-American Bund, but his main emphasis was communists.[21] He had an anti-labor reputation, and congressional support of the resolution was due, in fact, to anticommunism and the fear of communist penetration of New Deal agencies.[22] Most of the congressmen who voted for the creation of the committee were southern Democrats and Republicans who were not only anticommunists but were also concerned about the growth of organized labor.[23] Chaired by Dies, the committee introduced infamous practices that would be later associated with Senator Joseph R. McCarthy of Wisconsin (R):[24] Dies exaggerated, sought the sensational and held irresponsible proceedings (supported with minimal documentation), drew attention to the role of communists in the Congress of Industrial Organizations (CIO)[25] and named hundreds of organizations and newspapers as "Communistic," including the Boy Scouts; he frequently attacked members of the Roosevelt cabinet and administration, demanding their resignation, and publicly exposed names of federal employees he claimed were communists.[26]

The public and the press were very much aware of the Dies Committee's work and viewed it favorably. In January 1939, a poll found that 59 percent have heard of the committee's work, and by the end of that year, the figure rose to 81 percent.[27] In addition, in a survey conducted in December 1938, 74 percent of the public supported the Dies Committee's investigations, and public support remained above 60 percent throughout.[28] In 1938 the press was largely uncritical,[29] and although it later criticized the committee's methods, it also found many revelations as helpful.[30]

The Demand to Prohibit Subversive Expression of Fascists and Communists

Liberals, socialists and radicals campaigned against fascism and communism and favored restrictions on the right of "seditionists" to speak.

During the 1930s, liberals and radicals founded organizations to fight fascism. Indeed, liberal and left groups were the most fervent antifascists. Several were successful in recruiting significant support, and they issued newsletters, sponsored forums and organized demonstrations against fascists. Among them were: the Friends of Democracy, the Non-Sectarian Anti-Nazi League, the Mobilization for Democracy, the Council for Democracy, the American Council Against Nazi Propaganda and the Council Against Intolerance. Friends of Democracy, whose advisory board included Paul Douglas, had as its goal to expose Nazis and fascists. By 1939, Friends of Democracy put together 800 files on pro-Nazi and fascist groups.[31]

Veteran organizations, including the American Legion and the Veterans of Foreign Wars, conducted a campaign against fascism, especially against the German-American Bund, whom they demanded to be outlawed.[32]

Socialists combated communists. Already in 1919, the Socialist Party split from its left pro-Bolshevik factions.[33] Socialists attacked communism on its lack of democracy and rejected Lenin's Marxist views and the imposition of a communist party dictatorship.[34] On the labor front, in the mid-1930s, nearly every AFL affiliate prohibited membership of communists,[35] and leaders of certain CIO affiliates, such as the Amalgamated Clothing Workers Union and the Ladies Garment Workers Union, removed communists from their unions.[36]

American communism faced opposition from Trotskyists. Trotskyists were expelled from the American Communist Party (CPUSA) in 1929 when they sided against Stalin,[37] and Stalin's attacks against them brought support from some intellectuals: In the late 1930s the Committee for Cultural Freedom was formed, which opposed totalitarianism of both fascism and Soviet communism; its manifesto was signed by 140 intellectuals, led by John Dewey.[38]

In 1936 Roosevelt asked the FBI to broaden its investigations of fascist groups to include communist groups. The FBI director, J. Edgar Hoover, notified FBI offices to obtain information concerning subversive activities being conducted in the United States by communists and fascists advocating the replacement of the government by illegal methods. In 1938 Hoover updated Roosevelt that the FBI produced an index of 2,500 individuals engaged in subversive activities and the president approved a plan to expand FBI investigations.[39]

In the battle against fascism, leading liberals questioned the right of fascists to express their views. The fear of the spread of Hitler's fascism prompted them to lower tolerance of fascist propaganda. For example, the columnist Heywood Broun, backed by the editors of the *New Republic*, published in 1938 antipathy to a policy of free speech for everyone (urging civil libertarians to defend the underdog); political scientist Karl Lowenstein warned that absolute toleration of political free speech might lead to internal revolution and totalitarianism; and intellectual Lewis Mumford asked to restrict fascist material from the mails.[40]

The media in general, and not only liberal and radical publications, was antifascist. *Life* magazine, the *Saturday Evening Post* and the *New York Times* published photo-essays, stories and columns describing the fascist threat. *March of the Time* newsreels, radio newscasters and even Hollywood films emphasized it as well.[41]

In addition, polls showed that public opinion throughout the 1930s was inclined to denying freedom of speech and the press to communists.[42] And in June 1940, the month the Smith Act passed, according to a *Fortune* poll, 43 percent of Americans supported drastic action against communists in the United States.[43]

The signing of the Molotov-Ribbentrop nonaggression pact in August 1939, and the subsequent invasion of Poland by Germany and by the Soviet Union in September 1939, brought about a heightened scare of subversion from both communists and fascists, because of the alliance between the communist USSR and the fascist Nazi Germany. The CPUSA announced that the conflict with the Western allies was an imperialist war, and Americans now viewed communism and fascism mutually as totalitarian movements (Soviet communism as "red fascism" and Nazism as "brown bolshevism"). In February 1940, the American Civil Liberties Union (ACLU) decided to ban from its governing committees persons who were members of organizations that supported totalitarian regimes or by their public statements indicated support of totalitarian principles. In March 1940 Congress amended the Espionage Act of 1917 "to increase the penalties of peacetime violations," including Title XII section 3 regarding using the mails of the United States for the transmission of any matter declared to be nonmailable.[44]

The German annexation of Czechoslovakia a year earlier and the invasion of Norway in April 1940 prompted a fear that a "fifth column" might be at work in the United States. During the Spanish Civil War, a rebel general declared that while Franco's troops were advancing on Madrid in four columns, there was a "fifth column" of fascist supporters inside the city who would assault the Republican government from within. In Czechoslovakia Hitler used covert, organized Nazis, and in Norway secret Nazi followers sabotaged the mobilization of the Norwegian armed forces (some German troops came out from freighters in docked Norwegian ports) afterwards installing themselves as leaders of the government. This fear further intensified with the German invasion of Belgium and Holland on May 10, 1940, the astonishing speed of the Wehrmacht's advance, and the conquering of Paris on June 14, 1940. The fear was not necessarily of the German military machine but rather the belief that the French were defeated by internal subversion, by a fifth column of Nazi and communist sympathizers. In a May 1940 radio broadcast, President Roosevelt said that a "Trojan Horse" threatened the United States, and that same month in a message to Congress asking for increases in defense appropriations, he mentioned the "treacherous use of the Fifth Column." In the period following the Nazi conquest of Western Europe, citizen reports regarding subversives and spies exceeded 2,000 a day.[45]

Support for restricting subversive expression came not only from diverse organizations, congressmen and the White House but also from the intelligence community and the military, from the Navy Department and from the Justice Department, which was involved in drafting the act "to prohibit certain subversive activities" – the Smith Act.[46]

Legislation, Enforcement and Judgment on the Smith Act

On June 22, 1940, the House passed the Alien Registration Act – 382 in favor, 4 against and 45 not voting[47] – and on the same day, it was agreed to by the Senate[48] (see legislative account and analysis of deliberation in the following chapter). It is called the Smith Act, after its sponsor, Representative Howard W. Smith of Virginia (D). While the act required registration and fingerprinting of all resident aliens in the United States (and amended existing law for deportation of aliens), Title I, authored by Representatives Smith, McCormack and Sam F. Hobbs of Alabama (D),[49] in effect outlawed certain speech. Following is a summary of sections 1, 2 and 3 of Title I:

- Section 1 prohibited interfering with the loyalty, morale or discipline of the armed forces and made it unlawful to advise, counsel, urge or distribute any written matter that advises, counsels or urges insubordination by any member of the armed forces.
- Section 2 made it unlawful (1) to advocate, abet, advise or teach the necessity of overthrowing or destroying any government in the United States by force or violence; (2) to print, publish, edit, circulate or publicly display any written matter advocating, advising or teaching the necessity of overthrowing or destroying any government in the United States by force or violence; and (3) to organize, help organize or affiliate with any group that teaches, advocates or encourages the overthrow or destruction of any government in the United States by force or violence.
- Section 3 made it unlawful for anyone to conspire to commit any of the acts prohibited by the title.[50]

On June 28, 1940, President Roosevelt signed it into law,[51] in spite of protests from the ACLU, maintaining that the above sections did not amount to an inappropriate infringement of civil liberties considering the world conditions at that time.[52]

The first prosecution under the Smith Act was against twenty-nine leaders of the Socialist Workers Party (SWP) and the Local 544 of the Teamsters Union in Minneapolis. The SWP was a small Trotskyist party that controlled the Local 544 of the International Brotherhood of Teamsters. In 1934 they led a violent strike, controlling the streets of Minneapolis for a while, and only after the governor declared martial law was the conflict settled. Thereafter the Local 544's power grew, organizing a quarter of a million workers in an eleven-state area. With the likelihood of war increasing, so did government concerns about obstruction in the defense industry, because the SWP and Local 544 were hostile to the administration's mobilization efforts and refused to assist military preparedness. One SWP manifesto proclaimed that the people have their own war to fight (against the capitalist class). By the end of 1940, FBI director Hoover concluded that Local 544 was set out to control transportation in the Midwest, and in early 1941, he repeatedly warned President Roosevelt that Trotskyites and communists, through Local 544, planned to shut down more than 30 defense contractors. Consequently, Department of

Justice lawyers built a case in prosecuting them under the Smith Act. In a report in June 1941, acting Attorney General Francis Biddle wrote to the president that prosecution of Minneapolis Trotskyites would have a certain beneficial effect. In July 1941 the twenty-nine leaders of the SWP were indicted, charged with (1) conspiring to destroy the government of the United States by force and (2) committing acts intended to interfere with the discipline of the armed forces, and organizing and becoming members of groups whose purpose is to teach, advocate and encourage the overthrow of the government of the United States.[53]

In December 1941 eighteen of the defendants were found guilty on count two and were sentenced to over a year of imprisonment. Their appeal was unanimously rejected in September 1943 by the Circuit Court of Appeals. The Supreme Court denied review.[54]

In addition to the afore-mentioned prosecution, in June 1942, the government indicted twenty-six fascist leaders, charging them under both the Smith Act and the Espionage Act with conspiracy to undermine the morale of the armed forces. Those indicted included fascists described earlier, such as Pelley (founder of the Silver Shirts; already in jail, see below) and Winrod (the fundamentalist Protestant preacher) and others, such as the anti-Semitic demagogue Gerald L.K. Smith and Hans Diebel, a former Bund leader.[55] According to the indictment the defendants used organizations such as the German-American Bund and the Ku Klux Klan to implement their conspiracy. The government produced statements of the defendants charging the laws of the United States as corrupt and traitorous, describing Roosevelt as a pawn of Jews and communists, and supporting Germany, Italy and Japan.[56]

The trial was known as the "Great Sedition Trial" and received extensive cover by the press who initially supported the prosecution. However, as the defendants were a mixed crowd, some eccentric, proving that they acted together as part of a conspiracy was difficult. After reformulating the charges in 1943, the case continued into 1944, and in November of that year, the presiding judge suddenly died producing a mistrial. In 1946, after the war had ended, the government dropped the charges.[57]

The Espionage Act was also used throughout the war, and in total, approximately 200 persons were indicted under the Espionage Act and the Smith Act, including Pelly, who was sentenced in 1942 to fifteen years in prison.[58] The Espionage Act was also invoked for banning over seventy publications from the mail, including Coughlin's (the anti-Semitic fascist Catholic priest) journal, *Social Justice*, and SWP's journal, the *Militant*.[59]

With the outbreak of the Cold War immediately following World War II (see Chapter 6), the Smith Act was used against communists: in July 1948 the government indicted twelve CPUSA leaders, including its general secretary, Eugene Dennis, under the Smith Act of 1940 for advocating the necessity of overthrowing the government by force and violence.[60] The prosecution maintained that Leninist texts supported violent revolution and that the teachings of Marxism-Leninism were systematic advocacy of the overthrow of government. The presiding judge, Harold Medina, held that although the Smith Act did not prohibit abstract advocacy for overthrowing the government by unlawful means, it did prohibit the advocacy of action for that purpose. The jury found the defendants guilty, and Medina sentenced all except one to five years in prison. The U.S. Court of Appeals upheld the convictions.[61]

All the defendants appealed to the Supreme Court, which in 1951, in a 6-2 decision, upheld the convictions in *Dennis v. United States* Chief Justice Fred Vinson held that the Smith Act did not prevent discussion of ideas of Marxism-Leninism but did prohibit advocacy of violent revolution. He explained what "clear and present danger" meant:[62]

> Obviously, the words cannot mean that before the Government must act, it must wait until the putsch is about to be executed, the plans have been laid and the signal is awaited. If Government is aware that a group aiming at its overthrow is attempting to indoctrinate its members and to commit them to a course whereby they will strike when the leaders feel the circumstances permit, action by the Government is required.[63]

Immediately following the Supreme Court's decision, the FBI arrested a few dozen Communists Party leaders, and during the height of the Cold War, until 1957, the government prosecuted 145 people under the Smith Act, securing 108 convictions. In 1957 the Supreme Court agreed to hear the case against Oleta Yates and eleven other California communist leaders, who were convicted in 1951 of violating the Smith Act (*Yates v. United States*). In a 6-1 decision, the Court voted to remand the convictions (with orders to acquit five) because the evidence for advocacy of concrete action of violent overthrow (as opposed to advocacy of an abstract doctrine) was insufficient. Thereafter the government dismissed remaining charges and ceased to file prosecutions under the Smith Act.[64]

In sum, during the 1930s liberals, socialists, veterans, members of Congress and indeed the majority of Americans viewed fascism and communism as a real and daunting threat to the U.S. polity. Both ideologies were conceived as anti-American, and on the eve of World War II, several groups in society, including liberals, along with officials in the Justice Department, as well as congressmen, saw a need to restrict certain subversive expressions made by fascists and communists at that perilous time. The result was the legislation of the Smith Act and subsequent prosecutions and convictions (also upheld by the Supreme Court during the Cold War).

Thus the explanation on how such a law that restricts freedom of speech came about in a democracy like the United States, and how it was used during World War II and the Cold War. The next chapter will examine deliberation in Congress in order to assess the degree of its democratic legitimacy.

Notes

1 On the necessity to study political culture and political socialization to understand political functions (interest articulation, rule making and the rest), see Gabriel A. Almond, "Introduction: A Functional Approach to Comparative Politics," In *The Politics of Developing Areas*, Eds. Gabriel A. Almond and James S. Coleman (Princeton: Princeton University Press, 1960), 31.
2 John Earl Haynes, *Red Scare or Red Menace?: American Communism and Anticommunism in the Cold War Era* (Chicago: Ivan R. Dee, 1996), 6; Ellen Schrecker, "'Mere Shadows': The Early Cold War," In *Security v. Liberty: Conflicts Between Civil Liberties and National Security in American History*, Ed. Daniel Farber (New York: Russell Sage Foundation, 2008), 70; M. J. Heale *American Anticommunism: Combating the Enemy Within, 1830–1970* (Baltimore and London: The Johns Hopkins University Press, 1990), xi.
3 Haynes, 7.
4 Walter LaFeber, *America, Russia and the Cold War 1945–1996*, 8th ed. (New York: McGraw-Hill, 1997), 4.
5 Haynes, 7–8; Robert Griffith, "American Politics and the Origins of 'McCarthyism'," In *The Specter: Original Essays on the Cold War and the Origins of McCarthyism*, Eds. Robert Griffith and Athan Theoharis (New York: Franklin Watts, Inc., 1974), 6; Geoffrey R. Stone, *Perilous Times: Free Speech in Wartime from the Sedition Act of 1798 to the War on Terrorism* (New York: W.W. Norton & Company, 2004), 221–222. According to Murray Levin, although there indeed was a fear that a Bolshevik revolution "that would destroy property, church, home, marriage, civility, and the American way of life" was imminent, it was the product of political hysteria promoted by the "power elites of capitalism" to weaken the working class. Murray B. Levin, *Political Hysteria in America: The Democratic Capacity for Repression* (New York: Basic Books Inc., 1971), 29, 90.
6 Stone, 221–222; Haynes, 8.
7 Griffith, 6.
8 Haynes, 8–9; Griffith, 6. The U.S. Labor Department refused to deport those arrested without a hearing. Consequently, the majority was released – a few hundred were deported before the hearing requirement was initiated and approximately six hundred were departed afterwards Haynes, 9.
9 Haynes, 9; Griffith, 6–7; Stone, 224.
10 William R. Tanner and Robert Griffith, "Legislative Politics and 'McCarthyism': The Internal Security Act of 1950," In *The Specter: Original Essays on the Cold War and the Origins of McCarthyism*, Eds. Robert Griffith and Athan Theoharis (New York: Franklin Watts, Inc., 1974), 174.
11 Haynes, 17; Leo P. Ribuffo, *The Old Christian Right: The Protestant Far Right from the Great Depression to the Cold War* (Philadelphia: Temple University Press, 1983), xiii; Richard W. Steele, *Free Speech in the Good War* (New York: St. Martin's Press, 1999), 28, 70.
12 Stone, 259; Haynes, 20.
13 Ribuffo, 80–81, 105, 113, 117–119; Haynes, 20. In 1938 he entered the Republican primary for a U.S. Senate seat from Kansas (he was defeated).
14 Stone, 275–277; Haynes, 20–21.
15 Stone, 244, 246, 235; Haynes, 19–20; Steele, 28, 191.
16 Robert Justin Goldstein, *Political Repression in Modern America: From 1870 to 1976*. 2nd ed. (Urbana and Chicago: University of Illinois Press, [1978] 2001), 213–214; Steele, 30.
17 Haynes, 11, 15; Alan D. Harper, *The Politics of Loyalty: The White House and the Communist Issue, 1946–1952* (Westport: Greenwood Publishing Corporation, 1969), 13.

18 Goldstein, 213–215; Haynes, 64–65; Ribuffo, 71; Steele, 29–30.
19 See account of Representative McCormack, 76th Congress, 1st Session, *Congressional Record – House*, Vol. 84, 10374, July 28, 1939.
20 Haynes, 65; Goldstein, 240–241. Access to Soviet files in the mid-1990s revealed that in May 1938, shortly after the creation of the House Un-American Activities Committee, the Soviet NKVD accepted an offer from Dickstein to pass materials and data on fascists in exchange for a monthly payment. Although Dickstein was excluded from the Committee and his value declined in the view of his NKVD handlers (he was assigned the codename "Crook"), this relationship continued until February 1940. Dickstein later (1946–1954) served as justice on the New York State Supreme Court. Allen Weinstein and Alexander Vassiliev, *The Haunted Wood: Soviet Espionage in America – The Stalin Era* (New York: The Modern Library, 2000), 140–150.
21 Haynes, 66; Goldstein 241–242; Stone 245–246.
22 Heale, 119.
23 Ira Katznelson, *Fear Itself: The New Deal and the Origins of Our Time* (New York: Liveright Publishing Corporation, 2013), 329–330. Melvyn Dubofsky writes that in 1937, "trade unionism accomplished what it had failed to achieve during the previous past century" when organized labor signed collective bargaining contracts with General Motors and United States Steel. In addition, in 1937, unions recruited more than three million members and the total membership was over eight million. Melvyn Dubofsky, *The State and Labor in Modern America*. (Chapel Hill: The University of North Carolina Press, 1994), 137; Melvyn Dubofsky, "Introduction," In *American Labor Since the New Deal*, Ed. Melvyn Dubofsky (Chicago: Quadrangle Books, 1971), 12.
24 Griffith, 7.
25 Katznelson, 330. The Congress of Industrial Organizations (CIO) was a federation of unions that organized industrial workers. John L. Lewis, president of the United Mine Workers, formed the CIO – with communist assistance – in the mid-1930s, when he broke with the American Federation of Labor (AFL). Communists were later driven out. Ellen Schrecker, *Many Are the Crimes: McCarthyism in America* (Princeton: Princeton University Press, 1998), 27–28; Haynes, 12; Klehr, Harvey, Haynes, John Earl and Firsov, Fridrikh Igorevich, *The Secret World of American Communism* (New Haven and London: Yale University Press, 1995), 9, 12. In 1937, membership of CIO affiliates surpassed that of the AFL. Dubofsky, "Introduction," 12.
26 Stone, 246–247; Haynes, 66.
27 Steele, 37.
28 Stone, 248.
29 Goldstein, 244.
30 Stone, 248.
31 Ribuffo, 178–179; Haynes, 25.
32 Haynes, 24–25.
33 Goldstein, 140–141.
34 Haynes, 99–100.
35 David M. Oshinsky, "The CIO and the Communists," In *The Specter: Original Essays on the Cold War and the Origins of McCarthyism*, Eds. Robert Griffith and Athan Theoharis (New York: Franklin Watts, Inc., 1974), 119.
36 Oshinsky, 120–121.
37 Schrecker, *Many Are the Crimes*, 76. CPUSA – Communist Party of the United States of America; For a brief history of the American Communist Party, see Klehr et al., 4–14.
38 Haynes, 103–105.

39 Goldstein, 215, 247; Stone, 249.
40 Steele, 70–71; Ribuffo, 183–184; Haynes, 26–27.
41 Ribuffo, 181–182; Haynes, 23.
42 Griffith, 6, quoting Hadley Cantril, *Public Opinion, 1935–1946* (Princeton, 1946).
43 Katznelson, 333, quoting Hadley Cantril, *Public Opinion, 1935–1946* (Westport: Greenwood Press, 1951).
44 Haynes, 31, 34–35; Goldstein, 240, 261; Stone, 250; Ribuffo, 185; Steele, 42, 72. Amendment of Espionage Act: Act of March 28, 1940, chap. 72, *Statutes at Large of the United States of America*, Vol 54, Part 1, 79–80 (Washington: Government Printing Office, 1941).
45 Haynes, 18–19, 23; Steele, 74–77; Stone 251; Ribuffo, 185.
46 Steele, 81; Zechariah Chafee, *Free Speech in the United States* (Cambridge: Harvard University Press, 1967), 447, 450. Quote from Act of June 28, 1940, chap. 439, *Statutes at Large of the United States of America*, Vol. 54, Part 1, 670 (Washington: Government Printing Office, 1941). See also letter dated February 27, 1939, from Acting Secretary of the Navy Department to the Speaker of the House in which "The Navy Department recommends enactment" of proposed legislation to suppress attempts to incite members of the Army and Navy to disobedience (which has as its ultimate goal the overthrow of the U.S. government by force), 76th Congress, 1st Session, *Congressional Record - Senate*, Vol. 84, 2122, March 2, 1939.
47 76th Congress, 3rd Session, *Congressional Record – House*, Vol. 86, 9036, June 22, 1940. In actuality, the House voted on a conference report (a conference committee was set up a week earlier. See 76th Congress, 3rd Session, *Congressional Record – Senate*, Vol. 86, 8347, June 15, 1940, and *Congressional Record – House*, Vol. 86, 8426, June 17, 1940).
48 The Senate agreed to the conference report, without taking a roll call. 76th Congress, 3rd Session, *Congressional Record – Senate*, Vol. 86, 8952, June 22, 1940. See also Chafee, 440–441, ft. 1; 454, ft. 29.
49 Chafee, 442.
50 Section 4 allowed the removal of written material intended for use in violation of the Act, section 5a specified the penalty (fine and imprisonment) for violation and section 5b restricted employment by the United States of a convicted person. See Appendix B for full text of sections 1, 2 and 3. Act of June 28, 1940, chap. 439, *Statutes at Large of the United States of America*, Vol. 54, Part 1, 670 (Washington: Government Printing Office, 1941).
51 76th Congress, 3rd Session, *Congressional Record - House*, Vol. 86, 9126–9127, July 1, 1940.
52 Steele, 81; Stone, 252.
53 Steele, 129–133; Stone 255.
54 Steele, 138–140; Stone, 255.
55 Haynes, 30; Stone 273.
56 Stone, 621–622, ft. 179–180; Haynes, 31.
57 Stone, 273–275; Haynes 31. See Ribuffo, 193–213 and Steele, 223–224, 227–230 for a detailed account of the trial.
58 Stone, 275, 264–265.
59 Goldstein, 268; Stone, 277.
60 Stone, 396; Haynes, 163.
61 Haynes, 163–164; Stone, 397–399 (one defendant was sentenced to three years; Stone 652, ft. 328). The defendants appealed to the U.S. Court of Appeals, where Judge Hand upheld the convictions (the same judge that in World War I, after the New York Postmaster declared *The Masses* nonmailable, granted the editor's request for an injunction; except that his decision was reversed

by the court of appeals), asserting that the evidence showed that the defendants were engaged in a conspiracy to overthrow the government by force and adding that First Amendment concerns beliefs and allows fierce criticism but does not protect those who advocate violence. See Stone, 399–402. For a legal analysis of the trial and the U.S. Court of Appeals decision upholding the conviction, see Stone, 396–402.

62 Haynes, 164; Stone, 403–404.

63 Quoted in Stone, 404. Upon the Supreme Court's decision, the defendants fled (except for Dennis, who was already in prison for contempt of Congress); see Haynes, 165. For a full review of the court's decision and a criticism of it, see Stone, 402–411.

64 Stone, 411, 413–415. Besides a change in historical circumstances between 1951 and 1957 (see note 91 in Chapter 6), the composition of the Court also changed with four justices being replaced.

References

Almond, Gabriel A. "Introduction: A Functional Approach to Comparative Politics." *The Politics of Developing Areas*. Eds. Gabriel A. Almond and James S. Coleman, 3–64. Princeton: Princeton University Press, 1960.

Chafee, Zechariah. *Free Speech in the United States*. Cambridge: Harvard University Press, 1967.

Congressional Record: Proceedings and Debates of the 76th Congress First Session, Vol. 84. Washington: United States Government Printing Office, 1939.

Congressional Record: Proceedings and Debates of the 76th Congress Third Session, Vol. 86. Washington: United States Government Printing Office, 1940.

Dubofsky, Melvyn. *We Shall Be All: A History of the Industrial Workers of the World*. Chicago: Quadrangle Books, 1969.

Dubofsky, Melvyn. *The State and Labor in Modern America*. Chapel Hill: The University of North Carolina Press, 1994.

Goldstein, Robert Justin. *Political Repression in Modern America: From 1870 to 1976*. 2nd ed. Urbana and Chicago: University of Illinois Press, [1978] 2001.

Griffith, Robert. "American Politics and the Origins of 'McCarthyism'." *The Specter: Original Essays on the Cold War and the Origins of McCarthyism*. Eds. Robert Griffith and Athan Theoharis, 1–17. New York: Franklin Watts, Inc., 1974.

Harper, Alan D. *The Politics of Loyalty: The White House and the Communist Issue, 1946–1952*. Westport: Greenwood Publishing Corporation, 1969.

Haynes, John Earl. *Red Scare or Red Menace?: American Communism and Anticommunism in the Cold War Era*. Chicago: Ivan R. Dee, 1996.

Heale, M. J. *American Anticommunism: Combating the Enemy Within, 1830–1970*. Baltimore and London: The Johns Hopkins University Press, 1990.

Katznelson, Ira. *Fear Itself: The New Deal and the Origins of Our Time*. New York: Liveright Publishing Corporation, 2013.

Klehr, Harvey, Haynes, John Earl and Firsov, Fridrikh Igorevich. *The Secret World of American Communism*. New Haven and London: Yale University Press, 1995.

LaFeber, Walter. *America, Russia and the Cold War 1945–1996*. 8th ed. New York: McGraw-Hill, 1997.

Levin, Murray B. *Political Hysteria in America: The Democratic Capacity for Repression*. New York: Basic Books Inc., 1971.

Oshinsky, David M. "The CIO and the Communists." *The Specter: Original Essays on the Cold War and the Origins of McCarthyism*. Eds. Robert Griffith and Athan Theoharis, 116–151. New York: Franklin Watts, Inc., 1974.

Ribuffo, Leo P. *The Old Christian Right: The Protestant Far Right from the Great Depression to the Cold War*. Philadelphia: Temple University Press, 1983.

Schrecker, Ellen. *Many Are the Crimes: McCarthyism in America*. Princeton: Princeton University Press, 1998.

Schrecker, Ellen. "'Mere Shadows': The Early Cold War." *Security v. Liberty: Conflicts Between Civil Liberties and National Security in American History*. Ed. Daniel Farber, 67–94. New York: Russell Sage Foundation, 2008.

Statutes at Large of the United States of America, Vol. 54, Part 1. Washington: Government Printing Office, 1941.

Steele, Richard W. *Free Speech in the Good War*. New York: St. Martin's Press, 1999.

Stone, Geoffrey R. *Perilous Times: Free Speech in Wartime from the Sedition Act of 1798 to the War on Terrorism*. New York: W.W. Norton & Company, 2004.

Tanner, William R. and Griffith, Robert. "Legislative Politics and 'McCarthyism': The Internal Security Act of 1950." *The Specter: Original Essays on the Cold War and the Origins of McCarthyism*. Eds. Robert Griffith and Athan Theoharis, 172–189. New York: Franklin Watts, Inc., 1974.

Weinstein, Allen and Vassiliev, Alexander. *The Haunted Wood: Soviet Espionage in America – The Stalin Era*. New York: The Modern Library, 2000.

5 Congressional Deliberation on the Smith Act

Technically the Alien Registration Act was deliberated by Congress: Congressmen identified a problem (the threat of subversion by communists and fascists), initiated a legislative remedy (the restriction of subversive expression), congressional committees heard testimonies and submitted written reports and congressmen debated the proposed bill on the floor. However:

1. There was very little deliberation on sections 1 and 2 of the act – those restricting freedom of speech (Congress did spend time deliberating the provisions regarding registration, fingerprinting and deportation of aliens);
2. The little deliberation that was conducted on sections 1 and 2 was relatively shallow; that is, there wasn't that much serious consideration of proposals, in-depth examination of the issues at stake (e.g., the constitutionality of restricting freedom of speech) or significant investigation and clarification of strengths and weaknesses of arguments pro and con.

House and Senate Judiciary Committee Hearings and Deliberation

On March 20, 1939, Representative Howard Smith of Virginia (D) introduced H.R. 5138 – "a bill to make unlawful attempts to overthrow the Government of the United States;... to make unlawful attempts to interfere with the discipline of the Army and Navy; to require registration and fingerprinting of aliens [and for other purposes]." On the same day it was referred to the Committee on the Judiciary of the House.[1]

A subcommittee of the House Judiciary Committee held hearings on April 12 and 13, 1939 (a day and a half), during which it heard testimonies and collected statements.

The chief challenger of the provisions prohibiting to advocate the necessity of overthrowing the government by force and prohibiting to advise or distribute printed matter urging insubordination was the ACLU. Concerning the provisions prohibiting to advocate the necessity of overthrowing the government by force, the ACLU representative argued that unrestricted exercise of the right of free speech is essential to the "continuance of democracy."[2] In addition, punishing advocacy of a doctrine (putting into prison people who preach subversive doctrines) does not do away with the doctrine, because the doctrine is an outcome of conditions, and the "only way to get rid of the doctrine is to get rid of the conditions."[3] Therefore, it would be "unwise" for Congress to legislate against ideas.[4] The representative of the AFL stated that the AFL was "apprehensive" of these the provisions, and in reply to a question by Representative Samuel Hobbs of Alabama (D), concerning suggestions for amendments, he said that "an entire redraft" would be better.[5] The representative of the Maritime Unions of the CIO pointed out that the wording "by any other unlawful means" in certain sections (e.g., the bill stated that it would be unlawful for any person with intent to overthrow the government by force or violence "or by any other unlawful means" to distribute any written matter advocating that doctrine) was "superfluous" because the only way to overthrow a government of a country is by force or violence[6] (these words were later stricken out, see below).

Concerning the provisions prohibiting to advise or distribute printed matter urging insubordination, the ACLU, while recognizing that there may be a need for legislation that will prevent civilians to "stir up mutiny" (illegal for soldiers), it did not believe that there was any need for such action at that time "so as to require a bill as broad as the one here drawn," and the ACLU also had "grave" reservations about the interpretation and administration of any such bill.[7]

On the other hand, the American Legion, patriotic fraternities and societies, conservative organizations, congressmen as well as Representative Smith spoke in favor of the bill's enactment. Among other things, it was argued that the bill does not interfere with freedom of speech (it is constitutional),[8] the country is demanding some legislation that will stop subversive activities[9] and the object of the bill is "very salutary."[10]

The representatives of the Navy went into details concerning the provisions prohibiting to advise or distribute printed matter urging insubordination[11] and asked Congress to enact such legislation.[12] (The Navy addressed itself solely to these provisions; the Army Department fully concurred).[13] Besides supplying the subcommittee with the information that the secretary of state, the secretary of war and the attorney general had no objection to the bill's enactment,[14] the representatives of the Navy explained the need for it:

> organizations whose aims are considered inimical to those of the United States Government are attempting to influence, through subversive and seditious measures, the loyalty, morale, and discipline of the enlisted personnel of the Navy...[by] distribution of circulars and leaflets urging our men to violate the oath of allegiance, and

> by personal contact, both ashore and afloat, trying to influence adversely discipline[15] (and attempting to establish committees aboard Navy ships).

However, legally, the Navy was impaired, for example: the articles for the government of the Navy gave no jurisdiction over civilians; the section of the Criminal Code that made inciting to rebellion or insurrection punishable was inadequate because the handbills distributed ("by the agitators") never advocated open rebellion or insurrection (and didn't result in rebellion or insurrection); and section 3 of the Espionage Act, which covers these activities, is applicable only in time of war so it could not be invoked during the late 1930s.[16] In addition, the Navy representative refuted the arguments that the legislation is unconstitutional, that is, a violation of the First amendment and an abridgment of freedom of speech, citing decisions of the Supreme Court and elsewhere.[17]

According to Representative Smith, the Judiciary Committee "made it a continuing order of business for something like a month. [The] committee went over it day after day and considered it and… redrafted the measure."[18] When the bill was reported back to the House on June 29, 1939 (by Representative Samuel Hobbs of Alabama (D)),[19] section 2, which outlawed advocating the overthrow of the U.S. government by force or violence, was stricken out. But, *not* for substantial reasons concerning freedom of speech: it was stricken out merely because the exact same provision was passed as an amendment that Representative John McCormack of Massachusetts (D) offered to another bill in the House on June 5, 1939. Indeed Representative Smith regarded section 2 as "the very heart of the legislation" and explained to the House that when the bill was pending before the Committee on the Judiciary, "[Mr. McCormack], who is really the author of the language, obtained passage of substantially the same bill by attaching it as a rider to some other bill," and since it already passed the House, the Committee of the Judiciary was of the opinion that it should not be included in the measure. But as he was concerned that the Senate might not pass the measure, he asked to restore the provision.[20]

Actually, further to the antifascist and anticommunist atmosphere and demand to prohibit subversive expression across the nation (in the late 1930s as shown in the previous chapter) on the first day of session of Congress (January 3, 1939), several bills were introduced to make it a crime to advocate or promote the overthrow of the government of the United States by force or violence.[21] Half a year later, on July 19, 1939, Representative James Taylor of Tennessee (R) spoke on the issue of registration and fingerprinting of aliens, but his words were indicative of congressmen minds in general on the issue of subversion:

> There is no room in this country for such double allegiance as we saw demonstrated in Madison Square Garden, New York, recently when 18,000 members of the so-called German Bund assembled

> there and boldly acclaimed a European dictator, only to be followed a few nights later by 22,000 Communists who met in the same hall and praised the Soviet Government and the Third International. Mr. Speaker, these subversive influences are becoming more and more active and audacious every day – boring from within.... If we are worthy of the heritages handed down to us by those immortals who set up this Government by the sacrifice of free blood and treasure, we will awake from our lethargy and stamp out this menace to American democracy.[22]

Thus, ten days later, on July 29, 1939, at the request of Representative Smith, the House reinserted section 2 into the bill.[23]

In May 1940, a subcommittee of the Senate Judiciary Committee held half a day of hearings on the bill[24] (after the House debated on and passed the bill in July 1939, see below). Liberal organizations claimed that the bill was an abridgment of the right to free speech and unconstitutional, further elaborating that there's a difference between outlawing overt acts to overthrow the government and the advocacy of ideas (or the expression of moral convictions) that do not have a clear and present danger of being carried into effect.[25] To this a utilitarian claim was added: that it would be better to let people express their opinion and keep a subversive movement in the open, rather than driving them underground, which is dangerous.[26] Representatives Smith and Hobbs spoke on behalf of the bill. Both mentioned the need for the bill on the part of the armed forces,[27] and Representative Smith, in an answer to a question by Senator John Danaher of Connecticut (R) (a member of the subcommittee), rejected the claim that the bill violated that First Amendment.[28]

Most of the subcommittee's work was on redrafting the complex bill into a "harmonious whole."[29] Indeed Senator Thomas Connally of Texas (D), chairman of the Senate Subcommittee of the Committee of the Judiciary on H.R. 5138, when reporting the bill (report No. 1796), stated that the Senate Judiciary Committee "did not decide to change any substance of [the bill]," but "after consulting the departments and legislative counsel, [concluded that the measure] should be rewritten."[30] Nevertheless, the Senate Judiciary Committee did strike out the words "or by any other lawful means" in section 2 of the proposed bill, which came after the words "by force or violence." The original language made it unlawful to advocate overthrowing the government by force or violence "or by any unlawful means." The committee struck out these words because they were felt to be unclear and unnecessary.[31]

Debate on the Floor

The House began considering the Smith bill on July 19, 1939; debated it at length (over half a day) on July 28, 1939; and continued some more on

July 29, 1939. The Senate debated the bill on June 15, 1940. After a conference committee was set up, the House discussed the bill also on June 22, 1940.

As mentioned earlier, Congress did spend time and engage in a deliberation process on the aspects of the bill that concerned the registration, fingerprinting and deportation on aliens. However, as compared to that, there was relatively little deliberation on section 1, which prohibited interfering with the loyalty, morale or discipline of the armed forces and made it unlawful to advise, counsel, urge or distribute any written mater that advises, counsels or urges insubordination by any member of the armed forces; and there was almost no deliberation on section 2, which made it unlawful to advocate the necessity of overthrowing any government in the United States by force.

Section 1

The main argument against section 1 was that it infringes on freedom of speech, and a secondary argument was that it is unnecessary as there is no danger of military disaffection. These arguments were lumped together by Representative Emanuel Celler of New York (D) on both July 19 and 28, 1939:

> the bill is violative of our liberties and of the Bill of Rights. … I, too, want to scotch naval or military sedition. But, … [t]he bill is so broad and indefinite that it threatens freedom of speech and freedom of the press on all matters affecting the Army and the Navy.… Aside from all this, … [t]here is no danger of military disaffection.[32]
>
> I say the bill…goes too far… The testimony given before our committee did not show any inherent danger in the Army or the Navy because of any subversive activities. … There is no serious danger that would warrant the drastic remedies in title 1. A peace pronouncement, by a reputable organization, a peace manifesto, might be deemed a violation.… If somebody gets up on a public platform and says that he does not countenance and he deplores the use of troops in strikes, he might be held as violating section 1, title I, of this act.[33]

At one point Representative Edouard Izac of California (D) offered to strike out all of title I. He asked, rhetorically:

> Have we reached the point in this country when we can no longer depend on the boys you and I send to the Naval Academy and the Military Academy and to the training stations of this country and to the camps in the Army?… It is an absolute disgrace and insult to the type of young men we are bringing into the armed forces of this

> country today. They are of the highest type, in my opinion, that we have ever had

He added, "I do not take seriously the complaint of some of our intelligence officers that there is this danger because of some pamphlets that are being handed out when a boy goes on leave."[34]

According to Representative Vito Marcantonio of New York (American Labor Party), section 1 "properly gives the right to characterize [the bill] as a Gestapo bill," adding that

> The Army and Navy do not need this Gestapo law. The men of the Army and Navy are loyal. They are loyal to the United States and they are loyal to the democracy of this country. Court martial and military procedure can handle those who are disloyal.[35]

Representatives Herman Eberharter of Pennsylvania (D), Kent Keller of Illinois (D) and Phillip Ferguson of Oklahoma (D) echoed this line of reasoning. Eberharter said that there are

> plenty of statutes on the books now which are amply able to take care of any propaganda which may have any effect on the armed forces of this country. The passage of this bill, in my opinion, is a confession... that we do not have any confidence... in the personnel of [the armed forces]...[and] is a step away from our reliance on the Constitution of the United States and our own belief in the principles of democracy.

Keller observed, "We have already all the laws...that we need to protect our country" and that the Army and Navy "have been able to take care of themselves." Ferguson stated that the United States is "the last country in the world to maintain democratic institutions" and raise its armed forces by the volunteer method, and therefore men in the armed forces are patriotic and "do not need any censorship."[36]

Representative Donald O'Toole of New York (D) went so far as to offer an amendment prohibiting any person in the capacity of the Army or Navy from reading "the Bible and Congressional Record, while in said service," explaining that the amendment "is no more absurd than the crackpot legislation that is before us today" wishing to disclose to members of Congress "the foolishness of the so-called Smith bill" because under it "some fanatic might well term [the Bible] a propaganda inspirational book" adding,

> There is no doubt in my mind that in the very first section of this bill you are asking men ... of education, men of culture who are in the service of their country... [to] read only that which the Congress of the United States feels they are entitled to read.[37]

A concise assertion of the objection to the bill was made by Representative Thomas Ford of California (D): "I am opposed to this bill because I believe in the Bill of Rights, which refers to persons and guarantees to persons certain liberties which this bill seeks to deny. It is un-American, undemocratic, and, in my view, un-constitutional."[38]

However, the arguments' pro swarm over those con, and Representative Izac's suggestion to strike out title I was rejected.[39] Supporters of section 1 claimed that (1) it only limits certain speech, (2) damage is being done in the armed forces, (3) it is needed for national security in times of war and (4) it is needed to fight internal subversion and protect American democracy.

1. It only limits certain speech: Representative James Taylor of Tennessee (R), responding to Representative O'Toole's claim that the bill takes away the liberty of the members of the Army and Navy to read, disagreed and said that it "prevents advocates of communism from spreading propaganda among members of the armed forces… and prevents any effort to provoke insurrection or spread mutiny and sedition."[40] Likewise, exactly one day earlier, when the Senate discussed an essentially similar bill to that of section 1 of the Smith bill,[41] Senator David Walsh of Massachusetts (D) explained that the proposed legislation "does not infringe upon the rights of free speech or a free press.… It does, however, prevent persons from urging members of the armed forces to violate the laws and regulations by which they are governed."[42]
2. Damage is being done in the armed forces: Representative Smith reported to the House that section 1, which made it unlawful "to spread sedition through the Army and Navy of the United States," after having been lain dormant for several years (section 1 was substantially along the lines of a bill the Special Committee on Un-American Activity introduced in 1935 upon the request of the Navy Department)[43] was redrafted and sent to Congress by the Navy Department, and that at the House Judiciary Committee hearings, representatives of both the Army and Navy urged adoption of the measure. He quoted the representative of the Navy (Lieutenant Ira Nunn): "whereas the last time we came before Congress with this request we were forced to say there had been no apparent damage done, I am afraid now, gentlemen, that we have to report that damage is being done."[44]

Representatives William Blackney of Michigan (R), Charles Faddis of Pennsylvania (D) and John Robsion of Kentucky (R) reiterated this: Representative Blackney explained that the Army and Navy urged adoption of the bill "because the ill effect of allowing communistic propaganda to be circulated in the Army and Navy was already proving disastrous";[45]

Representative Faddis, opposing Representative Issac's suggestion to strike out title I, said:

> any man who has ever had the slightest acquaintance with an Army post knows there are detrimental influences near those post which are working at all times. … The same thing is true of naval stations.… [We] should protect them from being submitted to the influence of those who spread these subversive doctrines.[46]

Representative Robsion, favoring the objectives of the bill, said:

> Those in charge of our armed forces have become alarmed. They say that Communists and other organizations are flooding the ships, barracks, Army and Navy posts with subversive literature.… We are now spending approximately $2,000,000,000 annually to build up the [armed forces].… Millions are being spent every year to instruct our young men and women in our defense program.… Now why should we permit these Communists, anarchists, and other subversive groups to distribute their un-American and poisonous literature among our armed forces? We might as well take poisonous reptiles into our households and among our own wives and children.[47]

3. National security in times of war: This was best articulated by Representative Hobbs, who thought the bill was one of the most important bills that has ever been presented on Congress, making clear that

   > There is no security in this country for life, liberty, the pursuit of happiness, or property without adequate national defense. There can be no adequate defense as long as subversive influences threaten to undermine the loyalty and devotion of our fighting forces. … The officers testified before our committee that they were loath to ask for this provision in peacetime but that conditions had become worse, that propagandists were now gaining a foothold.[48]

   Representative Robsion also touched upon this issue when he spoke of the money being spent to build up the armed forces "to defend effectively our country if assailed."[49]
4. Fight internal subversion and protect American democracy: opposing Representative O'Toole's suggestion to prohibit any person in the capacity of the Army or Navy from reading the Bible, Representative John Schafer of Wisconsin (R) said that it "conforms to the principles and philosophies of the Communists" and declared, "We want no alien form of autocracy to supplant our democracy. We care not whether it be Nazi, Fascist, Communist, or any other brand."[50] Minutes before, Representative Clare Hoffman of Minnesota (R) saw

"no reason why there should be such great concern exhibited when the Congress attempts to protect, maintain, and keep as it is this Government of ours. When Congress seeks to prevent subversive activities."[51] And in opposition to Representative Izac's suggestion to strike out title I, Representative Faddis asserted that communists

> are working all the time to destroy our form of government. They maintain that the Bill of Rights should protect them in their activities to destroy this Government in order that they may replace it with a government of another type, but should their efforts succeed, the Bill of Rights would not last overnight in their hands.[52]

Section 2

When reintroducing section 2, which outlawed advocating the overthrow of the U.S. government by force or violence on July 29, 1939, Representative Smith explained that it was needed because while aliens are restricted from doing so, there was no such restriction on the books for American citizens:

> We have laws against aliens who advocate the overthrow of this Government by force, but do you know there is nothing in the world to prevent a treasonable American citizen from doing so?... This amendment makes it unlawful for any person, be he American citizen or alien, to advocate the overthrow of the Government of the United States by force.[53]

Representatives Lee Geyer of California (D) and John Hinshaw of California (R) – the only representatives to articulate fundamental arguments against the insertion of the section at that time – opposed it on the grounds that it was un-American, undemocratic and unfair. Representative Geyer explained that in opposing, he is "defending American principles" because "real Americanism" does not merely consist in saluting the flag, the emblem of democracy, as it goes by real Americanism "consists of being able, willing and anxious to defend fundamental principles," the Bill of Rights, which states that Congress shall make no law abridging the freedom of speech. He maintained that the amendment offered by Representative Smith denies the right to freedom of speech and appealed to his fellow congressmen:

> My colleagues, look well to your vote, lest under the guise of defending democracy you undermine its very foundations. You cannot preserve it by destroying it bit by bit, as this bill does. ... There is only one way to defend democracy, and that is to never allow it to be denied to anyone.[54]

Representative Hinshaw agreed and added that it is wrong to restrict the freedom of speech of American citizens since "perfectly good American citizens" might "in the heat of controversy," without intention of breaking the law, "express offhand [some word]" and be subjected to persecution, and thus he said, "I do not think it is right, I do not think it is fair."[55]

At this point Representative McCormack offered to insert the words "knowingly or willfully," that is, that it should be unlawful for any person to "knowingly or willfully" advocate overthrowing the Government of the United States by force or violence. He explained that if a

> good American citizen and who is distressed, who is out of employment, for example...got up and said something that might be construed as advocating the overthrow of government by force or violence, when he never meant it... [he should not] be subject to indictment.

On the other hand, "a Communist is one who intends knowingly or willfully to participate in any actions, legal or illegal... that will bring about the ultimate overthrow of government. He is the one we are aiming at."[56] Representative Smith accepted Representative McCormack's suggestion, and section 2 was reinserted into the bill 79-32.[57]

That was all that was discussed during July 1939 on the section that prohibited advocating the overthrow of the U.S. government by force or violence. When the Senate debated the Smith bill on June 15, 1940, and when the House discussed the bill on June 22, 1940, it was brought up again, when advocates of the bill spoke of the need to fight a "fifth column" and defended the bill because it only relates to those who advocate overthrow of the government by force.

Senator Thomas Connally of Texas (D), chairman of the Senate Subcommittee of the Committee of the Judiciary on H.R. 5138, when reporting the bill, said that the Committee of the Judiciary believes the bill will "assure the public that Congress is doing something about the so-called 'fifth column' and in correcting subversive activities."[58] As mentioned in the previous chapter, the invasion of Norway in April 1940 prompted a fear that a "fifth column" might be at work in the United States, a fear that further intensified with the German invasion of Belgium and Holland on May 10, 1940, and the astonishing speed of the Wehrmacht's advance. There was a belief that the French were being defeated by internal subversion – by a fifth column of Nazi and communist sympathizers. Not only did President Roosevelt say in a May 1940 radio broadcast that a "Trojan Horse" threatened the United States, and in a message to Congress, asking for increases in defense appropriations, he mentioned the "treacherous use of the Fifth Column," so did congressmen talk of the threat on several occasions. For example, on May 14, 1940, Representative Dickstein said that "Congress must think very seriously how and in what matter we can effectively dispose" of groups who are "damaging our democratic institutions," hurting the citizenry and undermining the government, asserting:

> There is such a thing as free speech and freedom of the press, but there should be some limit when these groups come in here for the sole purpose of spreading this propaganda which eventually they hope will undermine the confidence ...in our form of government.[59]

Senator Connally and Senator John Danaher of Connecticut (R) emphasized that the bill was aimed only at specific advocacy. Agreeing that section 2 was "probably the broadest provision in the bill," Senator Connally explained that

> it should not disturb anyone, because it relates only to those who advocate, not a change of the Government under constitutional process, not a change of the Government under democratic institutions, but the overthrow of the Government by force or violence.[60]

Similarly, Senator Danaher stated that he "would rather err [on the question of constitutionality] in favor of the public policy of sustaining the Government's right to protect itself" than protect the rights of an individual who had "criminal" and "unlawful" intent when undertaking to overthrow the government by force or violence.[61]

Finally, in support of both sections 1 and 2, Representative Hobbs and Representative Robert Ramspeck of Georgia (D) agreed that in fighting "Communist, Nazi, and Fascist organizations," the bill is constitutional and "efficacious."[62]

The sole congressman to speak against the bill in 1940 was Representative Vito Marcantonio of New York (American Labor Party), arguing that it is undemocratic:

> It seems to me that in a period as trying as is this period, the test of democracy lies in the ability of that democracy to maintain its liberties, to preserve those liberties, and to have more freedom rather than less freedom. ... [This bill] represents that philosophy of restricting liberty and freedom in America; and we restrict that liberty and freedom under the guise of protecting American democracy. I believe this is the most incongruous proposition I have ever heard. On the one hand you say that you want to preserve American liberty and you then attempt to preserve American liberty by destroying American liberty. You are curtailing democratic rights in America under the guise of trying to protect American democracy. You end, if you carry out your course, with no freedom and no democracy.... I take this position because I want to preserve American democracy....

> [Y]ou cannot preserve American democracy by destroying it, by curtailing it, or by limiting it.[63]

When asked about the right of democracy to protect itself, Representative Marcantonio replied: "There is no question about that. A democracy has a perfect right to protect itself," spies, saboteurs and anyone who engages in illegal activity should be immediately apprehended and severely punished, but "this legislation" does not "accomplish that end" and does not protect democracy, it only "undermine[s] American freedom" and destroys "the very thing you are trying to protect."[64]

Shortly after, the House voted on the bill: 382 in favor and 4 against.[65] On the same day the Senate agreed to it as well.[66]

Public Good and Persuasion

The overall picture on the matter of the public good is a mixed one. As noted earlier, there was little deliberation in Congress on sections 1 and 2 of the Smith Act, and in the little deliberation that was conducted, congressmen didn't urge deliberation on the common good. On the other hand, several of the arguments pro and con described earlier alluded to the common good and on one occasion a congressman directly framed support for the bill in terms of the welfare of the nation. This was done by Representative Hobbs, who asserted that "[the bill] is for the common weal. It will benefit every citizen and every good alien. It is in the interest of good government. It will make our beloved country a better place."[67]

There is little evidence that congressmen were persuaded regarding sections 1 and 2 of the Smith Act; that is, they either made up their minds after seeking information and considering arguments or changed their minds. On one occasion on June 28, 1939, Representative John Cochran of Missouri (D) stated that he intended to support the bill – that it was "all right to pass laws to protect our Army and Navy against those who intend to destroy our armed forces of the country" – but he was concerned that the bill would allow to prosecute "the boys in the Army and Navy" for minor violations. Representative Hobbs removed his fear by responding:

> We are assured by the Army and Navy that all misdemeanors and offenses of every kind and character... will be handled... by courts martial.... It is the propagandist, the one who is disseminating subversive influences, at whom this title is aimed.[68]

In sum, technically the Alien Registration Act was deliberated by Congress as congressional committees heard testimonies and submitted written reports, and debate was conducted in both chambers. However, the extent of deliberation on the provisions that restricted freedom of speech was relatively low, especially when compared to congressional deliberation on the Espionage Act: there wasn't any real exchange between opposing sides, there is little evidence that congressmen were persuaded on the merits of the bill, there wasn't any serious discussion on the significance of restricting the constitutional right to free speech, there was no notable support of arguments with evidence or information and the bill was only slightly changed as a result of committee and floor deliberation. Thus, the law carried a moderate level of democratic legitimacy.

Notes

1 76th Congress, 1st Session, *Congressional Record – House*, Vol. 84, 3013, March 20, 1939.
2 Crime to Promote the Overthrow of Government, *Hearing Before Subcommittee on the Judiciary, House of Representatives, 76th Congress 1st Session on H.R. 5138: April 12 and 13, 1939* (Washington: Government Printing Office, 1939), 7. (Hereafter cited April 1939 House Hearings.)
3 April 1939 House Hearings, 10 (referring also to the *Abrams* case).
4 April 1939 House Hearings, 11.
5 April 1939 House Hearings, 69.
6 April 1939 House Hearings, 38.
7 April 1939 House Hearings, 12.
8 Oral testimony of the representative of the American Coalition (of 115 patriotic societies), and written statement of the National Council, Junior Order United American Mechanics, April 1939 House Hearings, 83–84 and 94.
9 Representative Smith, April 1939 House Hearings, 73.
10 Representative James Taylor of Tennessee (R), April 1939 House Hearings, 92.
11 April 1939 House Hearings, 25–35.
12 April 1939 House Hearings, 35.
13 April 1939 House Hearings, 25, 36.
14 April 1939 House Hearings, 26.
15 April 1939 House Hearings, 28.
16 April 1939 House Hearings, 29–31.
17 April 1939 House Hearings, 31–35.
18 76th Congress, 1st Session, *Congressional Record – House*, Vol. 84, 9536, July 19, 1939.
19 76th Congress, 1st Session, *Congressional Record – House*, Vol. 84, 8343–8344, June 29, 1939. (Report No. 994).
20 76th Congress, 1st Session, *Congressional Record – House*, Vol. 84, 10452, July 29, 1939.
21 76th Congress, 1st Session, *Congressional Record – House*, Vol. 84, 22–30, January 3, 1939.
22 76th Congress, 1st Session, *Congressional Record – House*, Vol. 84, 9533, July 19, 1939.
23 76th Congress, 1st Session, *Congressional Record – House*, Vol. 84, 10452, 10454 July 29, 1939. 79 yeses, 32 no's.
24 Crime to Promote the Overthrow of Government, *Hearing Before a Subcommittee on the Judiciary, United States Senate, 76th Congress 3rd Session on H.R. 5138: May 17, 1940* (Washington: Government Printing Office, 1940). (Hereafter cited May 1940 Senate Hearings).
25 Testimony of representatives of the ACLU, the Descendants of the American Revolution (a liberal organization founded in 1938, not affiliated with the

Daughters of the American Revolution or the Sons of the American Revolution), the National Institute of Immigrant Welfare in New York City and the Civil Rights Federation of Detroit; May 1940 Senate Hearings, 48–50, 17–18, 66, 52.

26 Testimony of representatives of the ACLU, and the National Institute of Immigrant Welfare in New York City; May 1940 Senate Hearings, 50 and 66.

27 May 1940 Senate Hearings, 6, 12–13.

28 May 1940 Senate Hearings, 8. Adding that Congress passes many laws that have to stand the test of constitutionality in the courts and that the bill would not be an exception of that rule.

29 76th Congress, 3rd Session, *Congressional Record – Senate*, Vol. 86, 8345, June 15, 1940.

30 76th Congress, 3rd Session, *Congressional Record – Senate*, Vol. 86, 8340, June 15, 1940, 7818, June 10, 1940. Senator Connally stated that they called in a representative of the Drafting Service and worked

> some 2 weeks every day in putting the bill into shape. We called on the Department of Justice and had the Solicitor General with us. We called in the Commissioner of Immigration and Naturalization, and together we went over all the existing laws, and worked the new provisions into the existing laws, so as to make a harmonious whole.

Even the words "by force or violence" didn't appear in the subsection of section 2, which concerned organizing any group who advocates the overthrow of the government; that is, it didn't say that it was unlawful to do so "by force or violence" (of course these words were in the original bill); Senator John Danaher of Connecticut (R) opposed this in the subcommittee and the words "by force or violence" were added. 76th Congress, 3rd Session, *Congressional Record – Senate*, Vol. 86, 8344–8345, June 15, 1940.

31 "Recent Statutes: Recent Federal Legislation Against Subversive Influences," *Columbia Law Review* 41 (1941): 165, ft. 39. The initial wording of the section was published a number of times in the Congressional Record, for example: 76th Congress, 1st Session, *Congressional Record – House*, Vol. 84, 10355, July 28, 1939, and 10451–10452, July 29, 1939.

32 76th Congress, 1st Session, *Congressional Record – House*, Vol. 84, 9539, July 19, 1939.

33 76th Congress, 1st Session, *Congressional Record – House*, Vol. 84, 10373, July 28, 1939.

34 76th Congress, 1st Session, *Congressional Record – House*, Vol. 84, 10379, July 28, 1939.

35 76th Congress, 1st Session, *Congressional Record – House*, Vol. 84, 10370, July 28, 1939. Faithful to his views he added that

> you are putting into this bill the same tory political philosophy that this Congress has been legislating into law ever since its inception, a reactionary philosophy, a Bourbon philosophy that has crucified the unemployed of this Nation, assaulted the rights of American labor, a philosophy which is aimed at the Bill of Rights, a philosophy which will go down to the everlasting shame of the Seventy-sixth Congress.

He was applauded.

36 76th Congress, 1st Session, *Congressional Record – House*, Vol. 84, 10380–10381, July 28, 1939.

37 76th Congress, 1st Session, *Congressional Record – House*, Vol. 84, 10376, July 28, 1939.

38 76th Congress, 1st Session, *Congressional Record – House*, Vol. 84, 10370, July 28, 1939.

39 115-30, 76th Congress, 1st Session, *Congressional Record – House*, Vol. 84, 10382, July 28, 1939. Representative O'Toole's amendment concerning outlawing the reading of the Bible was, of course, rejected as well, 117-1, 76th Congress, 1st Session, *Congressional Record – House*, Vol. 84, 10378, July 28, 1939.

40 76th Congress, 1st Session, *Congressional Record – House*, Vol. 84, 9533–9534, July 19, 1939.

41 S. 1677–To make better provision for the government of the Army and the Navy of the United States by the suppression of attempts to incite members thereof to disobedience. 76th Congress, 1st Session, *Congressional Record – House*, Vol. 84, 9533.

42 76th Congress, 1st Session, *Congressional Record – Senate*, Vol. 8, 49360, July 18, 1939.

43 See account of Representative McCormack, who was chairman of the special committee, 76th Congress, 1st Session, *Congressional Record – House*, Vol. 84, 10374, July 28, 1939. For a discussion on the 1935 House hearings, see Chafee, 447–451.

44 76th Congress, 1st Session, *Congressional Record – House*, Vol. 84, 9536, July 19, 1939, 10382, July 28, 1939. He further stated that there was "some trouble" and Representative Celler interpreted this to mean that "there is no serious danger." Lieutenant Nunn stated:

> We are having some trouble, a little trouble, and… I believe that our comparative freedom from things of this kind can be laid directly to the high character and the intelligence of the men that make up our armed forces… but there exists a slight difficulty, which certainly will grow more if not corrected.

75th Congress, 1st Session, *Congressional Record – House*, Vol. 84, 10373, July 28, 1939, 9539, July 19, 1939.

45 76th Congress, 1st Session, *Congressional Record – House*, Vol. 84, 10365, July 28, 1939.

46 76th Congress, 1st Session, *Congressional Record – House*, Vol. 84, 10380, July 28, 1939.

47 76th Congress, 1st Session, *Congressional Record – House*, Vol. 84, 10366, July 28, 1939.

48 76th Congress, 1st Session, *Congressional Record – House*, Vol. 84, 10357, July 28, 1939.

49 76th Congress, 1st Session, *Congressional Record – House*, Vol. 84, 10366, July 28, 1939.

50 76th Congress, 1st Session, *Congressional Record – House*, Vol. 84, 10377, July 28, 1939.

51 76th Congress, 1st Session, *Congressional Record – House*, Vol. 84, 10377, July 28, 1939.

52 76th Congress, 1st Session, *Congressional Record – House*, Vol. 84, 10380, July 28, 1939.

53 76th Congress, 1st Session, *Congressional Record – House*, Vol. 84, 10452, July 29, 1939.

54 76th Congress, 1st Session, *Congressional Record – House*, Vol. 84, 10452–10453, July 29, 1939.

55 76th Congress, 1st Session, *Congressional Record – House*, Vol. 84, 10453, July 29, 1939. Representative Francis Walter of Pennsylvania (D) also opposed the amendment, but only because, as mentioned earlier, it was passed as an amendment that Representative McCormack offered to another bill in the House on June 5, 1939, therefore he called Representative Smith's request to

restore the provision "surplusage." 76th Congress, 1st Session, *Congressional Record – House*, Vol. 84, 10453–10454, July 29, 1939.

56 Adding that "the Government should have the burden of proving that a person 'knowingly or willfully' advocates the overthrow of government." 76th Congress, 1st Session, *Congressional Record – House*, Vol. 84, 10454, July 29, 1939.

57 76th Congress, 1st Session, *Congressional Record – House*, Vol. 84, 10454, July 29, 1939.

58 76th Congress, 3rd Session, *Congressional Record – Senate*, Vol. 86, 7818, June 10, 1940. Also, five days later he stated that the purpose of section 1 was to prevent "a 'fifth column' among our own troops and our own naval forces." 76th Congress, 3rd Session, *Congressional Record – Senate*, Vol. 86, 8342, June 15, 1940.

59 76th Congress, 3rd Session, *Congressional Record – House*, Vol. 86, 6113–6114, May 14, 1940.

60 76th Congress, 3rd Session, *Congressional Record – Senate*, Vol. 86, 8342, June 15, 1940.

61 76th Congress, 3rd Session, *Congressional Record – Senate*, Vol. 86, 8345, June 15, 1940.

62 76th Congress, 3rd Session, *Congressional Record – House*, Vol. 86, 9032–9033, June 22, 1940.

63 76th Congress, 3rd Session, *Congressional Record – House*, Vol. 86, 9034, June 22, 1940.

64 76th Congress, 3rd Session, *Congressional Record – House*, Vol. 86, 9034, June 22, 1940.

65 45 not voting. 76th Congress, 3rd Session, *Congressional Record - House*, Vol. 86, 9036, June 22, 1940. As mentioned in note 47 in Chapter 4, in actuality the House voted on a conference report that was set up a week earlier.

66 As mentioned in note 48 in Chapter 4, the Senate agreed to the conference report, without taking a roll call. 76th Congress, 3rd Session, *Congressional Record – Senate*, Vol. 86, 8952, June 22, 1940.

67 76th Congress, 1st Session, *Congressional Record – House*, Vol. 84, 10359, July 29, 1939.

68 76th Congress, 1st Session, *Congressional Record – House*, Vol. 84, 10357, July 28, 1939.

References

Columbia Law Review. "Recent Statutes: Recent Federal Legislation Against Subversive Influences." 41 (1941): 159–171.

Congressional Record: Proceedings and Debates of the 76th Congress First Session, Vol. 84. Washington: United States Government Printing Office, 1939.

Congressional Record: Proceedings and Debates of the 76th Congress Third Session, Vol. 86. Washington: United States Government Printing Office, 1940.

Crime to Promote the Overthrow of Government, *Hearing before Subcommittee on the Judiciary, House of Representatives, 76th Congress 1st Session on H.R. 5138: April 12 and 13, 1939*. Washington: Government Printing Office, 1939.

Crime to Promote the Overthrow of Government, *Hearing before a Subcommittee on the Judiciary, United States Senate, 76th Congress 3rd Session on H.R. 5138: May 17, 1940*. Washington: Government Printing Office, 1940.

Part IV

The Cold War – Anticommunism and the McCarran Act

6 The Second Red Scare, Anticommunist Demands and the Internal Security Act Enactment, Enforcement and Adjudication

In September 1950, at the height of the Cold War and three months after the opening of hostilities in the Korean Peninsula, Congress voted over President Truman's veto and passed what one political scientist has labeled "one of the most massive onslaughts against freedom of speech and association ever launched in American history"[1] – the Internal Security Act (sponsored by Senator Patrick A. McCarran of Nevada (D). This act,[2] among other things:

- prohibited any person to conspire or agree with any other person to perform any act that would substantially contribute to the establishment within the United States of a totalitarian dictatorship under foreign control;
- required "communist-action organizations" and "communist front organizations" to register with the attorney general and report names of their officers (in the case of communist-action organizations – names and addresses of members as well) and an accounting of moneys received (including sources) and expended (including purposes);
- declared unlawful for communist organizations to "transmit or cause to be transmitted" any publication through the mail unless it bears "Disseminated by _______, a Communist organization," or broadcast any matter over any radio or television station, unless such matter is preceded by the statement "The following program is sponsored by _______, a Communist organization"; and
- established a "Subversive Activities Control Board," composed of five members appointed by the president with the advice and consent of the Senate, to hold hearings and determine whether any organization that failed to register is a communist-action or communist front organization.

Hundreds of witnesses testified at the hearings of the Subversive Activities Control Board. In 1961, the Supreme Court upheld the registration requirement in *Communist Party of the United States v. Subversive Activities Control Board.*

What was the purpose of limiting freedom of speech during the Cold War in the United States by means of the Internal Security Act? How did it come about? What and whom did it serve, and how?

In what follows we shall see that political socialization processes in the United States have been geared toward anticommunism and that there existed – particularly in 1945–1950 – a real threat to U.S. national security. The subsequent section of this chapter surveys the forces in the American political system that advocated anticommunist policies during the Cold War, including elements in Congress and in the executive who supported the Internal Security Act. The final section reviews the major provisions of the Act itself and shows how it was enforced and then later judged upon by the courts who also upheld its constitutionality.

The Second Red Scare, 1945–1950

In June 1941, after Hitler violated the Molotov-Ribbentrop nonaggression pact and invaded the Soviet Union, American Communists ceased to oppose American involvement in World War II and supported American intervention,[3] and after the United States entered the war, Americans came to view the Soviet Union and American Communists favorably.[4]

However, most polls showed that more than half of Americans did not expect cooperation with the Soviet Union to continue after the war.[5] The repudiation of points agreed at Yalta ended the wartime alliance of the United States with the Soviet Union and brought about the beginning of the Cold War, along with a sense of fear among Americans and a transformation in the climate of American politics.[6]

After the war, the Soviet Union annexed Lithuania, Estonia, Latvia, half of Poland, parts of Romania and Finland and set up totalitarian regimes in Poland, Hungary, Czechoslovakia, Romania, East Germany and Bulgaria. A border of barbed wire, mine fields, watch towers and armed guards kept the people of Eastern Europe from fleeing communist control. This shocked many Americans and revived popular anticommunism. Churchill aptly applied the term "iron curtain." Additionally, Turkey was threatened by the Soviet Union, a civil war had broken out in Greece between communists and anticommunists and a severe European economic crisis was threatening to bring communist parties to power in Italy and France. President Truman responded in 1947 with the Truman Doctrine ("the policy of the United States to support free people who are resisting attempted subjugation by armed minorities or by outside pressure") and the Marshall Plan (massive American economic aid to Europe).[7] Concurrently, communists led by Mao Tse-tung were fighting for control in China.

At the same time as these events – the origins of the Cold War – unfolded, the American Communist Party (CPUSA)[8] reached a climax of political strength. Membership peaked at approximately 70,000; its newspaper's circulation (the *Daily Worker*) exceeded 20,000 on weekdays and 50,000 on Sundays; more than a dozen of other foreign-language newspapers maintained by the party circulated in the tens of thousands within immigrant communities; two publishing houses aligned with the party published more than a million books and pamphlets a year; a fraternal insurance company controlled by the party reached a membership of 185,000; and most importantly, within the labor movement, communist-aligned leaders represented roughly 1,370,000 unionists in the CIO, a quarter of the CIO's total.[9] The CPUSA's influence extended even beyond its members, owing to its front groups, including civil right organizations, student groups, peace groups, choral societies and professional organizations.[10] It had 1,700 neighborhood clubs, 3,000 job-related clubs and several hundred clubs for youth and students, in 600 American cities and towns.[11]

In 1947–1948, President Truman called communism godless, warned that the Soviet Union only understood the language of force and cautioned against the threat to American liberty. Such themes were absorbed by the American people, who began to view the world as divided between good and bad, in which the United States was defending freedom against communists.[12]

In this atmosphere, Americans believed that communists endangered the United States.[13] The CPUSA, with the beginning of the Cold War and the conversion of the Soviet Union into a major enemy, was seen as a threat to national security.[14] In 1946, according to a Gallop poll, outlawing the CPUSA was favored by 46 percent of respondents, and by 1949, the figure reached 68 percent.[15] Americans came to view the CPUSA as a fifth column, engaged in espionage and subversion.[16] Its conspiratorial tactics – it maintained a secret underground and made its members keep their association secret – increased its dangerous image.[17] FBI director J. Edgar Hoover accepted the fifth column paradigm and stressed along with others that the CPUSA was a covert-warfare agency, and its member's potential traitors engaged in espionage, sabotage and subversion.[18] During the Cold War the FBI collected information on the CPUSA (including by way of tapping phones and planting agents) and compiled files, and sometimes produced information in trials and hearings.[19]

There was real reason for these beliefs. Documents released after the collapse of the Soviet Union, in addition to the published Venona documents (deciphered KGB telegrams), have shown that hundreds of American Communists spied for the Soviet Union during the 1930s and 1940s, that the CPUSA was involved in their recruitment as well as in stealing American atomic bomb secrets and that three of the CPUSA's general secretaries (Jay Lovestone, 1927–1929; Earl Broder, 1932–1945; and Eugene Dennis, 1945–1959) personally participated in Soviet espionage against the United States.[20]

A number of espionage cases were exposed after World War II and played a major role in arousing anticommunism:[21] in the spring of 1945 federal authorities discovered that *Amerasia*, a journal on Asian politics and foreign policy, which was communist aligned (founded and funded in 1936 by patrons of the Communist Party and editors close to the party), possessed thousands of classified documents. A naval intelligence officer, a State Department official and the journal's editor were indicted, and two of them were convicted.[22] Following this case was the uncovering of a Soviet spy ring in Canada involved in stealing information from the joint American-British-Canadian atomic bomb project.[23] In August 1945, Elizabeth Bentley, a Soviet spy, turned herself in to the FBI and her statements exposed a Soviet espionage network in Washington, D.C. Her testimony in 1948 to the House Committee on Un-American Activities (HUAC) led to Whittaker Chambers, a senior editor for *Time* magazine who was a member of the Communist Party's secret apparatus and a Soviet spy, who testified and later provided evidence of a Soviet network in the State Department that led in January 1950 to the conviction of Alger Hiss, a former high-ranking American diplomat.[24] Early in 1949, it was discovered that Judith Coplon, a political analyst from a division at the Justice Department that worked with FBI counterintelligence, was a Soviet spy.[25] In addition, in February 1950, Klaus Fuchs, a British physicist who had been involved in the Manhattan Project, confessed to having passed atomic secrets to the Soviet Union when working in Los Alamos, and his confession led to the arrest of others, including Julius and Ethel Rosenberg, for atomic espionage in the summer of that year (after the Korean War broke out).[26]

A supplementary threat to espionage was the threat of subversion. The CPUSA wasn't an independent party, and it followed instructions from Moscow. Documents released from Moscow archives confirm that the CPUSA was supervised and financed by the Soviet Union: hundreds of Americans were sent to the Soviet Union for political and organizational training, the Soviet Union provided significant funding to the CPUSA that enabled the party to employ thousands of professional revolutionaries in the 1930s and 1940s and American Communist leaders traveled to Moscow to report to the Comintern and receive instructions for the American movement.[27] Moreover, documents show that one of the CPUSA's underground missions was to place communists in U.S. government agencies to influence policy.[28] During the late 1940s and early 1950s, accusations of such subversion were often made. In addition, there was a concern that in the case of war with the Soviet Union, the CPUSA might subvert the nation's military effort by advocating "revolutionary defeatism" – the Bolshevik policy of urging Russian soldiers in World War I to turn against their officers and join the revolution.[29]

An additional threat was that of sabotage, specifically strikes and work slowdowns with the intent to damage vital industries (power plants, water supplies, the pharmaceutical industry etc.) and interrupt maritime traffic. This threat especially concerned the Truman administration because in 1941, during the Nazi-Soviet nonaggression pact before the United States entered World War II, communists led shutdowns at two California aviation companies and at the Allis-Chalmers machine tool factory in Wisconsin. After an additional strike broke out at Allis-Chalmers in 1946, by communist-dominated United Automobile Workers Local 248, the memory of the earlier strike resonated, and thereafter, Allis-Chalmers was pointed out as an example of the threat of sabotage. [30]

How did the government respond? What actions did the government take to counter the threats to American national security? Among others, it took the following steps:

In March 1947, President Truman issued an Executive Order setting up a loyalty-security program for all federal civilian employees. This was "the domestic counterpart of the Truman Doctrine,"[31] intended to prevent communist infiltration into government.[32] The order stated that disloyal persons shall be refused or removed from federal employment, including "affiliation with or sympathetic association with" any association or movement designated by the attorney general as totalitarian, fascist, communist or subversive.[33]

In 1947 Congress passed the Taft-Hartley Act (which deals with the regulation of the labor movement), consisting a provision aimed at eradicating communists from the labor movement: to maintain the benefits and protection of federal law, union officials had to sign affidavits that have oaths stating that they were not members of the Communist Party or affiliated to it.[34] In 1950 the Supreme Court upheld the constitutionality of this provision, referring to the threat of subversion, specifically the danger of a political strike.[35]

In July 1948, as mentioned in Chapter 4, the government indicted twelve CPUSA leaders, including its general secretary, Eugene Dennis, under the Smith Act for advocating the overthrow of government by force;[36] all the defendants were convicted and sentenced to prison terms.[37]

Other prosecutions were conducted against communists. Federal prosecutors charged communists with charges such as conspiracy, perjury and contempt. These prosecutions did not only perform the classic functions of the criminal system – punishment and deterrent – they also had a political socialization function: they were part of a campaign to educate the American public about the evils of communism. Even though federal prosecutors wanted to secure convictions, for the purposes of rallying the nation against the threat of communism, indictments, and the publicity that went along with them, sufficed.[38]

Congress continued to conduct investigations, mostly through the House Committee on Un-American Activities (HUAC).[39] Investigations up to 1948 were by and large domestically related – communists in New Deal agencies (such as the Federal Theatre Project), trade unions and

Hollywood.[40] The investigation into Hollywood in 1947 fascinated the public. After hearing "friendly" (anticommunist) witnesses (including later President Ronald Reagan), "unfriendly" witnesses were called and ten screenwriters who refused to testify (maintaining that the committee's investigation violated the First Amendment) were cited for contempt of Congress and imprisoned.[41] After 1948, HUAC concerned itself with the internal security issues of espionage and subversion (including hearing, as mentioned earlier, Elizabeth Bentley and Whittaker Chambers, and also Alger Hiss).[42] Besides generating a great deal of information on communist activities,[43] HUAC also published over a million pamphlets on things Americans should know about communism.[44]

Senator McCarthy burst on stage in February 1950 after giving a speech on Lincoln Day in West Virginia, in which he criticized the Democrats for allowing China to fall to the communists and claimed to have a list of 205 concealed communists in the State Department. A Senate committee investigated McCarthy's charges and vindicated the Truman administration, but McCarthy received much publicity, took the offensive, became a leading anticommunist and, in speeches across America, talked about lapses in internal security.[45]

Plainly communism has never been popular in the United States, political socialization processes have been geared toward anticommunism and America's political culture is essentially anticommunist. With the Cold War turning into a "hot" one in Korea, it is not at all surprising that the McCarran Act was enacted in 1950.

Anticommunist Demands and the Internal Security Act

Groups in Society

Several groups in American society articulated anticommunism. In reality anticommunism came in numerous varieties, and the CPUSA's enemies were many, including ethnic groups, religious groups, conservatives from both political parties, left-wing intellectuals, socialists, liberals as well as businesspeople.[46]

During World War II, Stalin killed hundreds of thousands of Poles, annexed eastern Poland and deported over a million Poles to the Soviet Union. In 1944 the Polish American Congress was formed, an umbrella organization of 20,000 Polish groups, dedicated to American support for a free and independent Poland within its prewar boundaries. In January 1945 the Soviet Union disregarded the Polish government-in-exile and recognized the Polish National Liberation Committee as the provisional government of Poland, which set out on establishing a communist totalitarian state. As a consequence, in the years after Yalta, candidates for Congress in districts with a sizable Polish constituency had to be anticommunist. Indeed, the Democratic Party, by embracing anticommunism (and through President Truman's Cold War policies), managed to preserve the vote of millions of Polish Americans and other Eastern Europeans.[47]

Christians, in particular Protestant evangelists and Catholics, regarded communism as an enemy. Especially after World War II, with the apocalyptic nature of the Cold War, Protestant evangelical Christians shifted to viewing communism not just as a modern-secular threat but as a chief evil. The Church League of America produced anticommunist studies and pamphlets for fundamentalist preachers, and several small evangelical anticommunist organizations emerged.[48]

The Roman Catholic Church was historically opposed to communism, alienated by its atheism and by Lenin's 1922 attacks on believers.[49] Left-wing revolutionary violence in the Spanish civil war and persecution of Catholics in Eastern Europe, especially in Poland and Hungary, after World War II, heightened Catholic anticommunism and brought Catholics to regard anticommunism as a requisite of their faith.[50] By the middle of the twentieth century, Roman Catholics became the largest single religious community in America; the America Catholic Church, with more than 50,000 priests and nuns, possessed institutional power; and articles, lectures and sermons were directed to millions of people concerning the communist threat.[51] In addition, Catholic groups such as the Knights of Columbus, the Catholic War Veterans and the Association of Catholic Trade Unionists (ACTU) fought communism. The Knights of Columbus was a male fraternal order with more than a million members, and it, as well as the Catholic War Veterans, sponsored forceful anticommunist activities, including lobbying, propaganda and picketing.[52] The Association of Catholic Trade Unionists advocated the compatibility of Catholicism with unionism but vigorously fought communists within organized labor.[53]

The greater majority of the American labor movement was also anticommunist. Approximately five-sixths of organized labor was non-communist, and the majority was actively hostile to communists. The AFL in particular was anticommunist, believing in a philosophy of trade unionism; that is to say, the duty of unions is to advance the interest of their members by securing direct benefits to workers and are not to be subordinate to politics or part of a wider class war.[54] The major concern of its 1946 national convention wasn't work oriented but rather the infiltration of subversives in the State Department.[55]

Anticommunists could be found among liberals as well. Some were explicit and vocal in their anticommunism, such as G. Mennen Williams, governor of Michigan, and Franklin D. Roosevelt Jr., the president's son and a representative of New York. Others collaborated with anticommunists or otherwise did not take a stand against anticommunist activities, such as university and college presidents, the Americans for Democratic Action and the American Civil Liberties Union.[56]

Conservative businesspeople and veterans also voiced anticommunist demands. The United States Chamber of Commerce distributed pamphlets with the intent of exposing communists in government and in labor, including a pamphlet in 1948 titled "A Program for Community Anti-Communist Action." The American Legion was active at both the state and the federal levels: it lobbied for anticommunist legislation, including the Mundt-Nixon Communist Registration bill of 1947, the direct precursor of the Internal Security Act of 1950 (see below), and it campaigned against communists in Hollywood, radio and television, the government and other places.[57]

Anticommunist demands were reflected and amplified across the nation in numerous newspapers, including in the *New York Times* and in the *Washington Post*.[58] Indeed the general public opinion was anticommunist, with approximately 68 percent of Americans believing in 1948 the CPUSA should be banned.[59]

All the groups mentioned earlier, while having diverse interests and different agendas, did have one thing in common: they all sought to protect the nation against the threat of communism.[60] As we shall see in the next section, this too was the concern of many congressmen and members of the Truman administration.

Congress and the Administration and the Internal Security Act

Through the HUAC, Representatives Karl E. Mundt of South Dakota (R) and Richard Nixon of California (R) introduced in July 1947 a bill that would have required communist political organizations to register with the attorney general. The bill passed in the House of Representatives 319–58 (backed by both Republicans and Democrats), with only a small number of representatives speaking against it. The Senate Judiciary Committee held hearings on the Mundt-Nixon bill, but Congress adjourned for elections before it was brought to the floor. The Chairman of the Senate Judiciary Committee Alexander Wiley of Wisconsin (R) supported the bill and called for the election of a Republican Congress to promise its enactment, and the Republican Platform of 1948 endorsed legislation to expose the treasonable activities of communists.[61]

In 1949, Karl Mundt, now a senator, reintroduced the registration bill, joining forces with Senator Homer E. Ferguson of Michigan (R) and Senator Olin D. Johnston of South Carolina (D). In March 1950, in parallel to the Senate Judiciary Committee's favorable report on a Mundt-Johnston-Ferguson bill, Richard Nixon introduced a similar measure in the House.[62]

Elements in the Truman administration and Democrats in Congress did not oppose such bills in principle. Attorney General Tom Clark, an open anticommunist, agreed in 1948 that communists were dangerous and should be restricted but maintained that the registration requirement would be difficult to administer. The Justice Department, although opposing the registration requirement, supported since 1949 other restrictive bills, some of which were later included in the McCarran bill. Senator Hebert H. Lehman of New York (D) believed that the registration requirement would only drive the communists underground, and Senator Paul H. Douglas of Illinois (D) referred to the ineffectiveness of the McCarran bill due to expected delays in hearings, appeals and prosecutions.[63]

On June 25, 1950, the Korean War broke out. President Truman called the North Korean attack a major threat to national security and presented it as international aggression, directed by the Soviet Union. He committed American forces with General MacArthur in command. The transformation of the Cold War into a hot war, less than one year after the Soviet Union tested an atomic bomb, brought about fears of a third world war (along with the possibility of nuclear holocaust) and cemented anticommunist sentiment. More than 36,000 Americans died in the Korean War and over 100,000 were wounded. When Americans had brothers, fathers and friends being killed and wounded by communists, they became impatient and believed that domestic communism should be crushed.[64] On August 10, 1950, Senator McCarran introduced the internal security bill, integrating the Mundt-Nixon registration bill along with five other internal security proposals. In parallel, Representative John S. Wood of Georgia (D) introduced a similar measure in the House, which passed on August 29, 1950, with a vote of 354-20.[65]

At this point a coalition of liberal senators from the Democratic Party drafted an alternative proposal – an emergency detention bill – and received White House support for it (previously, on August 8, 1950, President Truman sent a special message to Congress on internal security countering the registration bill and suggesting measures to expand existing espionage, foreign agents registration and wiretap laws). The proposed bill authorized the president to declare an internal security emergency during which the attorney general could detain persons he had reason to believe would be engaged in sabotage, espionage or subversive activities. The rationale of the bill's supporter's was that it would be more effective in protecting national security by concentrating on sabotage and espionage, rather than propaganda (thus not restricting freedom of speech), and that a state of emergency would be rarely called upon. The proposal was co-sponsored by Democratic Senators Lehman, Douglas and five others from West Virginia, Minnesota, North Carolina, Tennessee and Connecticut. However, this strategy of opposing the internal security bill by proposing an alternative bill failed. In essence, the administration and senators admitted that the existing security procedures were insufficient in dealing with the threat communists posed to America's national security. After a series of votes and attempts by Majority Leader Senator Scott W. Lucas of Illinois (D) to amend the proposal,

Senators McCarran and Mundt and Representative Nixon came together with Senator Lucas and Senator Spessard Holland of Florida (D) and, along with the support of Senator Millard E. Tydings of Maryland (D), accepted an amendment that *added* the detention proposal to the internal security bill. This amended bill passed on September 12, 1950, with the support of many liberal Democratic senators and with only seven senators voting nay.[66]

Vice President Alben W. Barkley, as well as Senate and House leaders, including Speaker of the House, Representative Samuel T. Rayborn of Texas (D), House Majority Leader John W. McCormack of Massachusetts (D) and Senate Majority Leader Lucas, urged President Truman to sign the bill.[67] In spite of their advice, President Truman decided to veto it. His veto, however, was for the most part a condemnation of the bill on practical grounds. Truman in fact maintained that communism presented "real dangers" to American's free society, but "The bill would not hurt communists. Instead it would help them" because "it would seriously hamper the Federal Bureau of Investigation and our other security agencies" by "[requiring] the Department of Justice and its Federal Bureau of Investigation to waste immense amounts of time and energy attempting to carry out its unworkable registration provisions." The registration provisions

> "would in practice be ineffective, and would result in obtaining no information about communists that the FBI and our other security agencies do not already have. But in trying to enforce these sections, we would have to spend a great deal of time, effort, and money—all to no good purpose."

Truman elaborated by stating that

> "if an organization which the Attorney General believes should register does not do so, he must request a five-man "'Subversive Activities Control Board"' to order the organization to register. The Attorney General would have to produce proof that the organization in question was in fact a "'communist-action"' or a "'communist-front organization."' To do this he would have to offer evidence relating to every aspect of the organization's activities. The organization could present opposing evidence. Prolonged hearings would be required to allow both sides to present proof and to cross-examine opposing witnesses. To estimate the duration of such a proceeding involving the Communist Party, we need only recall that on much narrower issues the trial of the eleven communist leaders under the Smith Act consumed nine months. In a hearing under this bill, the difficulties of proof would be much greater and would take a much longer time."

In addition the "Board's decision could be appealed to the Courts." Truman added:

> "The fact is, the FBI already possesses very complete sources of information concerning the communist movement in this country. If the FBI must disclose its sources of information in public hearings to require registration under this bill, its present sources of information, and its ability to acquire new information, will be largely destroyed."

When all the provisions of the bill are considered together,

> "it is evident that the great bulk of them are not directed toward the real and present dangers that exist from communism. Instead of striking blows at communism, they would strike blows at our own liberties and at our position in the forefront of those working for freedom in the world."[68]

President Truman did have more than a few words to say regarding the infringement of basic freedoms. He stated, among other things, that the bill "would put the Government of the United States in the thought control business"; "[i]t would give Government officials vast powers to harass all of our citizens in the exercise of their right of free speech"; "the language of the bill is so broad and vague that it might well result in penalizing the legitimate activities of people who are not communists at all, but loyal citizens"; "[sections of the bill] move in the direction of suppressing opinion and belief. This would be a very dangerous course to take, not because we have any sympathy for communist opinions but because any governmental stifling of the free expression of opinion is a long step toward totalitarianism"; "[t]he course proposed by this bill would delight the communists, for it would make a mockery of the Bill of Rights and of our claims to stand for freedom in the world"; and that

> "Our position in the vanguard of freedom rests largely on our demonstration that the free expression of opinion, coupled with government by popular consent, leads to national strength and human advancement. Let us not, in cowering and foolish fear, throw away the ideals which are the fundamental basis of our free society."[69]

But by defending his veto on practical grounds (the bill would be ineffective and difficult to administer), and in fact stating that communists are dangerous, President Truman did not win any additional support at all. He was unsuccessful in persuading those who thought the nation needed more effective internal security legislation.[70] Within an hour, the House voted to override Truman's veto, 286-48. In the Senate, liberal Democrats led a sort of a filibuster in the hope that a delay would change the minds of other senators, but the Senate voted to override the veto 57-10. Every Republican voted to override, as well as the Senate leadership and the majority of Democrats. On September 23, 1950, the Internal Security Act became the law of the nation.[71]

The Internal Security Act, Enforcement and Adjudication

An Overview of the Internal Security Act

As mentioned earlier, the Internal Security Act required communist organizations to register with the attorney general and established a "Subversive Activities Control Board." In light of the discussion in the beginning of the chapter regarding the threat communism posed to the Unites States, it is interesting to note that the Act begins by stating the "necessity for legislation" (section 2). The necessity was noted as follows:

As a result of evidence adduced before various committees of the Senate and House of Representatives, the Congress hereby finds that:

> (1) There exists a world Communist movement which, in its origins, its development, and its present practice, is a world-wide revolutionary movement whose purpose it is, by treachery, deceit, infiltration into other groups (governmental and otherwise), espionage, sabotage, terrorism, and any other means deemed necessary, to establish a Communist totalitarian dictatorship in the countries throughout the world through the medium of a world-wide Communist organization...
>
> (6) The Communist action organizations so established and utilized in various countries, acting under such control, direction, and discipline, endeavor to carry out the objectives of the world Communist movement by bringing about the overthrow of existing governments by any available means, including force if necessary, and setting up Communist totalitarian dictatorships which will be subservient to the most powerful existing Communist totalitarian dictatorship. Although such organizations usually designate themselves as political parties, they are in fact constituent elements of the world-wide Communist movement and promote the objectives of such movement by conspiratorial and coercive tactics, instead of through the democratic processes of a free elective system or through the freedom-preserving means employed by a political party which operates as an agency by which people govern themselves.
>
> (7) In carrying on the activities referred to in paragraph (6), such Communist organizations in various countries are organized on a secret, conspiratorial basis and operate to a substantial extent through organizations, commonly known as "Communist fronts", which in

most instances are created and maintained, or used, in such manner as to conceal the facts as to their true character and purposes and their membership. One result of this method of operation is that such affiliated organizations are able to obtain financial and other support from persons who would not extend such support if they knew the true purposes of, and the actual nature of the control and influence exerted upon, such "Communist fronts"...

(15) The Communist movement in the United States is an organization numbering thousands of adherents, rigidly and ruthlessly disciplined. Awaiting and seeking to advance a moment...that overthrow of the Government of the United States by force and violence may seem possible of achievement, it seeks converts far and wide by an extensive system of schooling and indoctrination. ...The Communist organization in the United States... present a clear and present danger to the security of the United States and to the existence of free American institutions, and make it necessary that Congress, in order to provide for the common defense, to preserve the sovereignty of the United States as an independent nation, and to guarantee to each State a republican form of government, enact appropriate legislation recognizing the existence of such worldwide conspiracy and designed to prevent it from accomplishing its purpose in the United States.[72]

Accordingly, the Act, among other things:[73]

- prohibited any person to combine, conspire or agree with any other person to perform any act which would substantially contribute to the establishment within the United States of a totalitarian dictatorship under foreign control;
- required "communist-action organizations" (defined as organizations that are substantially directed, dominated or controlled by the foreign government or foreign organization controlling the world Communist movement – a worldwide revolutionary movement whose purpose is to establish a communist totalitarian dictatorship) and "communist front organizations" (defined as organizations directed by communist-action organizations and operating for the purpose of giving aid and support to the world Communist movement) to register with the attorney general and report names of their officers (in the case of communist-action organizations – names and addresses of members as well) and an accounting of moneys received (including sources) and expended (including purposes);
- barred members of registered communist organizations from government employment or employment in defense facilities;
- denied passports to members of communist organizations;
- declared unlawful for communist organizations to "transmit or cause to be transmitted" any publication through the mail unless it

bears "Disseminated by ________, a Communist organization," or broadcast any matter over any radio or television station, unless such matter is preceded by the statement "The following program is sponsored by _______, a Communist organization";

- established a "Subversive Activities Control Board," composed of five members appointed by the president with the advice and consent of the Senate, to hold hearings and determine whether any organization which failed to register is a communist-action or communist front organization (upon action by the attorney general); and
- authorized the president, in the event of an invasion, declaration of war by Congress or insurrection, to proclaim the existence of an "Internal Security Emergency," during which the president, acting through the attorney general, was authorized to apprehend and detain persons as to whom there was reasonable ground to believe that they would engage in, or probably will conspire with others to engage in, acts of espionage or of sabotage.

Enforcement

Although President Truman vetoed the Act, within a month of its enactment, he appointed members to the Subversive Activities Control Board (SACB), and one month later, in November 1950, Attorney General Howard McGrath petitioned the board to order the CPUSA to register as a "communist-action" organization.[74]

In April 1953 after conducting hearings and listening to testimonies (including a number of undercover FBI agents), the SACB ordered the Communist Party to register.[75] In the same month Attorney General Hebert Brownell petitioned the board to order twelve organizations to register as "Communist front" organizations.[76] Over the following three years, the attorney general petitioned the SACB to order over twenty organizations to register.[77] The Justice Department and the SACB during the Kennedy administration initiated a number of additional proceedings.[78] In its hearings, the SACB produced much evidence regarding covert communist activity at supposedly independent organizations but that were actually controlled by the CPUSA.[79]

With regard to the emergency detention provision, plans for detaining communists and sites for detention camps were prepared:[80] in 1952 Congress appropriated $775,000 to set up six detention camps in Arizona, Florida, Pennsylvania, Oklahoma and California.[81] In coordination with the Justice Department, the FBI compiled a list of dangerous persons (Security Index) to be arrested in a national emergency (the FBI had first prepared such a list in 1939, containing Nazis and fascists as well as communists). In 1950 the list totaled 12,000 people, and after the Internal Security Act was legislated, the list of "individuals who could potentially furnish financial or material aid" to the enemy was expanded and in 1955 totaled 26,000.[82]

In December 1950 the Senate established a special subcommittee of the Judiciary Committee known as the Senate Internal Security Subcommittee (SISS) to study and investigate (1) the administration, operation and enforcement of the Internal Security Act of 1950 and other laws relating to espionage, sabotage and the protection of the internal security of the United States and (2) the extent, nature and effects of subversive activities in the United States.[83] Its first chairman was Senator McCarran,[84] who, as stated, sponsored and pushed the Internal Security Act. The SISS was actually the Senate equivalent of the HUAC.[85] The subjects of its investigations during the 1950's included the formulation of U.S. foreign policy in the Far East (including investigation of the Institute of Pacific Relations); espionage by Soviet-bloc diplomats; subversion in the federal government, particularly in the Departments of States and Defense; immigration; communism in youth organizations; the television, radio and entertainment industry; the telegraph industry; passport policy; and subversive control of five labor unions.[86]

Adjudication

The Communist Party defied to register with the SACB and appealed to the courts who in the period of 1954–1961 repeatedly upheld the constitutionality of the Internal Security Act and the registration requirement. In June 1953 the CPUSA petitioned the Court of Appeals for the District of Columbia for a review, claiming that the Internal Security Act was unconstitutional, and in December 1954, the Court of Appeals overruled all the party's objections to the Act and the board's orders. The Communist Party appealed, and since the Court of Appeals failed to take into account allegations of perjury of three witnesses, in April 1956 the Supreme Court returned the case for reconsideration. The SACB then struck those testimonies from the record and again ordered the CPUSA to register.[87]

In June 1961, in *Communist Party of the United States v. Subversive Activities Control Board*, the Supreme Court upheld the constitutionality of the registration requirements of the Internal Security Act and ruled, 5-4, that the SACB's order to the CPUSA to register was justified.[88] The Supreme Court concluded that the SACB's determination that the CPUSA was a communist-action organization was correct and that it was substantially directed, dominated or controlled by a foreign government controlling the world Communist movement. In addition, the Internal Security Act did not violate the Constitution and the interests of national security justified requiring groups that threatened the government's existence to register. In delivering the opinion of the court, Justice Felix

Frankfurter wrote, with regard to the freedoms of expression and association protected by the First Amendment that:

> The Communist Party would have us hold that the First Amendment prohibits Congress from requiring the registration and filing of information, including membership lists, by organizations substantially dominated or controlled by the foreign powers controlling the world Communist movement and which operate primarily to advance the objectives of that movement: the overthrow of existing government by any means necessary and the establishment in its place of a Communist totalitarian dictatorship. We cannot find such a prohibition in the First Amendment. So to find would make a travesty of that Amendment and the great ends for the well-being of our democracy that it serves...
>
> On the basis of its detailed investigations Congress has found that there exists a world Communist movement, foreign-controlled, whose purpose it is by whatever means necessary to establish Communist totalitarian dictatorship in the countries throughout the world...that a Communist network exists in the United States; and that the agents of communism have devised methods of sabotage and espionage carried out in successful evasion of existing law...
>
> It is not for the courts to re-examine the validity of these legislative findings and reject them. ...They are the product of extensive investigation by Committees of Congress over more than a decade and a half. We certainly cannot dismiss them as unfounded or irrational imaginings. ...And if we accept them, as we must, as a not unentertainable appraisal by Congress of the threat which Communist organizations pose not only to existing government in the United States, but to the United States as a sovereign, independent nation – if we accept as not wholly unsupportable the conclusion that those organizations "are not free and independent organizations, but are sections of a world-wide Communist organization and are controlled, directed, and subject to the discipline of the Communist dictatorship of [a] ... foreign country," § 2 (5) – we must recognize that the power of Congress to regulate Communist organizations of this nature is extensive. "Security against foreign danger is one of the primitive objects of civil society," James Madison wrote in *The Federalist* (No. 41). "It is an avowed and essential object of the American Union. The powers requisite for attaining it must be effectually confided to the federal councils."...Means for effective resistance against foreign incursion – whether in the form of organizations which function, in some technical sense, as "agents" of a foreign power, or in the form of organizations which, by complete dedication and obedience to foreign directives, make themselves the instruments of a foreign power – may not be denied to the national legislature. "To preserve

its independence, and give security against foreign aggression and encroachment, is the highest duty of every nation, and to attain these ends nearly all other considerations are to be subordinated. It matters not in what form such aggression and encroachment come … ."

…

Of course, congressional power in this sphere, as in all spheres, is limited by the First Amendment. Individual liberties fundamental to American institutions are not to be destroyed under pretext of preserving those institutions, even from the gravest external dangers. But where the problems of accommodating the exigencies of self-preservation and the values of liberty are as complex and intricate as they are in the situation described in the findings of § 2 of the Subversive Activities Control Act – when existing government is menaced by a world-wide integrated movement which employs every combination of possible means, peaceful and violent, domestic and foreign, overt and clandestine, to destroy the government itself – the legislative judgment as to how that threat may best be met consistently with the safeguarding of personal freedom is not to be set aside merely because the judgment of judges would, in the first instance, have chosen other methods. Especially where Congress, in seeking to reconcile competing and urgently demanding values within our social institutions, legislates not to prohibit individuals from organizing for the effectuation of ends found to be menacing to the very existence of those institutions, but only to prescribe the conditions under which such organization is permitted, the legislative determination must be respected.[89]

Following this ruling, in December 1961 the CPUSA was indicted for refusal to register and afterward was fined $120,000 in the District Court.[90]

Epilogue

The diminishment of the extent of the communist threat on U.S. national security in the late 1950s brought with it a lessening of enforcement of the Internal Security Act[91] as well as a reversal in Supreme Court judgment. When the issue of registration returned to the Supreme Court in 1965, this time it ruled that such a requirement would be self-incrimination that could be used for other prosecutions and it violates the Fifth Amendment.[92] The ruling had the effect of emptying the SACB of its purpose and the SACB had little to do afterward.[93]

This chapter has shown that American political culture was historically anticommunist, and when the communist threat was high (the Cold War), various forces in the political system advocated anticommunist policies, and the government responded to the threat and to societal demands with a range of measures, including relevant legislation that restricted certain freedoms. The Internal Security Act was a direct response to the communist threat of subversion and espionage in 1945–1950 and limited the freedom of speech of American Communists who threatened to overthrow the American Republic and the ideals it stood for, among other ways, by requiring communist organizations to register with the attorney general.

The next chapter – by analyzing congressional deliberation on the enactment of the McCarran Act – deals with the major question: to what degree was such a law *democratically* legitimate?

Notes

1 Robert Justin Goldstein, *Political Repression in Modern America: From 1870 to 1976*. 2nd ed. (Urbana and Chicago: University of Illinois Press, [1978] 2001), 323. Quoted in Geoffrey R. Stone, *Perilous Times: Free Speech in Wartime from the Sedition Act of 1798 to the War on Terrorism* (New York: W.W. Norton & Company, 2004), 335.
2 Internal Security Act of 1950, *United States Statutes at Large*, Vol. 64, Part 1 (Washington: Government Printing Office, 1952), 987–1031.
3 John Earl Haynes, *Red Scare or Red Menace?: American Communism and Anticommunism in the Cold War Era* (Chicago: Ivan R. Dee, 1996), 35.
4 Stone, 322.
5 Melvyn P. Leffler, *A Preponderance of Power: National Security, the Truman Administration, and the Cold War* (Stanford: Stanford University Press, 1992), 14–15. Leffler concludes, "In other words, the American people retained a strong residue of animosity and suspicion toward the Bolshevik motherland."
6 Stone, 322–323; Haynes, 37; Robert Griffith, "American Politics and the Origins of 'McCarthyism'," In *The Specter: Original Essays on the Cold War and the Origins of McCarthyism*, Eds. Robert Griffith and Athan Theoharis (New York: Franklin Watts, Inc., 1974), 9.
7 Haynes, 37–40. See also Walter LaFeber, *America, Russia and the Cold War 1945–1996*. 8th ed. (New York: McGraw-Hill, 1997), 49–60. For an alternative view, that the Truman Doctrine wasn't a response to communist aggression but "the expression of a long-standing messianic anti-communistic antagonism that went looking for a situation," see Michael Parenti, *The Anti-Communist Impulse* (New York: Random House, 1969), 148.
8 Communist Party of the United States of America. For a brief history of the American Communist Party, see Klehr, Harvey, Haynes, John Earl and Firsov, Fridrikh Igorevich, *The Secret World of American Communism* (New Haven and London: Yale University Press, 1995), 4–14.
9 Haynes, 36. As mentioned in Chapter 4, the CIO was a federation of unions that organized industrial workers. John L. Lewis, president of the United Mine Workers, formed the CIO – with communist assistance – in the mid-1930s, when he broke with the American Federation of Labor (AFL). Communists were later driven out. Ellen Schrecker. *Many Are the Crimes: McCarthyism in America*. (Princeton: Princeton University Press, 1998), 27–28; Haynes, 12; Klehr et al., 9, 12.
10 Ellen Schrecker, "'Mere Shadows': The Early Cold War," In *Security v. Liberty: Conflicts Between Civil Liberties and National Security in American History*, Ed. Daniel Farber (New York: Russell Sage Foundation, 2008), 72–73.

11 Harvey Klehr, and John Earl Haynes, *The American Communist Movement: Storming Heaven Itself* (New York: Twayne Publishers, 1992), 108–109.
12 Stone, 324.
13 Ellen Schrecker, "McCarthyism: Political Repression and the Fear of Communism," *Social Research* 71 (Winter 2004): 1047.
14 Schrecker, *McCarthyism*, 1051.
15 David Caute, *The Great Fear: The Anti-communist Purge Under Truman and Eisenhower* (New York: Simon and Schuster, 1978), 215. And see discussion in next section on the groups in American society that articulated anticommunism.
16 Haynes, 63.
17 Schrecker, *Mere Shadows*, 71.
18 Haynes, 179; Schrecker, *McCarthyism*, 1051.
19 Haynes, 179–180; Klehr and Haynes, 129–130.
20 Schrecker, *McCarthyism*, 1051; Haynes, 198–199; Stone, 319–320.
21 Haynes, 15; Stone, 324.
22 Klehr and Haynes, 107; Haynes, 50–53.
23 M.J., Heale *American Anticommunism: Combating the Enemy Within, 1830–1970* (Baltimore and London: The Johns Hopkins University Press, 1990), 136; Stone, 324, Haynes, 55; Schrecker, *Mere Shadows*, 77.
24 Klehr and Haynes, 107; Haynes, 76–80; Heale, 148. Hiss accompanied President Roosevelt to the Yalta conference and was also a leading figure in the American delegation to the founding conference of the United Nations.
25 Haynes, 56–57; Schrecker, *Many Are the Crimes*, 175–176. She was caught handing over files to a Soviet diplomat.
26 Stone, 331; Heale, 151, 163; Haynes, 57–58. In 1953 the Rosenbergs were convicted and executed.
27 Haynes, 10.
28 Haynes, 14.
29 Schrecker, *Mere Shadows*, 74–75; Schrecker, *McCarthyism*, 1052.
30 Schrecker, *McCarthyism*, 1053–1055; Schrecker, *Mere Shadows*, 79–80.
31 Heale, 137.
32 Haynes, 169.
33 Ellen Schrecker, "Harry S. Truman, Executive Order 9385, March 21, 1947," In *The Age of McCarthyism: A Brief History with Documents*. 2nd ed. (Boston and New York: Bedford/St. Martin's, 2002), 174–175. This program very much affected American society during the Cold War as it became a foundation for anticommunism frenzy; Haynes, 169; Stone, 327. For criticism on the program and details on its upshots, see Haynes, 169–175; Schrecker, *McCarthyism*, 1062–1068; Schrecker, *Mere Shadows*, 84–85; Klehr and Haynes, 126; Stone, 326–327, 337–338, 343–352; Heale, 138.
34 Goldstein, 291; Haynes, 135; Klehr and Haynes, 116. In 1946 living costs rose sharply, the nation witnessed an unprecedented strike wave (in general, nonviolent) and antilabor sentiment in the general public and in the Congress elected that year was strong (Stone, 323; David M. Oshinsky, "The CIO and the Communists," In *The Specter: Original Essays on the Cold War and the Origins of McCarthyism*, Eds. Robert Griffith and Athan Theoharis (New York: Franklin Watts, Inc., 1974), 125–126; Melvyn Dubofsky, *The State and Labor in Modern America* (Chapel Hill: The University of North Carolina Press, 1994), 201). Melvyn Dubofsky, among others, views the Taft-Hartley Act as antilabor, Dubofsky, 199–208. But while many of the provisions were repressive, "the main thrust of Taft-Hartley was to *regulate* the labor movement...with regard to communists...the intent was *annihilation*" (italics in original), Goldstein, 291.

35 Schrecker, *Mere Shadows*, 80; Schrecker, *Many Are the Crimes*, 187.
36 Stone, 396; Klehr and Haynes, 127; Haynes, 163. The timing of the indictment – after Amerasia and the exposure of communist espionage, as well as the 1950 elections in sight – was not incidental: the Truman administration wanted to strengthen its anticommunist credentials. See Haynes, 163 and Stone, 397.
37 Haynes, 163–164; Stone, 397–398. At the height of the Cold War, between 1951 and 1957, a total of 145 communists were arrested and prosecuted under the Smith Act. Stone, 411.
38 Schrecker, *McCarthyism*, 1056–1058.
39 Set up in 1938 (see Chapter 4), the HUAC was yearly reauthorized by Congress from 1938 until 1945, and in 1946 a coalition of conservative Democrats and Republicans made it a permanent House committee. Schrecker, *Many Are the Crimes*, 91, Haynes, 69; throughout 1945–1951 (the 79th, 80th and 81st Congresses) there were a total of seventy investigations. Griffith, 13; Public hearing days of HUAC expanded from 11 during 1945–1946, to 52 during 1947–1948 and 115 during 1949–1950. Goldstein, 343; In 1945 HUAC's appropriation was $50,000 and by the 80th Congress (1947–1949), it increased $200,000. Heale, 140. Goldstein, 308.
40 Griffith, 14.
41 The "Hollywood Ten," Haynes, 70–73; Kleher and Haynes, 134; Stone, 327. There were communists in the Hollywood industry – communists helped found the Screen Writers Guild and were active in other unions – however, they were unsuccessful in bringing communist ideology into movies. Haynes, 70–71.
42 Griffith, 14; Haynes, 76–84.
43 Klehr and Haynes, 135; in 1947–1948 HUAC put together dossiers on 25,591 individuals and 1,786 organizations (and in total from 1945 to 1957 over 3,000 witnesses testified before HUAC). Stone, 355, 372.
44 Stone, 355.
45 Haynes, 144–146; Stone, 331–334. McCarthy continued to strike at the Truman administration, making wild accusations. In December 1954 his tactics of making inaccurate charges that lacked supporting evidence ran out, and with the Republicans in control of both Congress and the presidency, he was censured by the Senate. An alcoholic, he died in 1957 of cirrhosis of the liver (Haynes, 147–162). In light of the events of the Second Red Scare described earlier, leading up to 1950, and the anticommunism articulated by groups in American society, I agree with scholars such as Robert Griffith that Senator McCarthy was "the product of anti-Communist politics, not its progenitor" (Griffith, 16).
46 Schrecker, *McCarthyism*, 1043; Schrecker, *Mere Shadows*, 72; Haynes, 89; Heale, 133.
47 Haynes, 41–49.
48 Haynes, 89–92.
49 Donald F. Crosby, S. J., "The Politics of Religion: American Catholics and the Anti-Communist Impulse," In *The Specter: Original Essays on the Cold War and the Origins of McCarthyism*, Eds. Robert Griffith and Athan Theoharis (New York: Franklin Watts, Inc., 1974), 21; Haynes, 92, 89; Schrecker, *Mere Shadows*, 72.
50 Crosby, 22–27; Haynes, 92–93.
51 Haynes, 95, 92.
52 Crosby, 31–34; Haynes, 95; Griffith, 11.
53 Crosby, 35; Haynes, 96–97.
54 Haynes, 110–112; Schrecker, *Many Are the Crimes*, 69–70.
55 Oshinsky, 127.

56 Haynes, 40–41; Schrecker, *McCarthyism*, 1068–1071.
57 Griffith, 10–11; Heale, 139.
58 Heale, 139, 141; Griffith, 11; Stone, 318.
59 Caute, 215; Heale, 147.
60 Schrecker, *McCarthyism*, 1043.
61 William R. Tanner and Robert Griffith, "Legislative Politics and 'McCarthyism': The Internal Security Act of 1950," In *The Specter: Original Essays on the Cold War and the Origins of McCarthyism*, Eds. Robert Griffith and Athan Theoharis (New York: Franklin Watts, Inc., 1974), 176–177; Heale, 140.
62 Tanner and Griffith, 178. Hearings on Legislation to Outlaw Certain Un-American and Subversive Activities, *Hearing Before the Committee on Un-American Activities, House of Representatives, 81st Congress 2nd Session on H.R. 3903 and H.R. 7595: March 21,22,23 and 28, 1950* (Washington: Government Printing Office, 1948), 2170, 2311.
63 Tanner and Griffith, 179, 180, 181.
64 Athan Theoharis, "The Rhetoric of Politics: Foreign Policy, Internal Security, and Domestic Politics in the Truman Era, 1945–1950," In *Politics and Policies of the Truman Administration*, Ed. Barton J. Bernstein (New York: New Viewpoints, 1974), 215; Heale, 155; Stone, 334, Schrecker, *McCarthyism*, 1049; Klehr and Haynes, 132; United States Department of Veteran Affairs, *America's Wars* (Washington: Office of Public Affairs, May 2016), https://www.census.gov/history/pdf/va-veterans-62017.pdf [accessed: January 4, 2020].
65 Tanner and Griffith, 182–183; 81st Congress, 2nd Session, *Congressional Record –Senate*, Vol. 96, 12145, August 10, 1950; 81st Congress, 2nd Session, *Congressional Record –House*, Vol. 96, 12966, August 21, 1950; 81st Congress, 2nd Session, *Congressional Record –House*, Vol. 96, 13769–13770, August 29, 1950.
66 Tanner and Griffith, 182–185; Theoharis, 228; Heale, 156; Goldstein, 322; 81st Congress, 2nd Session, *Congressional Record –Senate*, Vol. 96, 14628, September 12, 1950.
67 Tanner and Griffith, 186; Stone, 335.
68 "Internal Security Act, 1950 – Veto Message from the President of the United States," 81st Congress, 2nd Session, *Congressional Record – House*, Vol. 96, 15629–15632, September 22, 1950.
69 "Internal Security Act, 1950 – Veto Message from the President of the United States," 81st Congress, 2nd Session, *Congressional Record – House*, Vol. 96, 15629–15632, September 22, 1950.
70 Theoharis, 228; Tanner and Griffith, 188.
71 Tanner and Griffith, 187–188; 81st Congress, 2nd Session, *Congressional Record – House*, Vol. 96, 15632–15633, September 22, 1950; 81st Congress, 2nd Session, *Congressional Record – Senate*, Vol. 96, 15726, September 23, 1950.
72 Internal Security Act of 1950, *United States Statutes at Large*, Vol. 64, Part 1 (Washington: Government Printing Office, 1952), 987–989.
73 Internal Security Act of 1950, *United States Statutes at Large*, Vol. 64, Part 1 (Washington: Government Printing Office, 1952), 987–1031. See Appendix C for the full text of sections 1–15 of Title I and of relevant sections of Title II.
74 Goldstein, 332; Caute, 170–171.
75 Caute, 171.
76 Goldstein, 339.
77 Caute, 172.
78 Goldstein, 418.
79 Haynes, 168.
80 Haynes, 169.

81 Goldstein, 324.
82 Goldstein, 324; Schrecker, *Many Are the Crimes*, 208; Haynes, 169. By 1958 the Security Index was reduced to its original number and in 1962 to ten thousand. Goldstein, 324.
83 "Senate Internal Security Subcommittee," Records of the Committee on the Judiciary and Related Committees, 1816–1968, In *Guide to the Records of the U.S. Senate at the National Archives (Record Group 46)*, http://www.archives.gov/legislative/guide/senate/chapter-13-judiciary-1947-1968.html#SISS [accessed: January 4, 2020].
84 Caute, 104; Heale, 160.
85 Haynes, 150.
86 "Senate Internal Security Subcommittee," Records of the Committee on the Judiciary and Related Committees, 1816–1968, In *Guide to the Records of the U.S. Senate at the National Archives (Record Group 46)*, http://www.archives.gov/legislative/guide/senate/chapter-13-judiciary-1947-1968.html#SISS [accessed: January 4, 2020]; Caute, 104.
87 Caute, 171.
88 Goldstein, 412; Caute, 172. See dissent of Chief Justice Warren and others in Paul L. Murphy *The Constitution in Crisis Times, 1918–1969* (New York: Harper & Row, Publishers, 1972), 373–374.
89 *Communist Party of the United States v. Subversive Activities Control Board.* 367 U.S. 1. Supreme Court of the United States. June 5, 1961. U.S. LEXIS 1934.
90 Caute, 564, ft. 28.
91 In 1953 the hot war in Korea ended and Stalin died. In Western Europe, the Marshall Plan had succeeded in restoring economic prosperity. Along with the establishment of the North Atlantic Treaty Organization, the fear of Western European states falling to the Soviet's lessened and Soviet expansionism was in check. In addition, Nikita Khrushchev proved less aggressive than Stalin. He met President Eisenhower in 1955 in Geneva and introduced the policy of "peaceful coexistence." It seemed that there was no immediate threat to the United States and anticommunism sentiment was significantly reduced. Klehr and Haynes, 140–141; Heale, 192–193. With the likelihood of war with the Soviet Union down, the Eisenhower administration, as well as Congress, deemed the detention plans as unnecessary. In 1956 the designated sites were sold or leased. Haynes, 169; Klehr and Haynes, 136; Goldstein, 403.
92 Klehr and Haynes, 135; Caute, 172, 38; *Albertson et al. v. Subversive Activities Control Board.* 382 U.S. 70. Supreme Court of the United States. November 15, 1965.
93 In 1968 Congress removed most of its nominal functions, and in 1973, together with the Nixon administration, it abolished the SACB by deleting it from the budget. Caute, 581 ft. 26; Haynes, 194; Goldstein, 500. The Supreme Court also ruled in 1967 that the provision of the Act that barred members of registered communist organizations from employment in defense facilities was unconstitutional in *United States v. Robel.* Stone, 416*n*; Goldstein, 424.

References

Caute, David. *The Great Fear: The Anti-communist Purge Under Truman and Eisenhower.* New York: Simon and Schuster, 1978.

Communist Party of the United States v. Subversive Activities Control Board. 367 U.S. 1. Supreme Court of the United States, June 5, 1961.

Congressional Record: Proceedings and Debates of the 81st Congress Second Session, Vol. 96. Washington: United States Government Printing Office, 1950.

Crosby, Donald F., "The Politics of Religion: American Catholics and the Anti-Communist Impulse." *The Specter: Original Essays on the Cold War and the Origins of McCarthyism*. Eds. Robert Griffith and Athan Theoharis, 18–38. New York: Franklin Watts, Inc., 1974.

Dubofsky, Melvyn. *The State and Labor in Modern America*. Chapel Hill: The University of North Carolina Press, 1994.

Goldstein, Robert Justin. *Political Repression in Modern America: From 1870 to 1976*. 2nd ed. Urbana and Chicago: University of Illinois Press, [1978] 2001.

Griffith, Robert. "American Politics and the Origins of 'McCarthyism'." *The Specter: Original Essays on the Cold War and the Origins of McCarthyism*. Eds. Robert Griffith and Athan Theoharis, 1–17. New York: Franklin Watts, Inc., 1974.

Haynes, John Earl. *Red Scare or Red Menace?: American Communism and Anti-communism in the Cold War Era*. Chicago: Ivan R. Dee, 1996.

Heale, M.J. *American Anticommunism: Combating the Enemy Within, 1830–1970*. Baltimore and London: The Johns Hopkins University Press, 1990.

Hearings on Legislation to Outlaw Certain Un-American and Subversive Activities, *Hearing before the Committee on Un-American Activities, House of Representatives, 81st Congress 2nd Session on H.R. 3903 and H.R. 7595: March 21,22,23 and 28, 1950*. Washington: Government Printing Office, 1950.

Klehr, Harvey and Haynes, John Earl. *The American Communist Movement: Storming Heaven Itself*. New York: Twayne Publishers, 1992.

Klehr, Harvey, Haynes, John Earl and Firsov, Fridrikh Igorevich. *The Secret World of American Communism*. New Haven and London: Yale University Press, 1995.

LaFeber, Walter. *America, Russia and the Cold War 1945–1996*. 8th ed. New York: McGraw-Hill, 1997.

Leffler, Melvyn P. *A Preponderance of Power: National Security, the Truman Administration, and the Cold War*. Stanford: Stanford University Press, 1992.

Murphy, Paul L. *The Constitution in Crisis Times, 1918–1969*. New York: Harper & Row, Publishers, 1972.

Oshinsky, David M. "The CIO and the Communists." *The Specter: Original Essays on the Cold War and the Origins of McCarthyism*. Eds. Robert Griffith and Athan Theoharis, 116–151. New York: Franklin Watts, Inc., 1974.

Parenti, Michael. *The Anti-Communist Impulse*. New York: Random House, 1969.

Schrecker, Ellen. *Many are the Crimes: McCarthyism in America*. Princeton: Princeton University Press, 1998.

Schrecker, Ellen. *The Age of McCarthyism: A Brief History with Documents*. 2nd ed. Boston and New York: Bedford/St. Martin's, 2002.

Schrecker, Ellen. "McCarthyism: Political Repression and the Fear of Communism." *Social Research* 71 (Winter 2004): 1041–1086.

Schrecker, Ellen. "'Mere Shadows': The Early Cold War." *Security v. Liberty: Conflicts Between Civil liberties and National Security in American History*. Ed. Daniel Farber, 67–94. New York: Russell Sage Foundation, 2008.

"Senate Internal Security Subcommittee," Records of the Committee on the Judiciary and Related Committees, 1816–1968, *Guide to the Records of the U.S.*

Senate at the National Archives (Record Group 46), <http://www.archives.gov/legislative/guide/senate/chapter-13-judiciary-1947-1968.html#SISS>.

Stone, Geoffrey R. *Perilous Times: Free Speech in Wartime from the Sedition Act of 1798 to the War on Terrorism*. New York: W.W. Norton & Company, 2004.

Tanner, William R. and Griffith, Robert. "Legislative Politics and 'McCarthyism': The Internal Security Act of 1950." *The Specter: Original Essays on the Cold War and the Origins of McCarthyism*. Eds. Robert Griffith and Athan Theoharis, 172–189. New York: Franklin Watts, Inc., 1974.

Theoharis, Athan. "The Rhetoric of Politics: Foreign Policy, Internal Security, and Domestic Politics in the Truman Era, 1945–1950." *Politics and Policies of the Truman Administration*. Ed. Barton J. Bernstein, 196–242. New York: Franklin Watts, Inc., 1974.

United States Department of Veteran Affairs, *America's Wars*. Washington, DC: Office of Public Affairs, May 2016, <https://www.census.gov/history/pdf/va-veterans-62017.pdf>.

United States Statutes at Large, Vol. 64, Part 1. Washington: Government Printing Office, 1952.

7 Congressional Deliberation on the McCarran Act

House and Senate Committee Hearings and Deliberation

In the case of the McCarran Act, the deliberative process actually began two years before floor debate, in congressional committee hearings and reports. The McCarran Act (and its direct precursors) was essentially discussed first in 1948, then in 1949 and finally in 1950:

- 1948: Recall from the previous chapter that Representative Karl E. Mundt of South Dakota (R) introduced in July 1947 a bill, formulated with Representative Richard Nixon of California (R), which would have required communist political organizations to register with the attorney general (in fact, with the Department of Justice. The bill also provided that communist printed matter be labeled). In February 1948, the Subcommittee on Legislation of the House Committee on Un-American Activities (HUAC) held hearings on this bill and on a bill introduced by Representative Gordon L. McDonough of California (R) (to make the practice of communism a treasonable act), and in April 1948 the committee reported a bill containing anti-sedition and registration provisions (the Mundt-Nixon bill). In May 1948 the bill passed the House (after being introduced by Representative Mundt) and the Senate Judiciary Committee held hearings on it, but the Senate committee did not report the bill and Congress adjourned for elections.[1]
- 1949: In March 1949, Karl Mundt, now a senator, along with Senator Olin Johnston of South Carolina (D), reintroduced a revised version of the Mundt-Nixon bill. In April and May 1949 a subcommittee of the Senate Judiciary Committee held hearings on this bill and one other sponsored by Senator Homer E. Ferguson of Michigan (R) and approved a version of the two bills, aka the Mundt-Johnston-Ferguson bill. This bill was introduced in the Senate in July 1949 by Senator Mundt, and after being referred to the Senate Judiciary Committee, it was reported favorably in March 1950.[2]
- 1950: In March 1950, Representative Nixon introduced a bill to protect against un-American and subversive activities, an analogous

> version of the Mundt-Johnston-Ferguson bill. From late March until early May 1950, the HUAC held hearings on this bill and on one other bill, introduced a year earlier by Representative John S. Wood of Georgia (D) (prohibiting federal employees, and individuals connected with national defense contracts, to be affiliated with the Communist Party). In August 1950, after a combination of these two bills was introduced by Representative Wood, the HUAC recommended it to pass.[3]

The following section analyzes the deliberation by the congressional committees. Public hearings were conducted; and external groups, individuals and law professors appeared and conveyed their views concerning the proposed legislation restricting freedom of speech. Indeed, original drafts were amended as a result of oral and written testimonies. However, the 1948 hearings were more deliberative than the others because, among other reasons, committee members were more keen on gathering information and considering arguments in order to make an evaluation and decide on the bills.

The 1948 HUAC Subcommittee Hearings

Nixon, as chairman of the subcommittee, presided over the hearings and at the outset spoke in a deliberative manner, saying that

> we have under consideration several bills which have been introduced that would curb or outlaw the Communist Party in the United States. It is the function of our subcommittee to study these proposals carefully, to conduct hearings, and to determine what, if any, legislative action should be referred … to the House.[4]

He further stated that the purpose of the committee hearings is to obtain answers to three questions: First, if American Communists constitute a real danger to national security; second, if present laws are adequate to cope with the danger, and if not, what new laws are necessary; and third, if there's any risk that adoption of the proposed legislation will impair "fundamental constitutional rights."[5]

Over the course of six days, the subcommittee heard and received over two dozen testimonies and statements (including from the representative of the Communist Party of the United States) arguing pro and con Representative McDonough's bill – to define communism and make the practice of communism a treasonable act – and Representative Mundt's bill – to require members of the Communist Party and organizations controlled by it to register with the Department of Justice as agents of a foreign principal and to provide that all printed matter distributed by such members and organizations be labelled in compliance with the legislation. While there was general consent that McDonough's bill was unconstitutional, there were diverse views concerning Mundt's proposal.

At the outset of the hearings, Mundt emphasized that his legislation "does not seek to deny to Communists or to supporters of Communist front organizations the right to speak and to publicize freely their views and opinions"; it does, however, "bring out of the black night of seductive secrecy the operations and activities of those conspiring to change the American way of life by stealth."[6] He reviewed evidence reported by the HUAC that the Communist Party was an agent of a foreign power and quoted Edgar Hoover's testimony before the HUAC from March 1947 that "The Communist Party of the United States is a fifth column if there ever was one."[7]

On the other hand, the general counsel for the American Civil Liberties Union (ACLU), Arthur Hays, stated, "Neither democratic principles nor practical expediency" can justify the proposals before the committee[8] declaring Mundt's bill unconstitutional: a bill of attainder, a denial of due process and an infringement of free speech, adding that it is specific legislation and not general, and it imposes penalties on individuals merely by their association and without any hearing.[9]

The attorney general of the United States, Tom Clark, did not give full support to the Mundt bill. While opposing communists and their ideology, he believed that the fight was "well on its way" and that victory was assured "by continued vigorous prosecutions" by the Department of Justice of subversive groups.[10] He told the committee not to "lose sight of the constitutional questions" when deliberating the legislation[11] and suggested the strengthening of existing statutes, including the Smith Act and the Espionage Act.[12]

The recurring opinion of experts in law who appeared before the subcommittee, however, was that communist activity threatens the destruction of civil rights;[13] the danger to democracy is imminent, clear, present and powerful;[14] and the way to deal with the threat was not to curb communists ideas, beliefs or speech but to aim legislation at their actions and activities.[15] Louis Waldman, a labor relations lawyer, presented ten facts as to the danger and proposed a program of exposure – a "Totalitarian Organizations Registration Law."[16] Adolf Berle, a Columbia law professor and former assistant secretary of state, thought that the Mundt bill came close to the solution because it relied on the principle of disclosure and suggested to add administrative machinery – that the attorney general has the power to subpoena witnesses, hold hearings, develop the facts and make an administrative finding on the basis of which registrations could be ordered.[17] Robert Maurer, a Georgetown University law professor, maintained that the courts would be expected to sustain the law if it was aimed at those acts and activities that are disclosed by legislative findings and the law is framed to protect the public interest.[18]

Subcommittee members attested to seriously considering arguments on the merits of the legislation and being persuaded – key deliberative elements. Thus Representative John McDowell of Pennsylvania (R) stated during the testimony of Robert Maurer that the purpose of the hearings is to get "you gentlemen down here – so we can assemble your thoughts. ... I will tell you frankly that I am sure the Congress is a long way from making up its mind on just how to tackle this problem."[19] Similarly, Nixon responded to Arthur Hays (ACLU) testimony by saying that "although we are in disagreement, I think you can see from the attitude of the committee today that we are attempting to find the proper laws in the American tradition to control what may to us appear to be somewhat more of a danger than appears to you."[20]

On April 30, 1948, the HUAC recommended passage of a newly redrafted bill (the Mundt-Nixon bill, introduced in the House by Representative Mundt), which incorporated suggestions brought up in the subcommittee hearings.[21] For example, it provided for administrative determinations, that is, enabled the attorney general to institute investigations to determine whether an organization is a communist political organization or a communist front organization (and provided that any organization may obtain judicial review of an order of the attorney general to register),[22] and it had an entire section on the necessity for legislation that contained the findings of Congress.[23]

Other sections were added as a result of the subcommittee hearings, including: making it unlawful to attempt, or facilitate, the establishment of a totalitarian dictatorship in the United States under foreign control (i.e., not just communist);[24] requiring that the registration with the attorney general of communist political organizations and communist front organizations be accompanied with a statement and names and addresses of their officers and an accounting of receipts and expenditures (thus forcing the Communist movement, in view of its foreign-directed character, to operate in the open rather than underground);[25] denying passports to members of communist political organizations (a means to fight the international communist conspiracy);[26] denying federal employment to members of communist political organizations (to protect the integrity of government itself);[27] and making it unlawful for registered communist organizations to broadcast any matter over the radio unless it is proceeded by a statement giving the name of the organization and the fact that it is communist.[28]

In its report, the HUAC explained that the Mundt-Nixon bill was adequate legislation. After a comprehensive analysis and study, it believed that the legislation was democratic and in accordance "with constitutional traditions." Other legislative proposals that effectively outlawed the Communist Party were rejected.[29]

On May 19, 1948, the Mundt-Nixon bill passed in the House of Representatives 319–58 (backed by both Republicans and Democrats), and later that month, the Senate Judiciary Committee held hearings on it.[30]

The 1948 Senate Judiciary Committee Hearings

The Senate Judiciary Committee began by hearing testimonies from Representative Nixon and from Donald Richberg, a Washington attorney who consulted the Subcommittee on Legislation of the HUAC on the drafting of the bill.[31] Their view was that the bill was an effective way to deal with the communist menace, as it would expose the Communist movement[32] and that the bill was constitutional. It was constitutional for many reasons, including the following: it didn't interfere with civil rights and didn't abridge freedom of speech or freedom of the press, because these freedoms are not unlimited and they can be curtailed when there is a clear and present danger ("freedom of speech has never meant freedom to say anything you wanted on any occasion");[33] it didn't specifically name the Communist Party nor declare communist political organizations illegal;[34] and innocent people were protected by means of the administrative procedure and judicial review sections of the bill.[35]

While other individuals and organizations joined the view that the bill was constitutional and urged its passing,[36] the majority who testified thought otherwise. Among the numerous arguments objecting the bill, were (1) section 4 made it unlawful to "attempt in any manner" the establishment of a totalitarian dictatorship in the United States; that is, it didn't limit overt acts, or limit speech advocating force and violence in face of clear and present danger, but it in effect outlawed peaceful, democratic advocacy of political change.[37] (2) A communist political organization was defined as having the characteristics of a political party that may be "reasonable to conclude" that it was under foreign control having regard to some or all of ten considerations, including "the expression of views," and support of the basic principles of communism as expounded by Marx and Lenin. Such loose definitions accounted to guilt by association, instead of punishing guilty individuals for illegal behavior, and also endangered any American organization (not only communistic).[38] (3) The bill gave too much power to the attorney general. He was to make administrative determinations and was empowered to order registration; afterward it became illegal, for example, to circulate mail that wasn't marked in a certain way, and refusal to register was a criminal act. Thus guilt was not proven in court but dependent on an attorney general's findings.[39] (4) The bill was the wrong way to go about solving the communist problem. Unemployment, lack of shelter, social inequality, racial discrimination and the like were the things that bred communism; what was needed was to remove those conditions and improve social security legislation, housing legislation, health insurance and so on.[40]

The Chairman of the Senate Judiciary Committee Alexander Wiley of Wisconsin (R) took a deliberative approach to the committee's activities. On the first day of the hearings, he incorporated into the record by reference the hearings before the subcommittee on legislation of the HUAC.[41] On the second day of the hearings, before opponents to the bill were to begin being heard, he asked the witnesses to ascertain, first, whether the bill was a practical answer to the problem; second, was it constitutional; and third, if it was neither, what constructive solution do they propose.[42] Additionally, at one point during the hearings, he pointed out that his office had at least 5,000 telegrams, most of them simply saying "kill the bill," but that in order for senators to make up their minds on the bill, they need more than that: they need information and they need to understand why someone is against the bill (further stating: "We want reason and judgment and law and facts").[43]

At the request of Senator Wiley, Attorney General Tom Clark wrote his views on the bill. He objected to the bill, explaining that "the measure might be held (notwithstanding the legislative finding of clear and present danger) to deny freedom of speech, of the press, and of assembly, and even to compel self-incrimination" and that it is "doubtful" if the "proposal will meet the requirements of due process under the fifth amendment" as it defines the nature and purpose of organizations by legislative fiat. He wrote, "I do not believe that sweeping new legislation of this type is required" and referred to his suggestions to strengthen existing legislation that he made to the HUAC subcommittee.[44]

The attorney general's opinion, as well as the opinions of others – in the words of Senator Wiley – "reflected generally the conclusion that there were constitutional objections to the bill," and so he consulted the Senate Judiciary subcommittee and, with counsel, produced a "revamped bill" that met the objections that were made.[45]

The revamped bill had numerous changes compared to the original. Among them: (1) Instead of making it unlawful to "attempt in any manner" the establishment of a totalitarian dictatorship, the prohibition now read "[to conspire] to perform any *act* which would substantially assist" in the establishment of a totalitarian dictatorship (emphasis added).[46] (2) The definition of a communist political organization and the considerations in determining whether an organization was such were narrowed.[47] (3) Rather having the attorney general investigate, hold hearings and make an administrative determination whether an organization that did not register is a communist political organization or a communist front organization, a Subversive Activities Board was to be established, composed by three members, appointed by the president with the Senate's consent, and the board was (upon the request of the attorney general) to conduct hearings, receive evidence and make determinations.[48]

As afore-mentioned, the Senate Judiciary Committee did not report the bill (and Congress adjourned for elections). In a statement before the

Senate on June 19, 1948, Senator Willey asked the revamped bill to be printed in the *Congressional Record* "so that it can have further study" and explained that the Mundt-Nixon bill arrived too late in the Senate, further elaborating that the committee "undertook to conscientiously consider all phases of the bill" to make sure "the civil liberties of every American were protected," and not "simply rubber stamp the House bill and send it to the Senate floor." The committee members emerged from the meetings with a firmer conviction that "the Communist threat must be met" and that lack of action on the Mundt-Nixon bill was merely due to the lack of time. In conclusion he stated: "However we despise communism, we love more our constitutional process of congressional government, and we will not forsake them even to meet the communist threat."[49]

The 1949 Senate Judiciary Subcommittee Hearings

From April 30, 1949, to June 10, 1949 (alternately), a subcommittee of the Committee on the Judiciary of the Senate held hearings on two similar bills to protect the United States against certain un-American and subversive activities, one introduced by Karl Mundt (who was now a senator) together with Senator Olin Johnston of South Carolina (D), and the other sponsored by Senator Homer E. Ferguson of Michigan (R).

These hearings did not possess the same deliberative nature as the two 1948 hearings. The chairman, Senator James Eastland of Mississippi (D), and subcommittee members did not take the deliberative approach of the chairmen and members of the House and Senate committees in 1948: they did not indicate that they wished to study proposals carefully, to gather information and to consider arguments on the merits of the legislation, including its practicality and constitutionality. Indeed, despite the chairman's declaration on the first day of the hearings that "We expect to give… every one a chance to be heard,"[50] some witnesses were not heard, among them the secretary of the American Labor Party and the secretary of the Progressive Party.[51] This was due to the subcommittee's rule that if a witness refuses to tell whether or not he is a communist and whether or not he has been a member of the Communist Party, he will not be permitted to testify.[52] Thus testimonies began with the subcommittee asking two questions: (1) "Are you or have you ever been a member of the Communist Party?" and (2) "Are you now or have you ever been a member of or affiliated in any way with any organization which has been cited by any governmental agency as a communist organization, a communist-front organization, or one substantially controlled, dominated or infiltrated by Communists?"

Witnesses contested these questions. The secretary of the American Labor Party, for example, said that the question "Are you now or have you ever been a member of the Communist Party?" imposes a political test on the right to testify. He wished to explain, but subcommittee member

Senator Herbet Romulus O'Conor of Maryland (D), who presided over the meeting, replied, "I will not permit you to do any such thing" adding "we are not interested in having your views if you are not willing to state categorically your answer to that question."[53]

The hearings commenced with the testimony of Senator Mundt, who began by explaining that communism is not an economic theory and the Communist Party is not a political party: communism is an international conspiracy that endangers freedoms in America.[54] The approach he proposed in the bill was of "exposure, identification, registration, and notification," explaining, "In that we have continued to permit communism to have freedom to meet, freedom to assemble, freedom of the press, freedom of the use of mail, freedom of the ballot, freedom to elect public officials to office."[55] Senator Ferguson also called the bill he proposed a registration bill and stated that the method in the bill is one of exposure: exposure of the "vast conspiracy of communism with which the Soviet Union has surrounded us" aimed at the destruction of free government. The bill was "a reasoned, effective means of facing up to that danger."[56]

Senator Mundt reviewed the bill and pointed out how it differed from the amended Mundt-Nixon bill produced by the Senate Judiciary subcommittee in the closing days of the Eightieth Congress.[57] For example, section 4, which made it unlawful to combine, conspire or agree with any other person to perform any act that would substantially facilitate in the establishment of a totalitarian dictatorship under foreign control ("the most controversial feature of the bill"), now read "unlawful for any person *knowingly* to combine, conspire or agree" (emphasis added). Senator Mundt explained that Congressman Nixon, fellow senators and himself put in the word "knowingly" because of the claim that a man might be innocent about what he was doing.[58] In response to Senator Eastland's questions, he further explained that under existing legislation (the Smith Act) it is only unlawful for any person to knowingly advocate the desirability of overthrowing the government by force or violence, whereas the proposed bill omits the necessity for force and violence and adds the aspect of a totalitarian dictatorship under foreign control. Hence the bill is needed.[59]

In the same section a provision was added that made it unlawful for employees of the United States to communicate any classified information obtained in the course of their official duties to any other person whom they have reason to believe to be a member of a communist organization. This was a response to espionage "which has been practiced in the high places of Government" and Mundt mentioned the case of Judith Coplon and the confessions of Elizabeth Bentley and Whittaker Chambers.[60]

Senator Mundt also pointed out newly added provisions aimed at protecting the innocent: for instance, although the attorney general would maintain two registers open for public inspection, one for communist political organizations and members and one for communist front organizations, individual names would not be revealed until thirty days have elapsed after the persons were notified, and if such a person requested his name to be removed from the list, the attorney general shall initiate an investigation and not make his name public for six months after receipt of such a request. And since, in addition, there was a right to appeal to the board and to the courts, the bill was constitutional.[61]

The proposed bills had support, for example, from veteran organizations,[62] but others, including the ACLU, the National Lawyers Guild, the CIO and Harvard professor Zechariah Chafee, argued against them. Some of the main reasons con were: (1) communists, who form one-twentieth of 1 percent of the U.S. population, do not constitute any conceivable threat, or clear and present danger, to American institutions and freedom.[63] (2) Any threat the Communist movement may pose to the security of the United States is already met by existing statutes, including the Espionage Act (which was, as mentioned in Chapter 6, amended in 1940 to increase the penalties of peacetime violations, including using the mails for transmission of any matter declared to be nonmailable) and the Smith Act (under which eleven leaders of the Communist Party were indicted in July 1948 for advocating the overthrow of government by force).[64] (3) Members and officers of communist organizations could be charged with violating section 4, regarding aiding the establishment of a totalitarian dictatorship; thus the very act of registration would infringe the constitutional privilege of the Fifth Amendment against self-incrimination.[65] (section 4 was also criticized as it punishes mere agreement, peaceful advocacy, as opposed to an overt act or act of violence.)[66] (4) The findings of Congress outlined in the section on the necessity for legislation convict people in advance rather than by judicial trial; therefore, the bills proposed are unconstitutional as bills of attainder.[67] (5) The bills seriously curtail freedom of speech, violate the First amendment and are therefore unconstitutional.[68] Concerning the section of the bill on the use of mails and radio, it was described as a license to talk, and a clear abridgment of freedom of speech because all communication was to be labeled, regardless of content.[69]

In March 1950, the Senate Judiciary Committee reported favorably a version of the two bills, aka the Mundt-Johnston-Ferguson bill. The committee rejected the arguments con. In its report, the committee analyzed the problem and reviewed the necessity for legislation as well as the inadequacies of existing law and the constitutionality of the bill.[70] Among other things, the committee concluded that "the Communist movement constitutes a threat to the security of the United States and to the American way of life,"[71] the committee's opinion was that existing statutes were ineffectual and that new legislation "is badly needed,"[72] the committee stated in its report that the legislation does not constitute a fiat because offenses defined in the bill require some act or failure to act and that the bill is not a bill of attainder since no provision punishes for acts already committed or prescribes punishment without conviction.[73]

Regarding the claim that registration would amount to an admission of liability under section 4 and thus would infringe the constitutional privilege against self-incrimination, a new paragraph was added that read "Neither the holding of office nor membership in any Communist organization by any person shall constitute a violation.... The fact of registration of any person...shall not be received in evidence against such person in any prosecution for any alleged violation."[74]

Concerning freedom of speech, the committee claimed that "while the freedoms guaranteed by the first amendment...are fundamental they are not in their nature absolute" and that the government may decline circulation of printed matter, which it regards injurious to the people so long as their transportation by means other than the mails is not forbidden.[75]

In sum, after referring to numerous court decisions and academic articles, ten years of work by the HUAC, "some 500 pages of testimony" before the House on the problem, "some 750 pages of testimony" before the Senate Judiciary Committee (500 in the 80th Congress and 250 in the 81st Congress), hundreds of witnesses, "50,000 pieces of mail" and consultation with "some of the best legal minds in America," the committee recommended the bill to pass.[76]

However, the committee members were not unanimous in their recommendation. Senator Carey Estes Kefauver of Tennessee (D) had "grave doubts as to the constitutionality in that in may violate guarantees of freedom of the press, speech, and individual liberty." He also had reservations as to certain provisions, especially in section 4. But, in order that the Senate may have an opportunity to consider the legislation – as a full discussion on the floor will reveal its weaknesses – he voted to report it.[77] Senator William Langer of North Dakota (R) voted against and submitted a minority report. He declared the bill a great threat to American liberties, a "product of hysteria and frantic, unthinking fear" and a "strike at the very foundations of democratic institutions – the right of the people to speak their minds, to hear every viewpoint on public questions, and to associate together freely to advance their common views."[78] Assessing the bill section by section, he called for its rejection.[79]

Five months later, after the outbreak of hostilities in Korea, on August 10, 1950, Senator Patrick A. McCarran of Nevada (D) introduced on omnibus bill, which included the Mundt-Johnston-Ferguson bill and four other bills (concerning deportation of aliens and the tightening up of certain espionage statues).[80]

The 1950 HUAC Hearings

The HUAC met from March 21, 1950, to May 4, 1950, alternately, for hearings on two bills: one introduced in March 1950 by Representative Nixon, which was analogous to the Senate Mundt-Johnston-Ferguson bill, and the other introduced a year earlier by Representative John S. Wood of Georgia (D), making it unlawful for federal employees, and for individuals employed in connection with national defense contracts, to be affiliated with the Communist Party.[81]

The 1950 HUAC hearings, yet again, did not possess the same deliberative nature as the two 1948 congressional hearings. In two aspects, they were even less deliberative compared to the 1949 Senate Judiciary Subcommittee hearings:

1. In contrast to all three hearings held thus far (1948 House, 1948 Senate, 1949 Senate), the sponsors of the legislation, Representatives Nixon and Wood, did not present the case and arguments pro their bills. While it is true that they were both members of the HUAC (Wood its chairman), the HUAC could have set up a subcommittee, just like it did in 1948: Mundt was a member of HUAC, but not of HUAC's subcommittee on legislation, and he did testify in 1948 to the subcommittee on the merits of his proposal. Alternatively, the HUAC didn't always meet in executive session; sometimes a subcommittee met to hear the testimonies.[82] So Representatives Nixon and Wood could have appeared before a subcommittee meeting and explain their legislative proposals, but they didn't.
2. There isn't evidence that members of the HUAC were open to arguments and ready to be persuaded. On the contrary, there were times when members of the HUAC reinforced the views of those who supported the Nixon bill or otherwise emphasized arguments in its support. For example, during the testimony of the representative of the American Veterans of World War II (AMVETS), Representative Harold Himmel Velde of Illinois (R) asked if he feels that the Nixon bill is an infringement upon freedom of thought, action and political belief, to which he replied, "I don't," and explained why. Representative Velde then continued, "In other words, we might be infringing on the rights of some, but by this legislation we will be protecting the rights of the great majority," to which he replied, "That is right," and Velde said, "I quite agree with you." Then Representative Bernard Kearney of New York (R) asked if he agrees that the Communist Party is not a political party but a revolutionary party dedicated to overthrowing the government by force and violence, to which the AMVETS representative replied, "Yes." Representative Kearney continued, "Do you further agree with me in my thoughts" that it is obligatory to protect the internal security of the country with legislation such as is proposed, to which he replied, "I definitely do."[83] In an another instance, Representative Wood challenged the illustration a witness gave that the proposed legislation was "somewhat akin to throwing the child out with the bath," suggesting instead that it is "designed to prevent having to burn down the barn to get rid of the rats."[84]

On one occasion, it seemed that the committee members paid lip service to the witnesses who were testifying: when the representative of the AFL testified in opposition to the Nixon bill, arguing that the bill's broad and loose definitions restrict the rights and liberty of free citizens and is disastrous to labor organizations,[85] Representative Moulder of Missouri (D) summarized the AFL's representative views, reflecting that the AFL representative is not opposed in principle to legislation to eliminate the dangers of un-American and subversive activities but the witness appeals "to the committee to conscientiously study the proposed legislation and to eliminate any provisions that might be based on passion or prejudice"; Representative Wood added that the "utmost diligence" would be given.[86] Nevertheless, and in contrast to earlier congressional committee deliberations, no provisions were "eliminated" in the bill reported.

The testimonies and statements pro and con the bills were similar to those heard and submitted before: for the most part veteran organizations voiced support, saying that the communist problem was grave, and the Nixon bill, which focused on exposure of communist conspirators, was the correct approach, as it was carefully drawn with safeguards to protect the innocent and did not restrain freedom of expression (which in any case is qualified to the public welfare).[87] On the other hand, generally liberals and those representing labor argued, among other things, that there was no imminent danger to warrant such bills, that there were already adequate laws on the statute books to deal with subversion and overthrow of the government through violence, that actions and not advocacy of beliefs should be made illegal and that the Nixon bill is a deviation from democracy as it curtails free speech and it is therefore unconstitutional.[88]

Despite the several arguments con, no significant amendments were made in Nixon's bill (besides integrating some provisions of the Wood bill) except for one: the term "communist political organization" was changed to "communist-action organization" to reflect the committee members' desire to control the conduct of carrying out ideas, and not sheer advocacy of an idea.[89]

On August 22, 1950, after a combination of the Nixon and Wood bills was introduced by Representative Wood (H.R. 9490), the HUAC reported it and recommended that it pass.[90] The HUAC report, similarly to the Senate Judiciary Committee report of March 1950, also analyzed the problem and described the necessity for the legislation. It differed in that the report was unanimous and no accommodations were made vis-à-vis the arguments against the bill. The report was committed after the outbreak hostilities in the Korean Peninsula and the committee did refer to that in its conclusion stating that the

> defense action is being opposed daily by those who are associated with the Communist organization of the United States… no one can

> at this time foresee when the foreign masters of these so-called spontaneous demonstrations will summon the all-out efforts of their disciples to permanently cripple and destroy our national defense.

It added that the legislation is "of supreme importance" to the national security of the United States in combating the clear and present danger of the communist organization.[91]

Chamber Deliberation

> I urge the Senate and I appeal to it to rise above the clamor, the hysteria, and the tensions of this time, and once again demonstrate to freedom-loving people all over the world that this body is the wisest and the most deliberative body in the world.
>
> Senator Hubert Huratio Humphrey, September 11, 1950

The Wood bill and the McCarran bill were extensively deliberated by Congress, and deliberation went about in the classic way: in both chambers, sponsors explained and defended the proposed legislation, others challenged them and responses were subsequently offered. The House of Representatives debated and passed the Wood bill on August 29, 1950, and the Senate debated the McCarran bill (alternately) for a period of six days, September 5–12, 1950. After conference of both chambers, the measure was further debated on September 20, 1950; and then again by the Senate on September 22, 1950, after it was vetoed by President Truman.

Launch of Floor Deliberation

President Truman contributed to congressional deliberation through a special message he sent to Congress on August 8, 1950. In it he acknowledged that there are periods, especially during war, when internal security laws need to be adjusted – laws are enacted that restrict individual liberty for the protection of the nation – and that the present period, when the United States is faced with the threat of the Communist movement, engaged in espionage, sabotage and other subversive acts, is one of those times. However, he answered the question of how to keep freedom secure against attack without, at the same time, unduly limiting individual rights, by recommending Congress to make certain amendments to existing espionage, foreign agent registration and national defense installation security laws, and to enact legislation permitting the attorney general to exercise supervision over aliens subject to deportation. He opposed the legislation pending before Congress, saying that it is so broad and vague in its terms that it endangered the freedoms of speech, press and assembly protected by the First Amendment and that some of its measures would in effect impose severe penalties for normal political activities on the part of certain groups. He declared it unnecessary (because communists would be repudiated by the people as they have always been), ineffective (because it is directed at normal political activity, whereas the dangers come from espionage, sabotage and destruction of government by violence – against laws already exist) and dangerous (because innocent or misguided people could be prosecuted) and cautioned against hysteria.[92]

A week and a half later, on August 17, 1950, the Senate Judiciary Committee reported favorably Senator McCarran's omnibus bill[93] (the HUAC report, mentioned earlier, in favor of passing the Wood bill was submitted on August 22, 1950[94]). The Senate committee report stated that principle changes were made (relative to the Mundt-Johnston-Ferguson bill, reported in March) to insure the constitutionality of the bill.[95] It is plausible that these were made in response to both President Truman's address and to the Senator Kefauver's and Senator Langer's reservations of the March Senate Judiciary Report. Two of those were: (1) In the first section, right after the title of the bill, the committee added that

> nothing in the act shall be construed to authorize, require, or establish military or civilian censorship or in any way to limit or infringe upon freedom of the press or speech as guaranteed – by the Constitution of the United States and that no regulation shall be promulgated under the act having that effect.[96]

(2) The term "Communist-controlled organization" was substituted for the term "Communist political organization" to remove "any implication of a congressional intent to curb legitimate activities of bona fide political parties."[97]

The committee recommendation to pass the McCarran bill was not unanimous. Senators Harvey M. Kilgore of West Virginia (D), Frank P. Graham of North Carolina (D) and William M. Langer of North Dakota (R) submitted minority views. While agreeing that the Communist movement presented a serious threat to internal security that "must be met with vigorous action," they claimed that the bill threatened "to create evils far more serious than those which it is supposed to remedy."[98] Except for modifications in existing law that were in line with President Truman's recommendations, they rejected, among others, the Mundt-Johnston-Ferguson provisions, including: (1) section 4, which prohibited all action that would contribute to the establishment of a totalitarian dictatorship, that is not only the use of force, thus it was "clearly unconstitutional" because "everyone is free to advocate even the most extreme changes in our form of government by the process of constitutional amendment."[99] (2) The labeling requirement (that literature distributed by communist organizations be marked "Disseminated by _______, a Communist organization) and the corresponding radio provision that applied to all publications and broadcasts regardless of their content, "no matter how innocent or meritorious," thus to "utterances on subjects protected by the first amendment."[100] (3) The standards to be applied by the Subversive Activities Control Board in determining whether an organization is communistic, which were too vague, thus giving "discretionary power" to the board which is "dangerous to freedom of speech and press."[101] The senators also wrote on the impracticality of the registration requirements in that they could not be enforced within "any reasonable period of time": failure to register is not punishable until the board has issued a final order – such an order may be issued only after a hearing, and the order is subject to judicial review. In the meantime, none of the real communist organizations will register.[102] And regarding the exclusion of members of communist organizations from government employment and denial of passports, the former was already accomplished by the president's loyalty-security program and the latter could be done under existing discretionary powers of the secretary of state.[103]

The presidents' message, alongside the Senate Judiciary Committee Report and the HUAC report recommending the Wood bill, set the stage for floor debate.

Exchange of Information and Arguments on the Floor

On September 5, 1950, Senator McCarran explained and defended his bill to the Senate; and on August 29, 1950, Representative Wood and his colleagues from the HUAC, Representatives Francis H. Case of South Dakota (R) and John McSweeney of Ohio (D), did the same in the House.

Senator McCarran took time to give an explanation of the bill, going through the provisions, the problem which prompted them and the way they offer a solution. At the outset he said that he intended "to go into the bill meticulously by way of explanation, so that the Senate may understand why each paragraph and each section is in the bill, and what each one means."[104] He highlighted the threat to the United States and to democracy: "the Communist fifth column in the United States is a clear and present danger...to all that we cherish in our democratic institutions,"[105] saying that the communists are working to destroy "the Nation from within" constituting "the most serious danger to the continuance of a free America."[106] Presenting data, he quoted J. Edgar Hoover, chief of the FBI, who said:

> Even though there are only 54,174 members of the [Communist] party, the fact remains that the party leaders themselves boast that for every party member there are 10 others who follow that party line and who are ready, willing, and able to do the party's work. In other words, there is a potential fifth column of 540,000 people.[107]

In general Senator McCarran emphasized that the bill is not the product of hysteria, nor has it been hastily conceived. It was carefully "drafted and redrafted" and is the product of years of study by various committees of Congress. The bill's provisions were "subjected to the closest scrutiny" by experts and "some of the ablest lawyers in the Nation" to the end that the legislation not only cope with "the Communist conspiracy in the United States" but be "in accord with our constitutional processes and conditions."[108]

Specifically, concerning the Mundt-Johnston-Ferguson provisions, Senator McCarran clarified the two "principal objectives" to be accomplished.[109] The first is to require registration of communist political organizations and their members and communist front organizations and their officers, the purpose of which is "to expose to the light of public opinion the Communist movement in the United States and thus protect the public against innocent and unwitting collaboration with it."[110] He emphasized that there is no provision that outlaws the Communist Party as such, the bill requires only registration, which "is no more than the law requires at the present time of legislative lobbyists," and that the provisions are constitutional.[111] The second principal objective is to declare certain acts to be a crime, for example, performing an act that would substantially contribute to the establishment within the United States of a totalitarian dictatorship under foreign control (section 4) and mailing publications for a communist organization without identifying the source.[112]

With regard to section 4, Senator McCarran "[pointed] out to the Senate that this particular provision of the bill above all others has been the object of the most bitter attack... that the provision is an abridgment of constitutional liberties." For that reason, the committee "made an extensive study of the constitutional issues," and he quoted Supreme Court decisions (including Justice Holmes in *Schenck v. United States*) in support of its constitutionality. Of course he explained the need for the provision: the Smith Act, which prohibited advocating the overthrow of the government by force, was inadequate because the present line of the Communist Party, in order to evade the statute, "is to avoid whenever possible the open advocacy of force and violence."[113] As to the labelling requirement, Senator McCarran rejected the charge that the bill restricts dissemination of opinions and suppression of ideas, adding that "The provision for labeling Communist propaganda for what it is cannot possibly be considered an interference with freedom of speech... we have the absolute right, under the Constitution, to make [the Communists] accept responsibility for the statements they make."[114]

In the House, Representative Case explained the Wood bill and in addition testified to its legislative history and committee deliberation, saying that Congress is dealing with the "most deliberative consideration of any bill" starting with the Mundt-Nixon bill passed by the House in 1948, public hearings held in 1950 after reintroduction of that bill by Representative Nixon and HUAC member's considerations in closed session. He pointed out the change made in the definition – as mentioned earlier "communist political organization" was changed to "communist-action organization" to reflect the committee members' desire to control the conduct of carrying out ideas, and not sheer advocacy of an idea – "an important change" in his view, because "in this legislation…we are not dealing with an ordinary party but…with a revolutionary party which deals in action" and is under foreign control.[115] Representative McSweeney referred to the common good by speaking about society and constitutional government:

> Now we are considering legislation which is designed to protect our Government and our people… today, we, as legislators, are trying conscientiously to preserve…[constitutional individual rights and] at the same time, to provide legislation that will keep that constitutional Government from being destroyed.[116]

Representative Wood, in the name of the committee, said that the legislation is "the nearest approach to the question which we could evolve without infringing upon the liberties and the freedom of thought and speech of the American people."[117]

Notwithstanding the explanations given by the sponsors of the legislation, it did have, as expected, opposition. Senator McCarran and Representative Wood were challenged with many arguments against the proposed legislation.

A predominant set of arguments con revolved around the curtailment of civil liberties, specifically the endangerment of free speech and the violation of the First Amendment:

- Senator Kefauver said that the bill "does violence" to the Constitution and to the Bill of Rights, and "endangers many of the basic rights we Americans hold so dear – freedom of speech, press, assembly, thought,"[118] noting that if the bill passes "we shall see innocent people prosecuted for what they say, what they read, and what they think."[119] Enacting the McCarran bill will "weaken our democracy… by trying to enforce conformity of thought, by doing away with freedom of speech."[120]
- Senator Herbert Lehman's of New York (D) "study" of the legislation indicated that the "bill represents the most dangerous and violent curtailment of our civil liberties of any legislation that has ever been proposed in the American Congress"[121] and would expose "people to the threat of political oppression by thought control."[122]
- Senator Hubert Humphrey of Minnesota (D) warned the Senate that the McCarran bill "may well seriously and drastically injure the

basic safeguards and the traditional liberties which have made our Nation the freest and most democratic in the world."[123]

- Congresspersons in the House named the bill averse to the Bill of Rights: Representative Abraham Multer of New York (D) said that the bill "destroys the Bill of Rights";[124] Representative Roy Wier of Minnesota (D) called the bill "objectionable" and "repugnant" to American traditions and of dubious constitutionality;[125] Representative Helen Gahagan Douglas of California (D) said the bill infringes on liberty and "crack(s) the sacred shell of democracy";[126] and according to Representative John Carroll of Colorado (D), many of the provisions in the bill could be "used to undermine the rights of all American citizens as guaranteed by the Bill of Rights."[127]
- Representative Vito Marcantonio of New York (American Labor Party) submitted that the registration and labeling provisions of the bill violate the Constitution, explaining that members of organizations may be subjected to "disabilities merely because of the views they advocate, regardless of how peaceable their conduct, their intent, and regardless of the absence of any incitement to unlawful action. Thus the first amendment, which guarantees freedom of speech and assembly, is violated."[128] Similarly, Representative Jacob Javits of New York (R) feared the bill

  > because it sets a precedent with regard to placing critically serious disabilities on people because of what they believe in.... As soon as Congress, as in this bill, starts to define ideas it does not like and then punish people for entertaining those ideas or belonging to organizations which entertain such ideas instead of punishing people for acts which they commit and are declared unlawful, a new and mischievous conception of our law has been created.[129]

  Representative Usher Lloyd Burdick of North Dakota (R) also told the House, "You cannot stop men from thinking by passing a law" and "If this bill becomes law every citizen will be afraid to speak his mind,"[130] and according to Representative Emanuel Celler of New York (D), the "[bill] will punish men for expressing ideas" and the registration provisions "offend" the first amendment.[131]

Proponents of the legislation responded to this set of arguments, claiming the legislation does not deny freedom of speech and is constitutional:

- Senator Mundt was explicit about what the "bill does not do":

  > It does not in any way deny anyone free speech, no matter how traitorous he may be. It does not deny freedom of assembly to anyone. The Communists can still have their meetings.... It does

> not deny the Communists the use of ballot.... It does not deny Communists the right to engage in every political propaganda activity in which they are now engaged. It simply forces them to do those things in the open.

Summarizing to those who say the bill goes too far, he pronounced "that the bill does not deny Communists freedom of speech, freedom of the press, freedom of the mails, freedom of movement, or freedom of assembly."[132]

- Responding to a direct question, Senator Spessard Holland of Florida (D) stated that he "does not think that freedom of thought and freedom of speech are in the slightest diminished by this measure."[133] Representative Edward deGraffenried of Alabama (D) also believed "the bill is constitutional"[134] and Representative Harold Velde of Illinois (R) claimed that the bill protects the freedoms guaranteed by the Constitution.[135]
- Concerning the argument on thought control by opponents of the legislation, Senator Herbert O'Conor of Maryland (D) described the bill as "directed toward the penalization of acts... not 'thoughts,' but 'acts' – which by their very nature are inimical to the safety and welfare of our country."[136] Senator Mundt challenged Senator Lehman "or any other Senator" to "quote a paragraph, a syllable, or a sentence anywhere in the bill which provided for thought policing... Quite the contrary is true.... We give Communists every single legitimate political privilege and freedom to function."[137]
- A couple of members of Congress underlined the notion that freedom of speech can be restricted under certain circumstances. Referring to three Supreme Court decisions, an academic article, constitutional lawyers and the Senate Judiciary Committee report from March 1950, Senator Alexander Wiley of Wisconsin (R) concluded that freedom of speech "does not comprehend the right to speak on any subject at any time"[138] and stated that the measure is constitutional.[139] Representative Kenneth Keating of New York (R) echoed this view in the House, also referring to academia and the Supreme Court:

  > It is...well recognized...that freedom of speech and of the press does not mean unbridled license to preach or publish any doctrine or contention, no matter how vicious, harmful, or subversive. These freedoms can and frequently have been held properly to be curtailed when there is a clear and present danger which the Government seeks to meet.[140]

Besides generally attacking the proposed legislation as unconstitutional and as an abridgement of freedom of speech, criticism was specifically directed at section 4 (prohibiting any person to combine, conspire or agree with any other person to perform any act that would substantially contribute to the establishment within the United States of a totalitarian dictatorship under foreign control) and the labeling provision (prohibiting communist organizations to transmit publications through the mail, or broadcast matter over the radio, without identifying the source) as abridging free speech:

Section 4 was, in Senator Kefauver's opinion, "the worst section of the bill" and has given many members of the Senate "a great deal of trouble." Among other reasons, he elaborated that "in section 4 the usual constitutional provision with respect to force and violence is not present. It covers any act which might include speaking, writing a letter, a conversation, or anything else."[141] Senator Frank Graham of North Carolina (D) concluded, "Since this provision is without the condition of the use of force and violence, it is in violation of the first amendment of the Constitution."[142] A question was also raised as to what act significantly contributes to the establishment of a totalitarian dictatorship: Senator Paul Douglas of Illinois (D) referred to the "vagueness of the phrase 'significantly contribute'. It does not read 'directly and predominantly contribute'. It merely says 'substantially'."[143] Senator Lehman described the provision

> as broad as all outdoors. Who is to determine what act might contribute to the establishment of a totalitarian dictatorship in the United States? There are those in this country who argue loudly and vehemently that public housing and rent control are substantial contributions to the establishment of a totalitarian dictatorship in the United States.[144]

After the bill returned from conference, Senator Kefauver recapitulated these ideas:

> "Any act" can be a speech. "Any act" can be reading a book. "Any act" can be anything.... What does "substantially contribute" mean?... Is speaking substantially contributing? Does a newspaper which prints an article "substantially contribute?".... The criteria of what constituted force and violence is left out of this section...they are necessary if the law is to meet the constitutional test.[145]

Senators Ferguson, Wiley and Mundt didn't leave these accusations unanswered. In a direct response to Senator Douglas, Senator Ferguson said that Senator Douglas omitted "two of the most important elements" in section 4: the factor of conspiracy and the fact that the totalitarian dictatorship must be under foreign control. Thus

> this section would prevent no person...as an individual, from expounding any doctrine whatsoever.... As for groups of individuals, it would not touch any group engaged in philosophical speculation...

> or activity of that nature, provided they did not enter into the prohibited element of conspiracy.[146]

Senator Ferguson attested that

> Section 4 (a) was the subject of the most intense study and deliberation for many hours and many days. In it, we say, for instance, that there must be a conspiracy to commit an act which would substantially aid in the establishment of a totalitarian government under [foreign control]. There must be an overt act...before [a man] could be prosecuted.[147]

Senator Wiley also asserted that under section 4 campaigns for political reform are not made unlawful; it's when communists undertake secret activities, then, by their actions, they "may be rendering substantial aid to an unlawful project."[148] As to the absence of the element of force and violence, Senator Ferguson explained:

> There are other ways of overthrowing a government than by force and violence. We learned that in Czechoslovakia. The force and violence comes afterwards, in order to consolidate and expand power and control...we are trying to do something about the kind of subversive acts that are really dangerous.

He added:

> [The communists'] technique is to gain control in some way by conspiracy...then afterward to use force and violence to retain [in power]. In view of that...technique, we propose to make it a crime to overthrow the government here, by acts which are short of force and violence.[149]

As to the labeling provision, Representative Marcantonio deemed it unconstitutional and a violation of the First amendment: "This section is a clear abridgment of freedom of speech and of the press, since it requires speech and writings to be invidiously labelled regardless of their contents."[150] A week later, Senator Lehman repeated this argument in the Senate stating, "The content of the literature or letter [to be labelled] will be immaterial."[151] The following day, Senator Mundt rejected that argument: he doesn't want censorship, and he's not concerned with content, adding that the bill does not deny "freedom of publication to anyone. It simply says to the Communists...'You have got to identify...publications sent through mails; you must show who it is who is responsible.'"[152]

In addition to general claims on the bill's unconstitutionality and specific arguments regarding section 4 and the labeling provision, opponents of the legislation alleged that the standards by which the Subversive

Activities Control Board was to determine whether an organization is communist are broad and vague and that the bill would result in "smearing" innocent persons and organizations, hurting, among others, labor organizations:

- Senator Lehman dubbed the standards "broad and vague" and voiced a few of them on the Senate floor:

  > "The extent to which," the bill says, "the organization fails to disclose or resists efforts as to obtain information as to its membership"... "The extent to which its meetings are secret"... Many labor unions keep their membership lists secret... hold meetings in secret and certainly resist efforts to obtain information as to their membership lists;
  >
  > ... one of the criteria the board shall use for determining whether an organization is a Communist front [is] "The extent of which the positions taken or advanced by it from time to time on matter of policy do not deviate from those of any Communist political organization...." This definition could lead to action against almost any organization which at any time has taken a stand for public housing, for fair employment practices. ... The Communist Party...has taken the same stand on these matters as have many good and patriotic Americans organizations.... Under the terms of the [bill], good American organizations – labor unions, church groups, and others – could be charged on this basis with being Communist fronts.[153]

- Senator Graham objected to the "indefiniteness of the phrase 'shall take into consideration the extent of which'" asking Senators to suppose an organization was formed to exclusively oppose the Truman Doctrine and the military-assistance program and had secret procedures, then there would be basis for determining a religious or pacifist organization as communist.[154]
- Senator Douglas specifically called the term "the extent to which" as vague explaining that "no definition is given to what extent, or how much of a given taint an organization must possess before it is labeled and branded." Thus the McCarran bill "can easily lead to the smearing of innocent persons" and "be used to smear innocent and basically patriotic organizations by branding them as Communist fronts... [because] the positions [they] took over a given period of time did not deviate from those of the Communist Party."[155]
- Several members of Congress lay emphasis on the point of deviation of positions on matter of policy from communism: for example, Senator Humphrey, who stated:

  > the Communist Party stands for rent control. How about all of us who believe in rent control? How about the tenants' association

> in my State, which has but one purpose, namely rent control?... Does that make the tenants' association in my State a Communist organization? ... there are many organizations that are worried. Organizations such as the American Federation of Labor and the Congress of Industrial Organization and the International Mechanics are worried.[156]

Senator Kefauver said:

> So if such persons were to organize for only 1 day, and if they were to oppose the Korean War or the Marshall Plan...that organization could be brought before the Board and could be termed a Communist-front organization, and every member of the organization would have to register.[157]

Representative Barratt O'Hara of Illinois (D) noted:

> Thus, under this measure we are asked to approve today, any church federation committee, any labor organization, any civic body, any group of American citizens of any character whatsoever, no matter how pure and lofty, could be by a board of five members...be branded as a Communist front for the one and only reason that it... had supported a Fair Employment Practice Act or rent controls.[158]

The allegations concerning the standards to determine whether an organization is Communist and the consequences were rejected by proponents of the legislation:

- Senator Mundt pointed out that according to the bill, a *communist-action* organization must be (1) substantially dominated by the foreign entity controlling the world Communist movement and (2) operating primarily to advance that movement; therefore "Obviously no one could bring within that kind of definition any labor union or any church group."[159]
- Both Senator Mundt and Senator Holland called the arguments made by opponents concerning the ease of determining an organization as a *communist-front* as "nonsense" and "ridiculous," explaining that in the bill, a communist-front organization was defined as being (1) under the control of a communist-action organization and (b) primarily operating for the purpose of giving aid to that organization, a communist foreign government, or the world Communist movement.[160] Proving that, according to Senator Holland, is "no small thing," and he asked the Senate rhetorically, "Does such a definition apply to the average church, to the average labor organization, to the average social club...?"[161] Moreover, as noted by Representative Nixon, Representative Francis Eugene Walter of Pennsylvania (D), Senator Ferguson and Senator Holland, according to the bill, the

Subversive Activities Control Board must take into account a total of four considerations in determining whether or not an organization is a communist front organization, not only the one standard concerning deviation of positions on matter of policy.[162]

– In addition, members of the House and Senate were asked to "realize" and "bear in mind" that the provisions in the measure for proceedings before the board, assure the organization the right to an open hearing, to present its case with the assistance of counsel, to present witnesses and offer evidence and to make a rebuttal. And the organization may appeal the board's findings to the courts.[163]

Besides, the substantial arguments averse the legislation discussed earlier, those opposing presented functional reasons against its enactment: (1) it is not needed, as the United States already has pertinent laws to safeguard security from subversive activities. (2) It is not effective – communists won't register; they'd be pushed underground, and furthermore the process for determining if an organization is communist is long, any enforcement of registration will take time. (3) It would obstruct FBI activities.

1. There are enough laws on the books to deal with espionage, sabotage and subversion; therefore there's no need for the proposed legislation. Senator Douglas asserted:

   > We already have the Foreign Agents Registration Act, the Immigration Act, the treason statute, the peacetime espionage laws, and the laws relating to sabotage of utilities. In addition to that, we have the Government loyalty program, and so on. Therefore, the idea that we are helpless in not true.[164]

   Several senators and members of the House drew attention to the conviction of communist leaders under the Smith Act, which was upheld by the U.S. Court of Appeals.[165] Senator Lehman tallied "more than 20 laws to control and penalize subversive activities."[166]
2. The measure is ineffective: Senator Humphrey declared, "I make the charge that the McCarran bill would practically drive the Communist Party and its members underground… Ten [McCarran] bills would never have caused Edith [Judith] Coplon to register. It would not have caused Alger Hiss to register."[167] Senator Douglas considered the bill "clumsy in operation" and "ineffective in detaining or exposing Communists" because "as long as an organization insists that it is not Communist-controlled or a Communist front, and carried its appeal upward though the successive steps of the administrative and legal processes, there is no final order and hence no obligation to register."[168] Producing figures and examples from a different field his conclusion was that "it would be 2, 3 or 4 years before a final order

could be obtained."[169] Other senators agreed that "hearings, trials, appeals and further appeals"[170] would take years[171] and would mean "delay, delay and delay."[172]

3. The bill would obstruct FBI activities: to prove that those who fail to register are communists, it would be necessary to disclose the identity of FBI undercover operatives and sources of valuable information in the Communist Party and subversive organizations, thus destroying their usefulness.[173]

Supporters of the proposed legislation disagreed that there were enough laws on the books, explaining that "we have some protection against some aspects of the problem. However, we do not have the machinery necessary to bring Communists out into the open so that they may be known to the public."[174] Senator Mundt pointed out that

> had we had but one Mundt-Ferguson bill enacted we would have had a much better means of both deterring and convicting [Alger Hiss]... since the FBI knew of his Communist background...at least the Attorney General would have been in a position... to have his name public.[175]

Advocates also disagreed that the bill would drive communists underground, as the Communist movement "is already underground... What we are trying to do is bring it out in the open"[176] by compelling registration and certain disclosures.[177] Agreeing that some communists will not register, Senator Mundt labeled the argument that a bill should be passed only when the Senate knows in advance that no one will violate it as "the silliest kind of an argument that can be made," just as counterfeiters are caught and go to jail, so will law enforcement proceed against violators of the McCarran Act.[178] Concerning slowness of administrative and legal procedures, Senators answered that the same applies to the enforcement of the Smith Act as well as other federal laws and that certain delays are inherent in concepts of Anglo-American justice.[179]

With regard to any hampering with FBI activities, Senator Holland commented that the FBI's hand is not forced by the bill and that those administering the law will determine "when, how and by what degrees" information will be disclosed.[180] Senator Ferguson added that the registration requirements of the bill will give the FBI specific "purpose for its surveillances in the Communist underground."[181]

Senators opposing the McCarran bill proposed instead an emergency detention bill,[182] which authorized the president to declare an internal security emergency during which the attorney general could detain persons he had reason to believe would be engaged in acts of espionage or sabotage. Their main argument was that the real dangers are sabotage and espionage (not "propaganda or political agitation"),[183] which their proposal directly addresses by laying down the rules in advance, in the event of an emergency "with respect to the detention of individuals who would sabotage the country in any and every way possible, if the opportunity were given them to do so"[184] (e.g., by poisoning water systems and blowing up bridges).[185] In addition, in the words of Senator Kefauver, it "does not get into the matter of thought control or curbing freedom of speech."[186]

Senators supporting the McCarran bill initially argued against the emergency detention proposal, arguing that (1) it doesn't meet the problem of communists running unidentified, and it doesn't bring communists into the open;[187] (2) it wasn't studied by the Senate Committee on the Judiciary, whereas the registration provisions have;[188] (3) it goes too far – for example, people are detained for thinking they will commit a crime, thus it "has no place in American traditions and...no justification...in American constitutional law."[189]

However, at one point Senator Douglas stated that if the proposal would be added to the pending measure "it might make an excellent additional feature."[190] And after the proposal to substitute the McCarran bill was defeated 50-23,[191] Senator McCarran proposed an amendment: to add at the end of the bill a new title, "emergency detention." He pronounced that he altered the text of the original proposal "to make it constitutional" so that senators would have a chance to vote on the detention question.[192] This amended bill passed 70-7.[193]

Public Good

As illustrated earlier, members of Congress framed arguments both pro and con the proposed legislation in terms of the public good, for example, concerning the communist threat to American institutions and to democracy, and in regard to free speech and to the bill's constitutionality.

In addition, senators signified the substantial influence the measure had on the public good and their responsibility to the public. On the first day of the debate in the Senate, Senator Lehman declared that the bills pending "before the United States Senate" are in a larger sense "before the Nation,"[194] and later he proclaimed that the Senate vote for the McCarran bill "was against the public interest and was against the best interests of our country."[195] Senator Wiley, calling the situation "serious," called for an "evaluation of our obligations as Senators representing our constituents and a nation of 155,000,000 persons."[196]

There was widespread agreement among members of both chambers of Congress that there was a need for anticommunist legislation to protect national security; they differed on what kind. Opponents underlined the threat from communists, "spies," "saboteurs" and "fifth columnists" and recognized the need to strengthen the internal security of the United

States, but they thought the pending legislation was not the right way to go about it.[197] In the words of Senator Humphrey:

> there is no argument as to the need for corrective legislation. The debate is over the manner and means of the legislation....We are divided...only as to the details and the nature of the legislation we need to meet the internal threat.[198]

The welfare of the nation in the face of war was also an argument articulated by supporters of the legislation. Representative Dayton Edward Phillips of Tennessee (R), for example, after the bill returned from conference, stated:

> American boys are facing deadly machine gun fire, mortars and tank warfare against Communists in Korea. They are giving their lives to save their homes and their people here at home. It is a well-known fact that we have Communist enemies in this country. This legislation will protect the American people against enemies at home.[199]

Persuasion and Call for Deliberation

During the floor debate in the Senate and the House of Representatives, there were numerous calls for and affirmation of deliberation, acknowledgment of understanding arguments and reaching a position and evidence of persuasion.

Both opponents and proponents of the legislation called for deliberation: In the House, Representative Barratt O'Hara of Illinois (D) talked about legislators' responsibility to "close study and analysis" of the bill and implored his colleagues to listen to his argument "with open minds" and be unafraid to act if he convinces them, and Representative Celler asked his colleagues to "give pause" adding, "This is a time for soberness and judgment, for solid, hard, and clear thinking."[200] Senator Humphrey appealed to the Senate "to take a few moments out for mediation" and asked "Members of the Senate...to think about what they are doing, before they vote for this bill."[201] Similarly, Senator Mundt, even though he was a principal drafter, after recognizing that the bill "is not perfect legislation," thought "it is important that we criticize and analyze the bill" given that "reasonable men may disagree."[202] Moreover, senators agreed on extending the debate and postponing voting to give the opportunity to those who "desire to speak" and "have speeches to make" regarding the bill.[203]

Several members of Congress revealed that they studied and understood the bill, talked about it with their colleagues, reached a position and deliberated: Senator Kilgore and Senator Wiley, for instance, on opposite sides vis-à-vis the McCarran bill, noted that they understood the bill's provisions, the arguments contra their own and that they considered alternatives (yet their position was either con or pro the bill);[204] Senator Mundt professed, "I have discussed the bill with [Senator Kilgore] many times. I am sure he is trying to struggle through his own thinking to know what he is to do about the bill. I know it is difficult to decide these things";[205] and Senator Holland affirmed that "numerous Members of the Senate, not serving on the committee concerned with this measure, have taken active part in its consideration, offering amendments which now make clearer and better certain portions of this measure."[206]

Two sections on the bill were modified as a result of deliberation on the Senate floor, thereby demonstrating persuasion: (1) on the first and second day of the floor debate, Senator Kefauver argued with reference to section 4 (a) (prohibiting acts that would substantially contribute to the establishment within the United States of a totalitarian dictatorship under foreign control), that "a person had a right to propose any kind of constitutional amendment he wanted to, regardless of whether it was advisable…[and that] could not be an unlawful act."[207] This matter troubled him because he wanted "to preserve to an American citizen or to a Member of the Senate or of House of Representatives the right to inaugurate any kind of constitutional amendment he wishes to."[208] A few days later he proposed an amendment to section 4 (a) – to insert that the subsection shall not apply to the proposal of a constitutional amendment. Senator McCarran and Senator Mundt agreed (after suggesting a change in language that was accepted by Senator Kefauver).[209] When the bill returned from conference, both Representative Wood and Senator McCarran pointed out this proviso in the bill.[210] Interestingly, on the same day, Senator Mundt, recalling the "colloquy" he had with Senator Kefauver during the debate (Senator Mundt didn't think that the introduction of a constitutional amendment could not be conceived as an unlawful act), disclosed that he went to Senator Kefauver and "personally" talked to him on the matter, subsequently not objecting to Senator Kefauver's amendment.[211] (2) Regarding Title II, the grounds upon which an internal security emergency could be declared were changed: originally, they included "imminent invasion" and a declaration by concurrent resolution of the Congress (the others being: invasion, declaration of war by Congress and insurrection in aid of a foreign enemy). During the debate, Senator Holland offered to strike those out, to bring the section "within the provisions of the Constitution."[212] The conferees agreed to this suggestion and narrowed the measure to include just the "three provisions."[213]

Senator McCarran and Representative Wood presented and explained the conference report and changes agreed upon, in addition to a statement accompanying the report that contained a "full explanation."[214]

Senator McCarran attested to deliberation and persuasion on the bill by proclaiming, "This bill is the product of many minds."[215] Among the changes compared to the original proposals that Representative Wood and Senator McCarran pointed out were: (1) the Senate provision in section 1 – "Nothing in this act shall be construed to authorize, require, or establish military or civilian censorship or in any way to limit or infringe upon freedom of the press or speech as guaranteed by the Constitution of the United States and no regulation shall be promulgated hereunder having that effect" – was written in the bill.[216] (2) As mentioned earlier, Senator Kefauver's proviso that subsection 4 (a) "shall not apply to the proposal of a constitutional amendment" was retained in Section 4.[217] (3) The words "per se" and "or of any other criminal statute" were added to the first sentence in subsection 4 (f) so that it now read "Neither the holding of office nor membership in any Communist organization by any person shall constitute *per se* a violation of subsection (a)...*or of any other criminal statute*,"[218] thus meaning that registration would not incriminate a person for violating the Smith Act. (4) Various changes were made in title II so that it was now constitutional and protective of "constitutional rights."[219]

Finally, support for the bill was bipartisan, and in a lesser respect so was opposition to it. As depicted earlier, in the Senate the proposal had support from both Democrats, such as McCarran, Holland and O'Conor, as well as Republicans, such as Mundt, Ferguson and Wiley; and in the House, the proposal had support from Democrats, such as Wood and McSweeny, as well as Republicans, such as Nixon, Velde and Case. Senator Holland called the measure a "product of bipartisan effort" in that senators from both sides of the aisle were "particularly actively associated" with it.[220] Additionally, opposition came not only from Democrats – in the Senate Kefauver, Lehman, Humphrey and others, and in the House Multer, Wier, Douglas and others – but also from Republicans – in the Senate Langer and in the House Javits and Burdick.

What's more, the vote wasn't partisan. The seventy years in the Senate in favor of the McCarran bill on September 12, 1950, were essentially split down the middle with thirty-eight Democrats and thirty-two Republicans;[221] and on August 29, 1950, when the House voted 354-20 in favor of the Wood bill, only two Republicans voted nay.[222] After the bill returned from conference, on September 20, 1950, the Senate voted 51-7 in favor, once again approximately half of the supporters Democrats and half Republicans;[223] and the House voted 313-20, with only one Republican voting nay.[224]

Veto, Reconsideration and Override

A veto by the president is a deliberative tool in several ways: first, as Hamilton explained in *Federalist* No. 73, "The oftener the measure is brought under examination, the greater the diversity in the situations of those who are to examine it, the less must be the danger of those errors which flow from want of due deliberation."[225] The legislature is not "infallible" and the executive veto increases the chances in favor of passing bad laws through "inadvertence."[226] The veto mechanism also "establishes a salutary check upon the legislative body, calculated to guard the community against...any impulse unfriendly to the public good."[227] Second, as Bessette points out, according to the Constitution, when the president vetoes a bill, he must formally give Congress reasons for doing so, and Congress in turn must reconsider the bill, (Article I, section 7), thus the presidential veto promotes argumentation and reasoning.[228]

On September 22, 1950, President Truman returned the proposed Internal Security Act of 1950 without his approval and "earnestly" requested Congress to reconsider its action.[229] In his veto message, he stated that he took this action "only after the most serious study and reflection and after consultation with the security and intelligence agencies of the Government."[230] Regarding the registration provisions, he repeated many of the arguments, including the functional arguments, that were voiced on the Senate and House floors: the language used is too broad and vague and might result in penalizing loyal citizens;[231] the criteria to be applied in determining if an organization is Communist endangers freedom of speech and assembly;[232] the United States already has on the books laws that give protection "from the real dangers of treason, espionage, sabotage, and actions looking to the overthrow of our Government by force and violence";[233] the operation of the bill would hamper the FBI, which will have to disclose sources of information in public hearings;[234] communist organizations won't register;[235] and all the proceedings will take time.[236]

Yet in addition President Truman did raise fundamental arguments regarding free speech: two of his "principal objections" to the bill were that "It would put the Government of the United States in the thought-control business" and that "It would give Government officials vast powers to harass all of our citizens in the exercise of their right of free speech."[237] Discussing the registration provisions (among the bill's "worst features") more fully, he pointed out:

> The basic error of these sections is that they move in the direction of suppressing opinion and belief.... In a free country, we punish men for crimes they commit, but never for the opinions they have... we would betray our finest traditions if we attempted, as this bill would attempt, to curb the simple expression of opinion.[238]

The House of Representatives promptly voted and passed the bill 286-48 without debate.[239] In contrast, the vote to override in the Senate was contested by the bill's opponents for almost twenty-four hours,[240] although their arguments were a prolonged repeat of what was previously articulated on the Senate floor.[241] The only new argument was that the president was commander-in-chief, responsible for protecting the nation's security, against enemies both foreign and domestic, and if he thinks the legislation is "unworkable," then the Senate should sustain his veto.[242] The bill's proponents believing it their "duty...to say a few words in rebuttal"[243] did that, with Senator McCarran "examining" the president's principal objections to the bill. Concerning "thought control," Senator McCarran did not like standing "on the Senate floor to take issue with the President of the United States" but "someone must have been misadvising the President," since the "bill contains no provisions that could properly be designated as thought control"; and concerning giving government officials powers to harass citizens in the exercise of their right to free speech, he maintained the president's charge misleading in that "[the] bill does not contain any actual authority to invade or impede the right of free speech"; therefore, it is no more true than in the administration of many other laws.[244]

Besides reconsidering the bill by way of argumentation as noted earlier, the president's veto had a certain persuasive effect. Senator Douglas and Senator Humphrey, for example, both voted on September 12, 1950, in favor of the McCarran bill in the "hope that the conference committee might eliminate some of the more dubious sections of the bill,"[245] didn't cast a vote on the bill after conference[246] but did vote with the small minority to uphold the president's veto on September 23, 1950 (the vote was 57-10 to override).[247] Senator Douglas explained his change in position due to, among other reasons, the "opportunity to reflect," the president's "compelling arguments," and he did so after "real travail and suffering of soul."[248] Senator Humphrey "reexamined" the decision he made, recognized the "mistake" he made and proclaimed that the president gave him the opportunity "to come clean" and vote his "convictions."[249]

In sum, the legislation that became the Internal Security Act of 1950 was extensively deliberated by Congress. First in House and Senate committees, where public hearings were conducted, committee members gathered information on the way to protect the United States against subversive activities, and amendments were made to the bills in question as a result of oral and written testimonies. Then in both chambers, where members of the House and Senate seriously exchanged reasoned arguments on the merits of the bill with intent to persuade as to what is the best legislative solution to the communist threat to the nation's security. Consequently the act was a democratically legitimate law.

Notes

1 Thomas I. Emerson and David Haber, *Political and Civil Rights in the United States: A Collection of Legal and Related Materials* (Buffalo: Dennis & Co., Inc., 1958), 412–413; William R. Tanner and Robert Griffith, "Legislative Politics and 'McCarthyism': The Internal Security Act of 1950," In *The Specter: Original Essays on the Cold War and the Origins of McCarthyism*, Eds. Robert Griffith and Athan Theoharis (New York: Franklin Watts, Inc., 1974), 176–177.
2 Emerson and Haber, 413; Tanner and Griffith, 178; Senate 81st Congress 2nd Session, Protection of the United States Against Un-American and Subversive Activities, *Report No. 1358*, March 21, 1950, 4–5.
3 Emerson and Haber, 413; Tanner and Griffith, 178; Hearings on Legislation to Outlaw Certain Un-American and Subversive Activities, *Hearing Before the Committee on Un-American Activities, House of Representatives, 81st Congress 2nd Session on H.R. 3903 and H.R. 7595: March 21,22,23 and 28, 1950* (Washington: Government Printing Office, 1948), 2170, 2311.
4 Hearings on Proposed Legislation to Curb or Control the Communist Party of the United States, *Hearings Before the Subcommittee on Legislation of the Committee on Un-American Activities, House of Representatives, 80th Congress 2nd Session on H.R. 4422 and H.R. 4581: February 5,6,9,10,11,19 and 20, 1948* (Washington: Government Printing Office, 1948), 1. (Hereafter cited 1948 House Hearings.)
5 1948 House Hearings, 3.
6 1948 House Hearings, 5.
7 1948 House Hearings, 5–10.
8 1948 House Hearings, 208.
9 1948 House Hearings, 211.
10 1948 House Hearings, 17.
11 1948 House Hearings, 18.
12 1948 House Hearings, 22–24.
13 See for example the testimony of Robert Milam (chairman of a special committee on the bill of rights of the American Bar Association, but speaking on his own behalf), 1948 House Hearings, 47.
14 Testimonies of Selma Borchardt, representing the Women's Bar Association of the District of Columbia, Louis Waldman, a labor relations lawyer, and James Burnham, a New York University law professor, 1948 House Hearings, 240, 106, 382.
15 Testimonies of Selma Borchardt and Robert Maurer, 1948 House Hearings, 242, 403.
16 1948 House Hearings, 106–107, 113.
17 1948 House Hearings, 256.
18 1948 House Hearings, 402.
19 1948 House Hearings, 407.
20 1948 House Hearings, 239.
21 House of Representatives 80th Congress 2nd Session, Protecting the United States Against Un-American and Subversive Activities, *Report No. 1844*, April 30, 1948. (Hereafter cited 1948 House Report No. 1844.) (Previously, on April 10, 1948, the subcommittee on legislation of the HUAC reported to the full committee that it found it advisable not to report the McDonough bill: Investigation of Un-American Activities in the United States, Committee on Un-American Activities, House of Representatives, Eightieth Congress Second Session, April 10, 1948, *Report of the Subcommittee on Legislation of the Committee on Un-American Activities on Proposed Legislation to Control*

Subversive Communist Activities in the United States (Washington: Government Printing Office, 1948)).

22 1948 House Report No. 1844, 11–12.

23 1948 House Report No. 1844, 7.

24 1948 House Report No. 1844, 8.

25 1948 House Report No. 1844, 2, 5.

26 1948 House Report No. 1844, 1, 5.

27 1948 House Report No. 1844, 1, 5.

28 1948 House Report No. 1844, 2, 11. Brought up in the hearings by Kenneth Parkinson, secretary of the District of Columbia Bar Association, 1948 House Hearings, 182.

29 1948 House Report No. 1844, 4–6.

30 Emerson and Haber, 412–413; Tanner and Griffith, 176–177.

31 Hearings Before the Committee on the Judiciary, United States Senate, Eightieth Congress Second Session, *H.R. 5852: An Act to Protect the United States Against Un-American and Subversive Activities: May 27, 28, 29 and 31, 1948* (Washington: Government Printing Office, 1948), 10, 33, 43. (Hereafter cited 1948 Senate Hearings.) Richberg also testified to the House Subcommittee in February, 1948 House Hearings, 59–85.

32 Thus allowing the American people to see whom they were associating with and make a fair choice whether to accept communism. 1948 Senate Hearings, 23–24, 43–44.

33 Quote of Richberg; Nixon handed a study on the constitutionality of the bill made by the Legislative Reference Service of the Library of Congress. 1948 Senate Hearings, 22–23, 34–35.

34 1948 Senate Hearings, 12, 34, 40, 46, 18.

35 1948 Senate Hearings, 11, 46.

36 Including Representative J. Hardin Peterson of Florida (D), veteran organizations (such as the American Legion, American Veterans of World War II (AMVETS) and the Marine Corps League) and the Special Committee on Bill of Rights of the American Bar Association. 1948 Senate Hearings, 47–50, 50–53, 65–67, 283–285, 447.

37 See, for example, testimonies and statements of Thomas I. Emerson, Yale University law professor, and of the ACLU, the American Jewish Congress and the Friends Committee on International Legislation. 1948 Senate Hearings, 171–172, 92, 343, 348, 352, 282.

38 See, for example, the testimonies and statements of Representatives Vito Marcantonio and Leo Isacson of New York (American Laborites); the American Federation of Labor (AFL); the National Lawyers Guild; the United Electrical, Radio, and Machine Workers of America, the Congress of Industrial Organizations (CIO); and the ACLU. 1948 Senate Hearings, 75–76, 57, 143–145, 147, 194, 467, 91. According to the ACLU and the AFL (as well as several other labor organizations), the entire bill had a "stultifying effect on freedom of discussion and freedom of association" and threatened labor organizations. 1948 Senate Hearings, 91, 141–146, 181, 381, 400.

39 See, for example, the testimonies and statements of the ACLU, the National Lawyers Guild and the Socialist Party. 1948 Senate Hearings, 87, 164, 242. Henry Wallace (candidate for president in the 1948 election, Progressive Party) declared during his testimony: "Never in the history of the United States has any public official been vested with such authority." 1948 Senate Hearings, 259.

40 See, for example, the testimonies and statements of the ACLU, the AFL, the Socialist Party and the International Longshoremen's and Warehousemen's Union. 1948 Senate Hearings, 89–90, 146, 241, 243, 402.

41 1948 Senate Hearings, 9.
42 1948 Senate Hearings, 69.
43 1948 Senate Hearings, 274–277.
44 1948 Senate Hearings, 422–425.
45 1948 Senate Hearings, 488.
46 1948 Senate Hearings, 491.
47 1948 Senate Hearings, 491, 496.
48 1948 Senate Hearings, 495–496.
49 Excerpt from Congressional Record in 1948 Senate Hearings, 488–489.
50 And that he is sure "that no member of the committee desires to report out a bill that would interfere with the liberties of the American people." Hearings before a Subcommittee on the Judiciary, United States Senate, Eighty-First Congress First Session, *S. 1194 and S. 1196: Bills to Protect the United States Against Certain Un-American and Subversive Activities: April 29, May 4, 6, 18, 19 and 20 And June 10, 1949* (Washington: Government Printing Office, 1949), 20. (Hereafter cited 1949 Senate Hearings.)
51 1949 Senate Hearings, 125, 216.
52 The chairman explaining that "it is a relevant question. It is something that we should know to be able to evaluate the testimony before the committee." 1949 Senate Hearings, 20.
53 1949 Senate Hearings, 125.
54 1949 Senate Hearings, 21–23. This was reiterated by Senator Ferguson, who testified that communism is not an economic philosophy yet a conspiracy aimed directly at representative government, and by Senator Johnston, who said that communism is an organized movement striving for monopolistic control of the world; 1949 Senate Hearings, 65, 151. The view was also expressed by the representative of the American Legion ("Communism is not a political party. It is an organized international conspiracy...directed from Moscow") and by Donald Richberg; 1949 Senate Hearings, 115, 217. At the end of his testimony, Senator Mundt listed fifteen "facts" that characterize communism and the activities of the Communist Party; 1949 Senate Hearings, 61–64.
55 1949 Senate Hearings, 26. 1949 Senate Hearings, 72, 67.
56 1949 Senate Hearings, 72, 67, 73, 78.
57 1949 Senate Hearings, 25.
58 1949 Senate Hearings, 28.
59 1949 Senate Hearings, 55.
60 1949 Senate Hearings, 23.
61 1949 Senate Hearings, 44–48, 57.
62 Veterans of Foreign Wars of the United States, American Veterans of World War II and the American Legion; 1949 Senate Hearings, 78–83, 83–86, 114–120.
63 1949 Senate Hearings, 241–242, 239, 172–173, 158, 104.
64 1949 Senate Hearings, 158, 170–171, 239–241, 234–235, 135, 138.
65 1949 Senate Hearings, 167–168, 248.
66 1949 Senate Hearings, 103,110, 236, 127, 141, 165–167, 247–248.
67 1949 Senate Hearings, 237, 168, 99.
68 1949 Senate Hearings, 94, 234, 137, 243.
69 1949 Senate Hearings, 109, 138, 243.
70 As mentioned earlier, the bill reported was initially introduced in the Senate in July 1949 by Senator Mundt. Senate 81st Congress 2nd Session, Protection of the United States Against Un-American and Subversive Activities, *Report No. 1358*, March 21, 1950, 4–5. (Hereafter cited 1950 Senate Report No. 1358.) Emerson and Haber, 413; Tanner and Griffith, 178.

71 1950 Senate Report No. 1358, 5.
72 1950 Senate Report No. 1358, 7.
73 1950 Senate Report No. 1358, 9, 20.
74 1950 Senate Report No. 1358, 2.
75 1950 Senate Report No. 1358, 21, 27.
76 1950 Senate Report No. 1358, 4–5, 16–29, 1.
77 1950 Senate Report No. 1358, 29–30.
78 1950 Senate Report No. 1358 Part 2, 1.
79 1950 Senate Report No. 1358 Part 2, 2–10.
80 81st Congress, 2nd Session, *Congressional Record – Senate*, Vol. 96, 12145, August 10, 1950; Senate 81st Congress 2nd Session, Protecting the Internal Security of the United States, *Report No. 2369*, August 17, 1950, 3.
81 Emerson and Haber, 413; Tanner and Griffith, 178; Hearings on Legislation to Outlaw Certain Un-American and Subversive Activities, *Hearing Before the Committee on Un-American Activities, House of Representatives, 81st Congress 2nd Session on H.R. 3903 and H.R. 7595: March 21,22,23 and 28, 1950* (Washington: Government Printing Office, 1948), III, 2170, 2311. (Hereafter cited 1950 House Hearings.)
82 There was a total of ten meetings; four were held by a subcommittee (March 23, 1950; March 28, 1950; May 2, 1950 and May 3, 1950).
83 1950 House Hearings, 2160–2161.
84 1950 House Hearings, 2209.
85 1950 House Hearings, 2163–2167.
86 1950 House Hearings, 2171.
87 1950 House Hearings, 2127–2131, 2136, 2141–2142, 2151–2152, 2159–2160.
88 1950 House Hearings, 2174–2177, 2180–2181, 2185, 2190, 2198, 2212, 2217, 2228, 2232–2242, 2253–2161, 2277–2279, 2286–2288, 2293, 2319–2323.
89 Statement of Representative Francis Case (R) of South Dakota, 81st Congress, 2nd Session, *Congressional Record – House*, Vol. 96, 13731, August 29, 1950.
90 House of Representatives 81st Congress 2nd Session, Protection of the United States Against Un-American and Subversive Activities, *Report No. 2980*, August 22, 1950. (Hereafter cited 1950 House Report No. 2980.)
91 1950 House Report No. 2980, 6.
92 81st Congress, 2nd Session, *Congressional Record – House*, Vol. 96, 12018–12020, August 8, 1950.
93 81st Congress, 2nd Session, *Congressional Record – Senate*, Vol. 96, 12693, August 17, 1950. As mentioned earlier, Senator McCarran introduced on omnibus bill on August 10, 1950, which included the Mundt-Johnston-Ferguson bill and four other bills (concerning deportation of aliens and the tightening up of certain espionage statues). 81st Congress, 2nd Session, *Congressional Record – Senate*, Vol. 96, 12145, August 10, 1950; Senate 81st Congress 2nd Session, Protecting the Internal Security of the United States, *Report No. 2369*, August 17, 1950, 3. (Hereafter cited 1950 Senate Report No. 2369.)
94 81st Congress, 2nd Session, *Congressional Record – House*, Vol. 96, 13062, August 22, 1950.
95 1950 Senate Report No. 2369, 3.
96 1950 Senate Report No. 2369, 3.
97 1950 Senate Report No. 2369, 4. In conference, the conferees agreed to the term of the Wood bill – "Communist-action organization," 81st Congress, 2nd Session, *Congressional Record – Senate*, Vol. 96, 15185, September 20, 1950; 81st Congress, 2nd Session, *Congressional Record – House*, Vol. 96, 15236; September 20, 1950.

98 1950 Senate Report No. 2369, Part 2, 2.
99 1950 Senate Report No. 2369, Part 2, 5.
100 1950 Senate Report No. 2369, Part 2, 10–11.
101 1950 Senate Report No. 2369, Part 2, 7–8.
102 1950 Senate Report No. 2369, Part 2, 8–9.
103 1950 Senate Report No. 2369, Part 2, 10.
104 81st Congress, 2nd Session, *Congressional Record – Senate*, Vol. 96, 14170, September 5, 1950.
105 81st Congress, 2nd Session, *Congressional Record – Senate*, Vol. 96, 14171, September 5, 1950.
106 81st Congress, 2nd Session, *Congressional Record – Senate*, Vol. 96, 14186, September 5, 1950.
107 81st Congress, 2nd Session, *Congressional Record – Senate*, Vol. 96, 14171, September 5, 1950.
108 81st Congress, 2nd Session, *Congressional Record – Senate*, Vol. 96, 14170–14171, September 5, 1950.
109 The following day, on September 6, 1950, Senator Mundt discussed "the exact purposes and the precise purport of the proposed legislation" concentrating on these provisions, 81st Congress, 2nd Session, *Congressional Record – Senate*, Vol. 96, 14231–14232, 14237, 14245–14246, September 6, 1950.
110 81st Congress, 2nd Session, *Congressional Record – Senate*, Vol. 96, 14174, September 5, 1950.
111 81st Congress, 2nd Session, *Congressional Record – Senate*, Vol. 96, 14174, September 5, 1950.
112 81st Congress, 2nd Session, *Congressional Record – Senate*, Vol. 96, 14174, September 5, 1950.
113 81st Congress, 2nd Session, *Congressional Record – Senate*, Vol. 96, 14174–14175, September 5, 1950.
114 81st Congress, 2nd Session, *Congressional Record – Senate*, Vol. 96, 14185, September 5, 1950.
115 81st Congress, 2nd Session, *Congressional Record – House*, Vol. 96, 13730–13731, August 29, 1950.
116 81st Congress, 2nd Session, *Congressional Record – House*, Vol. 96, 13733, August 29, 1950.
117 81st Congress, 2nd Session, *Congressional Record – House*, Vol. 96, 13730, August 29, 1950.
118 81st Congress, 2nd Session, *Congressional Record – Senate*, Vol. 96, 14597, 14596, September 12, 1950.
119 81st Congress, 2nd Session, *Congressional Record – Senate*, Vol. 96, 15195–15196, September 20, 1950.
120 81st Congress, 2nd Session, *Congressional Record – Senate*, Vol. 96, 15200, September 20, 1950.
121 81st Congress, 2nd Session, *Congressional Record – Senate*, Vol. 96, 14194, September 5, 1950.
122 81st Congress, 2nd Session, *Congressional Record – Senate*, Vol. 96, 14189, September 5, 1950.
123 81st Congress, 2nd Session, *Congressional Record – Senate*, Vol. 96, 14457, September 11, 1950.
124 81st Congress, 2nd Session, *Congressional Record – House*, Vol. 96, 13734, August 29, 1950.
125 81st Congress, 2nd Session, *Congressional Record – House*, Vol. 96, 13739, August 29, 1950.
126 81st Congress, 2nd Session, *Congressional Record – House*, Vol. 96, 13748, August 29, 1950.

127 81st Congress, 2nd Session, *Congressional Record – House*, Vol. 96, 15292, September 20, 1950.
128 81st Congress, 2nd Session, *Congressional Record – House*, Vol. 96, 13759, August 29, 1950. After the bill returned from conference, he summarized that the bill destroys the liberties of the American people, undermines the Constitution, substitutes "fascism and tyranny" for "democratic precepts" and kills "the America of the American revolution." 81st Congress, 2nd Session, *Congressional Record – House*, Vol. 96, 15288, September 20, 1950.
129 Which every minority must fear from. 81st Congress, 2nd Session, *Congressional Record – House*, Vol. 96, 13743, August 29, 1950.
130 81st Congress, 2nd Session, *Congressional Record – House*, Vol. 96, 13768, August 29, 1950.
131 81st Congress, 2nd Session, *Congressional Record – House*, Vol. 96, 13722–13723, August 29, 1950. The legislation being unconstitutional and against the "Bill of Rights" 81st Congress, 2nd Session, *Congressional Record – House*, Vol. 96, 13723, 13724, August 29, 1950.
132 81st Congress, 2nd Session, *Congressional Record – Senate*, Vol. 96, 14246, September 6, 1950.
133 81st Congress, 2nd Session, *Congressional Record – Senate*, Vol. 96, 15249, September 20, 1950.
134 81st Congress, 2nd Session, *Congressional Record – House*, Vol. 96, 13746, August 29, 1950.
135 81st Congress, 2nd Session, *Congressional Record – House*, Vol. 96, 13742, August 29, 1950.
136 81st Congress, 2nd Session, *Congressional Record – Senate*, Vol. 96, 14257, September 6, 1950.
137 81st Congress, 2nd Session, *Congressional Record – Senate*, Vol. 96, 14236, September 6, 1950.
138 81st Congress, 2nd Session, *Congressional Record – Senate*, Vol. 96, 14299–14230, September 7, 1950.
139 81st Congress, 2nd Session, *Congressional Record – Senate*, Vol. 96, 14297, September 7, 1950.
140 81st Congress, 2nd Session, *Congressional Record – House*, Vol. 96, 13749, August 29, 1950.
141 81st Congress, 2nd Session, *Congressional Record – Senate*, Vol. 96, 14611, September 12, 1950.
142 81st Congress, 2nd Session, *Congressional Record – Senate*, Vol. 96, 14445, September 8, 1950. In a statement Senator Harvey Kilgore of West Virginia (D) prepared that was printed in the Congressional Record, he also called section 4 "unconstitutional." 81st Congress, 2nd Session, *Congressional Record – Senate*, Vol. 96, 14537, 14539, September 11, 1950.
143 81st Congress, 2nd Session, *Congressional Record – Senate*, Vol. 96, 14414, September 8, 1950.
144 81st Congress, 2nd Session, *Congressional Record – Senate*, Vol. 96, 14192, September 5, 1950.
145 81st Congress, 2nd Session, *Congressional Record – Senate*, Vol. 96, 15198, September 20, 1950.
146 81st Congress, 2nd Session, *Congressional Record – Senate*, Vol. 96, 14438, September 8, 1950.
147 81st Congress, 2nd Session, *Congressional Record – Senate*, Vol. 96, 14439, September 8, 1950.
148 81st Congress, 2nd Session, *Congressional Record – Senate*, Vol. 96, 14300, September 7, 1950.

149 81st Congress, 2nd Session, *Congressional Record – Senate*, Vol. 96, 14612, 14614, September 8, 1950. Senator Mundt pointing out that the "Communist line changes from time to time from force and violence over to espionage, infiltration, and subversion, and a great many other techniques and devices which are not accompanied by forced and violence." 81st Congress, 2nd Session, *Congressional Record – Senate*, Vol. 96, 14613, September 8, 1950.

150 81st Congress, 2nd Session, *Congressional Record – House*, Vol. 96, 13746, 13759, August 29, 1950.

151 81st Congress, 2nd Session, *Congressional Record – Senate*, Vol. 96, 14192, September 5, 1950.

152 81st Congress, 2nd Session, *Congressional Record – Senate*, Vol. 96, 14235, 14246, September 6, 1950.

153 81st Congress, 2nd Session, *Congressional Record – Senate*, Vol. 96, 14192–14193, September 5, 1950.

154 81st Congress, 2nd Session, *Congressional Record – Senate*, Vol. 96, 14445, September 8, 1950, 14531, September 11, 1950.

155 81st Congress, 2nd Session, *Congressional Record – Senate*, Vol. 96, 14409, 14412, September 8, 1950.

156 81st Congress, 2nd Session, *Congressional Record – Senate*, Vol. 96, 14489, September 11, 1950.

157 81st Congress, 2nd Session, *Congressional Record – Senate*, Vol. 96, 15194, September 20, 1950.

158 81st Congress, 2nd Session, *Congressional Record – House*, Vol. 96, 13766, August 29, 1950. See also Representative Marcantonio's and Representative Celler's remarks earlier that same day, 81st Congress, 2nd Session, *Congressional Record – House*, Vol. 96, 13735, August 29, 1950.

159 81st Congress, 2nd Session, *Congressional Record – Senate*, Vol. 96, 14236, September 6, 1950.

160 81st Congress, 2nd Session, *Congressional Record – Senate*, Vol. 96, 14236, September 6, 1950, 15247, September 20, 1950.

161 81st Congress, 2nd Session, *Congressional Record – Senate*, Vol. 96, 15247, September 20, 1950.

162 81st Congress, 2nd Session, *Congressional Record – House*, Vol. 96, 13764, August 29, 1950; 81st Congress, 2nd Session, *Congressional Record – Senate*, Vol. 96, 14530–14531, September 11, 1950, 15248, September 20, 1950.

163 Senator Ferguson, Representative Nixon and Senator Holland, 81st Congress, 2nd Session, *Congressional Record – Senate*, Vol. 96, 14538, September 8, 1950, 15247–15248, September 20, 1950; 81st Congress, 2nd Session, *Congressional Record – House*, Vol. 96, 13764–13765, August 29, 1950.

164 81st Congress, 2nd Session, *Congressional Record – Senate*, Vol. 96, 14431, September 8, 1950.

165 Including Senator Humphrey 81st Congress, 2nd Session, *Congressional Record – Senate*, Vol. 96, 14463 (and 14481–14482), September 11, 1950; Senator Douglas 81st Congress, 2nd Session, *Congressional Record – Senate*, Vol. 96, 14404 and 14431, September 8, 1950; Senator Lehman 81st Congress, 2nd Session, *Congressional Record – Senate*, Vol. 96, 14190, September 5, 1950; Representative Javits 81st Congress, 2nd Session, *Congressional Record – House*, Vol. 96, 13743, August 29, 1950; and Representative Sidney Richard Yates of Illinois (D) 81st Congress, 2nd Session, *Congressional Record – House*, Vol. 96, 15294, September 20, 1950.

166 81st Congress, 2nd Session, *Congressional Record – Senate*, Vol. 96, 14190, September 5, 1950.

167 81st Congress, 2nd Session, *Congressional Record – Senate*, Vol. 96, 14461, September 11, 1950. Others argued the same, including Senator Lehman 81st Congress, 2nd Session, *Congressional Record – Senate*, Vol. 96, 14190, September 5, 1950, and 15188, September 20, 1950; Senator Douglas 81st Congress, 2nd Session, *Congressional Record – Senate*, Vol. 96, 14407, September 8, 1950; Senator Scott Wike Lucas of Illinois (D) 81st Congress, 2nd Session, *Congressional Record – Senate*, Vol. 96, 14584, September 12, 1950; and Representative Yates 81st Congress, 2nd Session, *Congressional Record – House*, Vol. 96, 15293, September 20, 1950. A supplemental argument that Communist organizations would "stymie action by changing their names" was made by Senator Douglas, 81st Congress, 2nd Session, *Congressional Record – Senate*, Vol. 96, 14410–14411, September 8, 1950.

168 81st Congress, 2nd Session, *Congressional Record – Senate*, Vol. 96, 14411, 14407, September 8, 1950. See 81st Congress, 2nd Session, *Congressional Record – Senate*, Vol. 96, 14409–14410, 14407, September 8, 1950 for a detailed description of the processes.

169 81st Congress, 2nd Session, *Congressional Record – Senate*, Vol. 96, 14411, September 8, 1950. Representative Celler had the same understanding 81st Congress, 2nd Session, *Congressional Record – House*, Vol. 96, 13723, August 29, 1950.

170 Senator Lehman, 81st Congress, 2nd Session, *Congressional Record – Senate*, Vol. 96, 14192, September 5, 1950.

171 See also Senator Graham, 81st Congress, 2nd Session, *Congressional Record – Senate*, Vol. 96, 14446, September 8, 1950; Senator Humphrey 81st Congress, 2nd Session, *Congressional Record – Senate*, Vol. 96, 14485, September 11, 1950; Senator Kilgore, 81st Congress, 2nd Session, *Congressional Record – Senate*, Vol. 96, 14538, September 11, 1950; and Senator Lucas, 81st Congress, 2nd Session, *Congressional Record – Senate*, Vol. 96, 14584, September 12, 1950.

172 Senator Humphrey, 81st Congress, 2nd Session, *Congressional Record – Senate*, Vol. 96, 14463, September 11, 1950.

173 Senator Kilgore, 81st Congress, 2nd Session, *Congressional Record – Senate*, Vol. 96, 14420, September 8, 1950; Senator Lucas, 81st Congress, 2nd Session, *Congressional Record – Senate*, Vol. 96, 14584, 14585, September 12, 1950; and Senator Lehman 81st Congress, 2nd Session, *Congressional Record – Senate*, Vol. 96, 15188, September 20, 1950. Senator Lehman and Representative Carroll also claimed that the bill's registration provisions would divert FBI time, efforts and attention from "detecting real threats" to "the shadow of Communist registration," 81st Congress, 2nd Session, *Congressional Record – Senate*, Vol. 96, 14190, 14192, September 5, 1950, 81st Congress, 2nd Session, *Congressional Record – House*, Vol. 96, 15292, September 20, 1950.

174 Senator Holland, 81st Congress, 2nd Session, *Congressional Record – Senate*, Vol. 96, 14431, September 8, 1950.

175 81st Congress, 2nd Session, *Congressional Record – Senate*, Vol. 96, 14500, September 11, 1950.

176 Senator Ferguson, 81st Congress, 2nd Session, *Congressional Record – Senate*, Vol. 96, 14535, September 11, 1950.

177 Senator Wiley, 81st Congress, 2nd Session, *Congressional Record – Senate*, Vol. 96, 14297, September 7, 1950.

178 81st Congress, 2nd Session, *Congressional Record – Senate*, Vol. 96, 142–34, 14233, September 6, 1950. Senator Ferguson adding at a later date, "I have never heard anyone use the argument that because people say they will not

obey a law it should not be passed." "If everyone obeyed ethics and always did the proper things, we should not be compelled to pass criminal laws." 81st Congress, 2nd Session, *Congressional Record – Senate*, Vol. 96, 14534, September 11, 1950.

179 Senator Holland, 81st Congress, 2nd Session, *Congressional Record – Senate*, Vol. 96, 14431, September 8, 1950, and Senator Ferguson, 81st Congress, 2nd Session, *Congressional Record – Senate*, Vol. 96, 14436, September 8, 1950.

180 81st Congress, 2nd Session, *Congressional Record – Senate*, Vol. 96, 14430–14431, September 8, 1950.

181 81st Congress, 2nd Session, *Congressional Record – Senate*, Vol. 96, 14535, September 11, 1950. Asking rhetorically with reference to limiting the FBI's usefulness, "What are police investigations for…if they are not to be used as the basis of prosecutions[?]"

182 Initially introduced on August 17, 1950, by Senator Warren Grant Magnuson of Washington (D), Senator Lucas, Senator Francis John Myers of Pennsylvania (D), Senator Kilgore, Senator Kefauver, Senator Theodore Francis Green of Rhode Island (D), Senator Douglas, Senator Humphrey, Senator Graham and Senator Lehman (S. 4061) 81st Congress, 2nd Session, *Congressional Record – Senate*, Vol. 96, 12963, August 17, 1950; and then on September 6, 1950, introduced as an amendment in the nature of a substitute to the McCarran bill by Senator Kilgore, Senator Douglas, Senator Humphrey, Senator Lehman, Senator Graham, Senator Kefauver and Senator William Benton of Connecticut (D) (S. 4130) 81st Congress, 2nd Session, *Congressional Record – Senate*, Vol. 96, 14299, September 6, 1950.

183 Senator Douglas 81st Congress, 2nd Session, *Congressional Record – Senate*, Vol. 96, 14405, September 8, 1950. See also 81st Congress, 2nd Session, *Congressional Record – Senate*, Vol. 96, 14405, 14411, 14416, 14417, 14418–14419, 14422, 11427, September 8, 1950.

184 Senator Lucas 81st Congress, 2nd Session, *Congressional Record – Senate*, Vol. 96, 14577, September 12, 1950.

185 Senator Millard Evelyn Tydings of Maryland (D) 81st Congress, 2nd Session, *Congressional Record – Senate*, Vol. 96, 14621, September 12, 1950, and Senator Douglas, 81st Congress, 2nd Session, *Congressional Record – Senate*, Vol. 96, 14411, September 8, 1950.

186 81st Congress, 2nd Session, *Congressional Record – Senate*, Vol. 96, 14597, September 12, 1950. See also Senator Douglas's remarks 81st Congress, 2nd Session, *Congressional Record – Senate*, Vol. 96, 14401–14402, 14405, 14419, 14427, September 8, 1950.

187 Senator Holland 81st Congress, 2nd Session, *Congressional Record – Senate*, Vol. 96, 14427–14429, September 8, 1950; Senator O'Conor 81st Congress, 2nd Session, *Congressional Record – Senate*, Vol. 96, 14597, September 12, 1950.

188 Senator Ferguson 81st Congress, 2nd Session, *Congressional Record – Senate*, Vol. 96, 14436, September 8, 1950 and 14585, 14622, September 12, 1950; Senator McCarran 81st Congress, 2nd Session, *Congressional Record – Senate*, Vol. 96, 14593, September 12, 1950; and Senator O'Conor 81st Congress, 2nd Session, *Congressional Record – Senate*, Vol. 96, 14597, September 12, 1950.

189 Senator Ferguson 81st Congress, 2nd Session, *Congressional Record – Senate*, Vol. 96, 14528, September 11, 1950. See also his remarks at 81st Congress, 2nd Session, *Congressional Record – Senate*, Vol. 96, 14425–14426, 14439, September 8, 1950, and 81st Congress, 2nd Session, *Congressional Record – Senate*, Vol. 96, 14585–14586, September 12, 1950; and Senator Mundt 81st Congress, 2nd Session, *Congressional Record – Senate*, Vol. 96,

14440, September 8, 1950, and 81st Congress, 2nd Session, *Congressional Record – Senate*, Vol. 96, 14499, September 11, 1950; and Senator McCarran 81st Congress, 2nd Session, *Congressional Record – Senate*, Vol. 96, 14548, September 11, 1950.

190 81st Congress, 2nd Session, *Congressional Record – Senate*, Vol. 96, 14431, September 8, 1950.

191 81st Congress, 2nd Session, *Congressional Record – Senate*, Vol. 96, 14606, September 12, 1950.

192 81st Congress, 2nd Session, *Congressional Record – Senate*, Vol. 96, 14623, September 12, 1950. For example, the grounds upon which an internal security emergency could be declared were changed (see further in the section on "Persuasion and Call for Deliberation").

193 81st Congress, 2nd Session, *Congressional Record – Senate*, Vol. 96, 14628, September 12, 1950.

194 81st Congress, 2nd Session, *Congressional Record – Senate*, Vol. 96, 14189, September 5, 1950.

195 81st Congress, 2nd Session, *Congressional Record – Senate*, Vol. 96, 15188, September 20, 1950 (going on to quote from correspondence he received and from newspaper editorials, to support his conviction).

196 81st Congress, 2nd Session, *Congressional Record – Senate*, Vol. 96, 14300, September 7, 1950.

197 Representative Douglas 81st Congress, 2nd Session, *Congressional Record – House*, Vol. 96, 13748, August 29, 1950; Representative Carroll 81st Congress, 2nd Session, *Congressional Record – House*, Vol. 96, 15292, September 20, 1950; Senator Kefauver 81st Congress, 2nd Session, *Congressional Record – Senate*, Vol. 96, 15191, September 20, 1950; Senator Lucas 81st Congress, 2nd Session, *Congressional Record – Senate*, Vol. 96, 14577, 14584, 14585, September 12, 1950; Senator Graham 81st Congress, 2nd Session, *Congressional Record – Senate*, Vol. 96, 14445, September 8, 1950; and Senator Lehman 81st Congress, 2nd Session, *Congressional Record – Senate*, Vol. 96, 14189–14190, September 5, 1950.

198 81st Congress, 2nd Session, *Congressional Record – Senate*, Vol. 96, 14457, September 11, 1950. See also 81st Congress, 2nd Session, *Congressional Record – Senate*, Vol. 96, 14422, September 8, 1950.

199 81st Congress, 2nd Session, *Congressional Record – House*, Vol. 96, 14582, September 14, 1950. See also Representative Clarence J. Brown of Ohio (R) 81st Congress, 2nd Session, *Congressional Record – House*, Vol. 96, 13724, August 29, 1950; Representative Edward Herbert Rees of Kansas (R) 81st Congress, 2nd Session, *Congressional Record – House*, Vol. 96, 13741, August 29, 1950; Representative Errett Power Scrivner of Kansas (R) 81st Congress, 2nd Session, *Congressional Record – House*, Vol. 96, 13742, August 29, 1950; and Senator Mundt 81st Congress, 2nd Session, *Congressional Record – Senate*, Vol. 96, 14237, 14243, 14248, 14252–14253, September 6, 1950.

200 Representative O'Hara 81st Congress, 2nd Session, *Congressional Record – House*, Vol. 96, 13765, August 29, 1950 and Representative Celler 81st Congress, 2nd Session, *Congressional Record – House*, Vol. 96, 13723, August 29, 1950. Representative Douglas asked to "legislate with reason" 81st Congress, 2nd Session, *Congressional Record – House*, Vol. 96, 13748, August 29, 1950.

201 81st Congress, 2nd Session, *Congressional Senate – Senate*, Vol. 96, 14489, September 11, 1950. Earlier urging the Senate and appealing to it "to rise above the clamor, the hysteria, and the tensions of this time, and once again demonstrate...that this body is the wisest and most deliberative body in the world." 81st Congress, 2nd Session, *Congressional Senate – Senate*, Vol. 96, 14457, September 11, 1950.

202 81st Congress, 2nd Session, *Congressional Senate – Senate*, Vol. 96, 14232, 14231, September 6, 1950. He also attested to doing just that in the public sphere: "I have been participating in that kind of discussion for over 30 months, in over a dozen radio forums, in over half a hundred public forums on platforms... and in articles in the press." 81st Congress, 2nd Session, *Congressional Senate – Senate*, Vol. 96, 14232, September 6, 1950.

203 81st Congress, 2nd Session, *Congressional Record – Senate*, Vol. 96, 14385–14390, September 7, 1950. Remarks of Senator Humphrey 81st Congress, 2nd Session, *Congressional Record – Senate*, Vol. 96, 14259, September 6, 1950, and Senator Lucas 81st Congress, 2nd Session, *Congressional Record – Senate*, Vol. 96, 14386, September 7, 1950.

On the importance of timing issues in the deliberative process of a political assembly, see John Uhr, *Deliberative Democracy in Australia: The Changing Place of Parliament* (Melbourne: Cambridge University Press, 1998), 219–224. Paul Quirk notes the influence opportunities for criticism and rebuttal have on the quality of deliberation in Congress, Paul J. Quirk, "Deliberation and Decision Making," In *The Legislative Branch*, Eds. Paul J. Quirk and Sarah A. Binder (New York: Oxford University Press, 2005), 324.

204 See, for example, Senator Kilgore 81st Congress, 2nd Session, *Congressional Senate – Senate*, Vol. 96, 14498, September 11, 1950, and Senator Wiley 81st Congress, 2nd Session, *Congressional Senate – Senate*, Vol. 96, 14297, September 7, 1950, and 15191, September 20, 1950. See also Representative Keating 81st Congress, 2nd Session, *Congressional Record – House*, Vol. 96, 13749, August 29, 1950, and Senator Stennis 81st Congress, 2nd Session, *Congressional Record – Senate*, Vol. 96, 14186, September 5, 1950.

205 81st Congress, 2nd Session, *Congressional Record – Senate*, Vol. 96, 14235, September 6, 1950.

206 81st Congress, 2nd Session, *Congressional Record – Senate*, Vol. 96, 15220, September 20, 1950.

207 81st Congress, 2nd Session, *Congressional Record – Senate*, Vol. 96, 14238, September 6, 1950. And see 81st Congress, 2nd Session, *Congressional Record – Senate*, Vol. 96, 14198–14199, September 5, 1950.

208 81st Congress, 2nd Session, *Congressional Record – Senate*, Vol. 96, 14239–14240, September 6, 1950.

209 81st Congress, 2nd Session, *Congressional Record – Senate*, Vol. 96, 14612–14614, September 12, 1950.

210 81st Congress, 2nd Session, *Congressional Record – House*, Vol. 96, 15286, September 20, 1950, 81st Congress, 2nd Session, *Congressional Record – Senate*, Vol. 96, 15185, September 20, 1950.

211 81st Congress, 2nd Session, *Congressional Record – Senate*, Vol. 96, 15195, September 20, 1950.

212 81st Congress, 2nd Session, *Congressional Record – Senate*, Vol. 96, 14592, September 12, 1950.

213 81st Congress, 2nd Session, *Congressional Record – Senate*, Vol. 96, 15187, September 20, 1950. In fact, imminent invasion and a declaration by concurrent resolution of the Congress were already absent from the "altered" text of Title II that Senator McCarran introduced on September 12, 1950 (81st Congress, 2nd Session, *Congressional Record – Senate*, Vol. 96, 14623–14624, September 12, 1950).

214 81st Congress, 2nd Session, *Congressional Record – Senate*, Vol. 96, 15185–15188, September 20, 1950, and 81st Congress, 2nd Session, *Congressional Record – House*, Vol. 96, 15265–15287, September 20, 1950.

215 81st Congress, 2nd Session, *Congressional Record – Senate*, Vol. 96, 15185, September 20, 1950.

216 81st Congress, 2nd Session, *Congressional Record – House*, Vol. 96, 15279–15280, September 20, 1950, and 81st Congress, 2nd Session, *Congressional Record – Senate*, Vol. 96, 15185, September 20, 1950.

217 81st Congress, 2nd Session, *Congressional Record – Senate*, Vol. 96, 15185–15186, September 20, 1950, and 81st Congress, 2nd Session, *Congressional Record – House*, Vol. 96, 15280, 15286, September 20, 1950.

218 81st Congress, 2nd Session, *Congressional Record – House*, Vol. 96, 15280, September 20, 1950.

219 81st Congress, 2nd Session, *Congressional Record – Senate*, Vol. 96, 15186, September 20, 1950, and 81st Congress, 2nd Session, *Congressional Record – House*, Vol. 96, 15287, September 20, 1950.

220 81st Congress, 2nd Session, *Congressional Record – Senate*, Vol. 96, 15250, September 20, 1950.

221 81st Congress, 2nd Session, *Congressional Record – Senate*, Vol. 96, 14628, September 12, 1950.

222 81st Congress, 2nd Session, *Congressional Record – House*, Vol. 96, 13769, August 29, 1950.

223 81st Congress, 2nd Session, *Congressional Record – Senate*, Vol. 96, 145260, September 20, 1950.

224 81st Congress, 2nd Session, *Congressional Record – House*, Vol. 96, 15297–15298, September 20, 1950.

225 Jay, Hamilton, James, Madison, and John, Jay. *The Federalist Papers*. Ed. Clinton Rossiter with an introduction and notes by Charles R. Kesler (New York: Signet Classic, 2003), 442.

226 *Federalist* No. 73, 442.

227 *Federalist* No. 73, 441.

228 Joseph M. Bessette, *The Mild Voice of Reason: Deliberative Democracy & American National Government* (Chicago: The University of Chicago Press, 1994), 29. Article I, section 7 of the Constitution states that if the president does not approve of a bill presented to him by the House of Representatives and the Senate,

> he shall return it, with his Objections to that House in which it shall have originated, who shall enter the Objections at large on their journal, and proceed to reconsider it. If after such Reconsideration two thirds of that House shall agree to pass the Bill, it shall be sent, together with the Objections, to the other House, by which it shall be likewise be reconsidered.

229 81st Congress, 2nd Session, *Congressional Record – House*, Vol. 96, 15629, September 22, 1950.

230 81st Congress, 2nd Session, *Congressional Record – House*, Vol. 96, 15629, September 22, 1950.

231 81st Congress, 2nd Session, *Congressional Record – House*, Vol. 96, 15629, September 22, 1950.

232 81st Congress, 2nd Session, *Congressional Record – House*, Vol. 96, 15630, September 22, 1950.

233 81st Congress, 2nd Session, *Congressional Record – House*, Vol. 96, 15629, September 22, 1950.

234 And waste the FBI and Department of Justice "immense amounts of time and energy attempting to carry out its unworkable registration provisions." 81st Congress, 2nd Session, *Congressional Record – House*, Vol. 96, 15629, 15631, September 22, 1950.

235 And that "The idea of requiring Communist organizations to divulge information about themselves... is about as practical as requiring thieves to

register with the sheriff." 81st Congress, 2nd Session, *Congressional Record – House*, Vol. 96, 15630, September 22, 1950.

236 81st Congress, 2nd Session, *Congressional Record – House*, Vol. 96, 15630, September 22, 1950.

237 81st Congress, 2nd Session, *Congressional Record – House*, Vol. 96, 15629, September 22, 1950.

238 81st Congress, 2nd Session, *Congressional Record – House*, Vol. 96, 15630, September 22, 1950.

239 81st Congress, 2nd Session, *Congressional Record – House*, Vol. 96, 15632–15633, September 22, 1950.

240 Starting 5:00 pm September 22, 1950, see Senator Douglas's, Senator Ferguson's and Senator Mundt's remarks 81st Congress, 2nd Session, *Congressional Record – Senate*, Vol. 96, 15674, 15718, 15723, September 23, 1950.

241 See, for example, Senators Humphrey, Lehman, Kefauver, Graham 81st Congress, 2nd Session, *Congressional Record – Senate*, Vol. 96, 15522–15524, 15710–15712, 15717, 15535–15536, 15689–15690, 15694–15696, 15545, 15550–15551, 15554–15556, September 22, 1950, and Senators Langer, Douglas and James Edward Murray of Montana (D) 81st Congress, 2nd Session, *Congressional Record – Senate*, Vol. 96, 15661, 15674–15678, 15681, 15685–15686, September 23, 1950.

242 Senators Humphrey, Lehman, Kefauver 81st Congress, 2nd Session, *Congressional Record – Senate*, Vol. 96, 15523, 15535, 15550, September 22, 1950, and Senator Langer 81st Congress, 2nd Session, *Congressional Record – Senate*, Vol. 96, 15658–15659, September 23, 1950.

243 Senator Ferguson 81st Congress, 2nd Session, *Congressional Record – Senate*, Vol. 96, 15719, September 23, 1950.

244 81st Congress, 2nd Session, *Congressional Record – Senate*, Vol. 96, 15722–15723, September 23, 1950.

245 Senator Douglas 81st Congress, 2nd Session, *Congressional Record – Senate*, Vol. 96, 15674, September 23, 1950, and see Senator Humphrey 81st Congress, 2nd Session, *Congressional Record – Senate*, Vol. 96, 15525, September 23, 1950.

246 81st Congress, 2nd Session, *Congressional Record – Senate*, Vol. 96, 15260, September 20, 1950.

247 81st Congress, 2nd Session, *Congressional Record – Senate*, Vol. 96, 15726, September 23, 1950.

248 81st Congress, 2nd Session, *Congressional Record – Senate*, Vol. 96, 15674, 15680, September 23, 1950.

249 81st Congress, 2nd Session, *Congressional Record – Senate*, Vol. 96, 15525, September 23, 1950.

References

Bessette, Joseph M. *The Mild Voice of Reason: Deliberative Democracy & American National Government*. Chicago: The University of Chicago Press, 1994.

Congressional Record: Proceedings and Debates of the 81st Congress Second Session, Vol. 96. Washington: United States Government Printing Office, 1950.

Emerson, Thomas I. and Haber, David. *Political and Civil Rights in the United States: A Collection of Legal and Related Materials*. Buffalo: Dennis & Co., Inc., 1958.

Hamilton, Jay, Madison, James and Jay, John. *The Federalist Papers*. Ed. Clinton Rossiter with an introduction and notes by Charles R. Kesler. New York: Signet Classic, 2003.

Hearings before the Committee on the Judiciary, United States Senate, Eightieth Congress Second Session, *H.R. 5852: An Act to Protect the United States Against Un-American and Subversive Activities: May 27, 28, 29 and 31, 1948.* Washington: Government Printing Office, 1948.

Hearings Before a Subcommittee on the Judiciary, United States Senate, Eighty-First Congress First Session, *S. 1194 and S. 1196: Bills to Protect the United States Against Certain Un-American and Subversive Activities: April 29, May 4, 6, 18, 19 and 20 And June 10, 1949.* Washington: Government Printing Office, 1949.

Hearings on Legislation to Outlaw Certain Un-American and Subversive Activities, *Hearing before the Committee on Un-American Activities, House of Representatives, 81st Congress 2nd Session on H.R. 3903 and H.R. 7595: March 21,22,23 and 28, 1950.* Washington: Government Printing Office, 1950.

Hearings on Proposed Legislation to Curb or Control the Communist Party of the United States, *Hearings before the Subcommittee on Legislation of the Committee on Un-American Activities, House of Representatives, 80th Congress 2nd Session on H.R. 4422 and H.R. 4581: February 5, 6, 9, 10, 11, 19 and 20, 1948.* Washington: Government Printing Office, 1948.

Quirk, Paul J. "Deliberation and Decision Making." *The Legislative Branch.* Eds. Paul J. Quirk and Sarah A. Binder, 314–348. New York: Oxford University Press, 2005.

Tanner, William R. and Griffith, Robert. "Legislative Politics and 'McCarthyism': The Internal Security Act of 1950." *The Specter: Original Essays on the Cold War and the Origins of McCarthyism.* Eds. Robert Griffith and Athan Theoharis, 172–189. New York: Franklin Watts, Inc., 1974.

Uhr, John. *Deliberative Democracy in Australia: The Changing Place of Parliament.* Melbourne: Cambridge University Press, 1998.

Conclusion

During war, democracies tend to curb freedom of speech. In this book I examined the phenomena of legislation by a national legislature restricting freedom of speech during war and asked under what circumstances is such legislation democratically legitimate.

Although the literature of war and emergency powers show that abridgment of rights during war should be legitimized in law by the national legislature after deliberation,[1] the literature does not explain the conditions under which the legislation of such laws can be considered democratically legitimate. And while deliberative democracy theory offers an answer to the question of legitimacy of legislation in democratic political systems – a democratically legitimate law is produced in a process of public discussion and debate in which participants reason on the common good – the theory of deliberative democracy put forward by theorists such as Jürgen Habermas[2] is poorly suited for the real world: we live in large-scale democratic countries, and it is impossible for all the citizens in a country to participate in an ideal deliberative process.

Regarding deliberative democracy as an aspect of representative democracy and not as a substitute for it,[3] I proposed an alternative normative account of deliberative democracy that focuses on the deliberations of a national legislature in regard to the circumstances legislation restricting freedom of speech during war can be considered democratically legitimate. This account provides that legislation restricting freedom of speech during war can be considered democratically legitimate if members of a national legislature deliberated well; that is, during the process of discussion and debate, they reasoned on the public good, seriously considered information and arguments and sought to decide and to persuade as to the best legislative solution. I term this "Legislative Deliberative Democracy."

I use five criteria to measure legislative deliberation: committee hearings, debate in both chambers, exchange of information and arguments on the floor, framing arguments in terms of the public good and persuasion. Laws restricting freedom of speech during war carry a higher degree of democratic legitimacy when members of a democratic government's national legislature, the representatives of the people, duly deliberate on them. The higher the extent of deliberation, the more legitimacy is attached to the legislation.

Using the criteria mentioned earlier to measure legislative deliberation, I researched four times of crisis in which the American national Congress enacted federal acts restricting freedom of speech and evaluated the extent of congressional deliberation: the Espionage Act of 1917, which is still on the books and prohibits, when the United States is at war, to incite disloyalty in the armed forces and obstruct enlistment; the Sedition Act of 1918, which prohibited, during war, language provoking resistance to the United States; the Alien Registration Act of 1940 (the Smith Act), introduced in Congress on the eve of World War II, which prohibited advocating the necessity of overthrowing the government by force and was enforced both in World War II and in the course of the Cold War; and the Internal Security Act of 1950 (the McCarran Act), which was legislated at the height of the Cold War to "protect the United States against certain un-American and subversive activities" and required Communist organizations to register with the attorney general. I evaluated the extent of congressional deliberation on these acts and thus of the degree of their democratic legitimacy. Following is a table summarizing the empirical findings:

	Espionage Act	Sedition Act	Smith Act	McCarran Act
Committee Hearings	✓	✗	✓	✓
Debate in both Chambers	✓	✓̵	✓	✓
Exchange on the Floor	✓	✓	✓̵	✓
Public Good	✓	✓̵	✓̵	✓
Persuasion	✓	✓̵	✓̵	✓

Figure 8.1 Summary of Empirical Findings: Congressional Deliberation on Acts Restricting Freedom of Speech during War

The Espionage Act and the McCarran Act were extensively deliberated by Congress. In the case of Espionage Act, congressmen took the bill under serious consideration, displayed sensitivity to the issue of free speech and narrowed the bill, drafting its provisions as to impair free speech during war to a minimum they thought was necessary for the safety of nation. In the case of the McCarran Act, House and Senate committee members gathered information on the way to protect the United States against subversive activities, amendments were made as a result of oral and written testimonies and, on the floor, members of the House and

Senate exchanged reasoned arguments with the intent to persuade as to what is the best legislative solution to the Communist threat to the nation's security. Consequently, the Espionage Act and the McCarran Act can be considered democratically legitimate measures.

On the other hand, the Sedition Act and the Smith Act were only moderately deliberated and therefore carry a lower level of democratic legitimacy. In the case of the Sedition Act, public hearings were not held at a congressional committee, the House scantily deliberated the pending bill and arguments in both chambers were only occasionally framed in terms of the common good while an underlying current in the arguments that were advanced was that of an unreflective and war-frenzied public voice. In the case of the Smith Act, the extent of deliberation on the provisions that restricted freedom of speech was relatively low; there wasn't any real exchange between opposing sides, no serious discussion on the significance of restricting the constitutional right to free speech or notable support of arguments with evidence or information; and the bill was only slightly changed as a result of committee and floor deliberation.

The Democratic Legitimacy of Legislative Restrictions on Freedom of Speech in Other Democracies during War

In times of war other national legislatures of democracies besides the United States passed laws that restricted freedom of speech. This phenomenon can be seen in different modern constitutional government systems, parliamentary as well as presidential, and in countries with an unwritten constitution besides a written one. Britain has a parliamentary system and an unwritten constitution, and the British experience in World War I and World War II is a case in point.

On August 8, 1914, the British Parliament passed what Rossiter called "perhaps the most radical parliamentary enactment in the history of England, indeed in all the history of constitutional government" – the Defence of the Realm Act (DORA).[4] This statute gave the British government the power to issue regulations "for securing the public safety and the defense of the realm" and to authorize trial by court martial in numerous economic and political spheres, including regulations designed "to prevent the spread of false reports or reports likely to cause disaffection to His Majesty or to interfere with the success of His Majesty's forces by land or sea."[5]

Several regulations were issued that enabled the government to censure the press and restrict freedom of speech. For example, Defence of the Realm Regulation (DRR) 27 prohibited to spread "by word of mouth or in writing" false reports and statements likely to cause disaffection, DRR 42 prohibited sedition and DRR 51a empowered the government to authorize the seizure of prohibited documents.[6] During the war, news was censured and raids were conducted against persons and organizations.[7]

On the eve of World War II, on August 24, 1939, the British Parliament passed an act similar to DORA, entitled the Emergency Powers (Defence) Act. This act empowered the government to make regulations necessary "for securing the public safety, the defence of the realm, the maintenance of public order and the efficient prosecution" of war, including regulations for "the detention of persons whose detention appears to the secretary of state to be expedient in the interests of the public safety or the defence of the realm."[8]

Regulation 18B gave the home secretary the authority to detain any person "to be of hostile origin or associations" or a member of an organization that is either "subject to foreign influence" or has associations with persons in sympathy with any "Power with which His Majesty is at war."[9] By the end of 1941 almost 1,800 detention orders had been made and members of fascist groups were arrested.[10] This regulation effectively suppressed speech as most people who would have made anti-war expressions either refrained from doing so or were detained.[11] Furthermore, Regulations 39A, 39B and 39BA made it a crime to seduce persons from duty and cause disaffection, make "false statements" and publish reports that are "likely to cause alarm or despondency."[12] In addition, the press was censured by means of Regulations 2C and 2D, which determined that "systematic publication of matter…calculated to forment opposition" to successful prosecution of war (including newspapers) is an offense. As a result, Communist publications were suppressed (before the Soviet Union joined the Allies).[13]

But was this legislation democratically legitimate? By examining deliberation in the British Parliament, we can trace an answer. After the bills were introduced, what debate was conducted at the committee stage, and how were the original drafts of the bills amended?[14] Did both the House of Commons and the House of Lords deliberate? If only one chamber of Parliament considered a bill and hastily voted on it, we would view the extent of deliberation on the act as lower as opposed to broad deliberation by both chambers. Was there an exchange of information and arguments between legislators who supported the bills and others? Were the arguments framed in terms of the public good, and how so? For example, did Members of Parliament and Lords discuss the meaning of restricting freedom of speech in Britain, the constitutionality of such legislation and why was it needed at that time? Were they persuaded in one way or another concerning the need to restrict speech during war? How was the original legislation proposed amended and in what way? The higher the extent of deliberation in the British Parliament, the more legitimacy is attached to the above-mentioned legislation.

Thus, the normative framework of Legislative Deliberative Democracy proposed in this book may be of use to examine the democratic legitimacy of laws restricting freedom of speech during war in various democratic nations.

In addition, the normative framework can be used to examine the democratic legitimacy of laws undermining other civil liberties during war. I chose to focus in this book on laws restricting freedom of speech because freedom of speech is such a fundamental right in a democracy, usually enshrined in a constitution. Robert Dahl defined freedom of expression as one of six political institutions of modern representative government – required for effective participation, an enlightened understanding of government actions and to influence the agenda of government decisions.[15] Indeed, we cannot imagine a democracy without freedom of speech. But of course, the Legislative Deliberative Democracy normative framework could certainly be used to examine the democratic legitimacy of laws undermining other civil liberties during war (e.g., freedom of assembly).

Legislative Deliberative Democracy and the War on Terror: The Case of Limiting Freedom of Speech Online in the United States to Combat ISIL

Modern terrorism targets potential supporters, among other audiences, through the Internet. One study identified eight different ways terrorists use the Internet, including recruiting and mobilizing supporters to play an active role in support of terrorist activities. For example, potential recruits receive anti-American propaganda and training manuals on how to be a terrorist. Another use of the Internet is information sharing, including on how to execute attacks.[16]

ISIL (or ISIS) is a skilled user of modern online platforms, including Facebook, Twitter, Telegram, and WhatsApp. Using the Internet, ISIL has encouraged individuals to conduct terrorist acts in the United States.[17] In other words, ISIL has encouraged "lone wolf" terrorism.[18] In this case, lone-wolf terrorism refers to an individual who becomes radicalized as a result of jihadist literature online.[19] Examples of such attacks on U.S. soil include the following: in December 2015, a married couple murdered fourteen people during a Christmas party at the California San Bernardino County Department of Public Health; in June 2016, a terrorist murdered forty-nine people at an Orlando gay nightclub; and in November 2017, a terrorist rammed his car and stabbed people at Ohio State University.[20] Over a fifth of the terrorist plots in the United States between 2014 and March 2017 were conducted by "virtual entrepreneurs" communicating digitally with ISIL.[21]

In the 2016 presidential campaign, both Republican and Democratic candidates voiced views in regard to limiting freedom of speech online. Donald Trump (R) said:

> We're losing a lot of people because of the Internet. And we have to do something. … maybe in certain areas, closing that Internet up in some way. Somebody will say, "Oh freedom of speech, freedom of speech." These are foolish people.

And Hillary Clinton (D) said:

> Resolve means depriving jihadists of virtual territory. … They are using websites, social media, chat rooms and other platforms to celebrate beheadings, recruit future terrorists, and call for attacks. We should … figure out how we disrupt them. … You're going to hear all of the usual complaints, you know, freedom of speech, et cetera. But if we truly are in a war against terrorism … then we've got to shut off their means of communicating.[22]

In addition, some legal scholars have brought up the need to reconsider existing understandings on free speech,[23] including one proposal to limit freedom of speech by making it illegal to access websites that glorify or support ISIL; to distribute links to videos, images or text taken from those websites; and to encourage people to access such websites.[24]

Even as ISIL has lost physical ground, it continues to inspire individuals to strike against the United States via its online activity, and it uses the Internet to advocate violent action.[25] Thus, the issue of limiting freedom of speech online in the fight against ISIL is of continued relevance. This question – that of balancing our desire to preserve the fundamental right of freedom of speech with the need to limit it under certain circumstances in order to defend ourselves and effectively fight jihadist terrorism – is one that everyone in a democratic society should care about.

In conclusion, this book addresses questions that matter in the democratic world. When democracies face war, how can they impede freedom of speech, including freedom of speech online, yet still remain democracies?

The views described previously by jurists and politicians are of value. However, the policy recommendation for democratic leaders in the United States deriving from this book is as follows: any abridgement of freedom of speech online must be instituted by Congress, and only through genuine deliberation in Congress – where the people's representatives during the process of discussion and debate reason on the public good, seriously consider information and arguments and seek to decide and to persuade as to the best legislative solution to the danger of ISIL web propaganda – can a law restricting online freedom of speech be democratically legitimate.

Notes

1 See for example Clinton L. Rossiter, *Constitutional Dictatorship: Crisis Government in the Modern Democracies* (Princeton: Princeton University Press, 1948), 296, 300, 302.

2 Jürgen Habermas, "Three Normative Models of Democracy," *Constellations* 1 (1994): 1–10; Jürgen Habermas, *Between Facts and Norms: Contributions to a Discourse Theory of Law and Democracy*, trans. William Rehg (Cambridge: The MIT Press, 1996), especially 296–308 (originally published in German in 1992).

3 See similar perspectives in Joseph M. Bessette, *The Mild Voice of Reason: Deliberative Democracy & American National Government* (Chicago: The University of Chicago Press, 1994); and in John Uhr, *Deliberative Democracy in Australia: The Changing Place of Parliament* (Melbourne: Cambridge University Press, 1998).

4 Rossiter, 153. The act was passed four days after war was declared (and one day after the Home Secretary asked the Commons to pass it). See Cornelius P. Cotter, "Constitutionalizing Emergency Powers," *Stanford Law Review* 382 (1953): 384.

5 Defence of the Realm Consolidation Act, 1914, 5 Geo V, c8. The original act was amended and the consolidated act enlarged the categories of offenses, Cotter, 385–386; Rossiter, 153.

6 Great Britain and Alexander Pulling. *Defence of the Realm Acts and Regulations: Passed and Made to July 31st 1915* (London: Printed for Fredrick Attenbury, King's printer of acts of Parliament and under authority of His Majesty's Stationary Office, by Darling & Son, Ltd, 1915), 25–26, 32, 34–35; Rossiter, 166; Brock Millman, "HMG and the War Against Dissent, 1914–18," *Journal of Contemporary History* 40 (2005): 422.

7 Millman, 422.

8 Emergency Powers (Defence) Act, 1939, 2 & 3 Geo VI, c62. The act was amended twice to increase government powers, Rossiter, 187; Cotter, 405.

9 Great Britain, *Defence Regulations: Being Regulations Made Under the Emergency Powers (Defence) Acts, 1939 and 1940, Printed as Amended up to and Including 15th January, 1941.* 7th ed. (London: His Majesty's Stationary Office, 1941), 39–40; Rossiter, 197.

10 Charles Townshend, *Making the Peace: Public Order and Public Security in Modern Britain* (Oxford: Oxford University Press, 1993), 125; Cotter, 408–409.

11 Rossiter, 198.

12 Great Britain, *Defence Regulations*, 93–94, 96–97; Rossiter, 199.

13 Great Britain, *Defence Regulations*, 11–13; Rossiter, 199.

14 In the case of the original Defence of the Realm Act, after the first reading of the bill, the Home Secretary moved that the House resolve itself into a committee on the bill, and it was immediately read a second time and reported without amendment (see Harold M. Bowman, "Martial Law and the English Constitution," *Michigan Law Review* 15 (December 1916): 94, including his quote of the Parliamentary debate). In other words, there was no committee deliberation on DORA.

15 Robert A. Dahl, *On Democracy* (New Haven and London: Yale University Press, 2000), 85–86, 96–97.

16 Gabriel Weimann, *How Modern Terrorism Uses the Internet* (Washington: United States Institute of Peace Special Report 116, March 2004), 1–10. The other six ways terrorists use the Internet according to Weimann are psychological warfare, propaganda, data mining (gathering information), fundraising, networking and planning and coordination.

17 Daniel Byman, *An Intelligence Reserve Corps to Counter Terrorist Use of the Internet* (Hoover Working Group on National Security, Technology and Law, Aegis Series Paper No. 1810, July 2018), 1, 4; Seamus Hughes and Alexander Meleagrou-Hitchens, "The Threat to the United States from the Islamic State's Virtual Entrepreneurs," *CTC Sentinel* 10 (March 2017): 1–2, available at https://ctc.usma.edu/the-threat-to-the-united-states-from-the-islamic-states-virtual-entrepreneurs/ [accessed: January 3, 2020].

18 Daniel Byman, "How to Hunt a Lone Wolf: Countering Terrorists Who Act on Their Own," *Foreign Affairs* 96 (March/April 2017): 102.

19 Sajjan M. Gohel, "The Internet and Its Role in Terrorist Recruitment and Operational Planning," *CTC Sentinel* 2 (December 2009): 15, available at https://ctc.usma.edu/the-internet-and-its-role-in-terrorist-recruitment-and-operational-planning/ [accessed: January 3, 2020].
20 Byman, *How to Hunt a Lone Wolf*, 96, 98–99.
21 Hughes and Meleagrou-Hitchens, 1, 6–7.
22 David Post, "Protecting the First Amendment in the Internet Age," *Volokh Conspiracy Washington Post*, 21 December 2015, https://www.washingtonpost.com/news/volokh-conspiracy/wp/2015/12/21/protecting-the-first-amendment-in-the-internet-age/?utm_term=.c621071a412a [accessed: January 4, 2020].
23 And other jurists think otherwise. Erik Eckholm, "ISIS Influence on Web Prompts Second Thoughts on First Amendment," *New York Times*, 27 December 2015, http://www.nytimes.com/2015/12/28/us/isis-influence-on-web-prompts-second-thoughts-on-first-amendment.html?_r=0 [accessed: January 4, 2020].
24 Providing graduated penalties for violations. Eric Posner, "ISIS Gives Us No Choice but to Consider Limits on Speech," *Slate*, December 15, 2015, http://www.slate.com/articles/news_and_politics/view_from_chicago/2015/12/isis_s_online_radicalization_efforts_present_an_unprecedented_danger.html [accessed: January 4, 2020].
25 Nathan A. Sales, U.S. Department of State Acting Undersecretary for Civilian Security, Democracy and Human Rights, "After the Caliphate: A New Global Approach to Defeating ISIS," *Remarks: The Brooking Institution*, April 30, 2019, https://www.state.gov/after-the-caliphate-a-new-global-approach-to-defeating-isis/ [accessed: January 4, 2020]; Joseph L. Votel, Cristina Bembenek, Charles Hans, Jefferey Mouton and Amanda Spencer, "#Virtual Caliphate: Defeating ISIL on the Physical Battlefield is Not Enough," *Center for a New American Security*, January 12, 2017, available at https://www.cnas.org/publications/reports/virtual-caliphate [accessed: January 4, 2020].

References

Bessette, Joseph M. *The Mild Voice of Reason: Deliberative Democracy & American National Government*. Chicago: The University of Chicago Press, 1994.

Bowman, Harold M. "Martial Law and the English Constitution." *Michigan Law Review* 15 (December 1916): 93–126.

Byman, Daniel. "How to Hunt a Lone Wolf: Countering Terrorists Who Act on Their Own," *Foreign Affairs* 96 (March/April 2017): 96–105.

Byman, Daniel. *An Intelligence Reserve Corps to Counter Terrorist Use of the Internet* (Hoover Working Group on National Security, Technology and Law, Aegis Series Paper No. 1810, July 2018): 1–16.

Cotter, Cornelius P. "Constitutionalizing Emergency Powers." *Stanford Law Review* 382 (1953): 382–417.

Dahl, Robert A. *On Democracy*. New Haven and London: Yale University Press, 2000.

Eckholm, Erik. "ISIS Influence on Web Prompts Second Thoughts on First Amendment." *New York Times* 27 December 2015. <http://www.nytimes.com>.

Gohel, Sajjan M. "The Internet and Its Role in Terrorist Recruitment and Operational Planning," *CTC Sentinel* 2 (December 2009): 12–15.

Great Britain. *Defence Regulations: Being Regulations Made Under the Emergency Powers (Defence) Acts, 1939 and 1940, Printed as Amended up to and Including 15th January, 1941.* 7th ed. London: His Majesty's Stationary Office, 1941.

Great Britain and Pulling, Alexander. *Defence of the Realm Acts and Regulations: Passed and Made to July 31st 1915.* London: Printed for Fredrick Attenbury, King's printer of acts of Parliament and under authority of His Majesty's Stationary Office, by Darling & Son, Ltd, 1915.

Habermas, Jürgen. "Three Normative Models of Democracy." *Constellations* 1 (1994): 1–10.

Habermas, Jürgen. *Between Facts and Norms: Contributions to a Discourse Theory of Law and Democracy.* trans. William Rehg. Cambridge: The MIT Press, 1996.

Hughes, Seamus and Meleagrou-Hitchens, Alexander. "The Threat to the United States from the Islamic State's Virtual Entrepreneurs," *CTC Sentinel* 10 (March 2017): 1–8.

Millman, Brock. "HMG and the War Against Dissent, 1914–18." *Journal of Contemporary History* 40 (2005): 413–440.

Posner, Eric. "ISIS Gives Us No Choice but to Consider Limits on Speech." *Slate*, 15 December 2015. <http://www.slate.com>.

Post, David. "Protecting the First Amendment in the Internet Age." *Volokh Conspiracy Washington Post*, 21 December 2015. <https://www.washingtonpost.com/news/volokh-conspiracy>.

Rossiter, Clinton L. *Constitutional Dictatorship: Crisis Government in the Modern Democracies.* Princeton: Princeton University Press, 1948.

Sales, Nathan A., U.S. Department of State Acting Undersecretary for Civilian Security, Democracy and Human Rights. "After the Caliphate: A New Global Approach to Defeating ISIS." *Remarks: The Brooking Institution*, April 30, 2019. <https://www.state.gov/after-the-caliphate-a-new-global-approach-to-defeating-isis/>.

Townshend, Charles. *Making the Peace: Public Order and Public Security in Modern Britain.* Oxford: Oxford University Press, 1993.

Uhr, John. *Deliberative Democracy in Australia: The Changing Place of Parliament.* Melbourne: Cambridge University Press, 1998.

Votel, Joseph L., Bembenek, Cristina, Hans, Charles, Mouton, Jefferey and Spencer, Amanda. "#Virtual Caliphate: Defeating ISIL on the Physical Battlefield Is Not Enough." *Center for a New American Security*, January 12, 2017. <https://www.cnas.org>.

Weimann, Gabriel. *How Modern Terrorism Uses the Internet.* Washington DC: United States Institute of Peace Special Report 116 (March 2004): 1–10.

Appendices

Appendix A

Relevant sections of the Espionage Act and of the Sedition Act

Following is the full text of relevant sections of the Espionage Act of June 15, 1917, and of the Sedition Act (Act to amend section 3, title I of the Espionage Act) of May 16, 1918:[1]

Espionage Act

Title I, Section 3

Whoever, when the United States is at war, shall willfully make or convey reports or false statements with intent to interfere with the operation or success of the military or naval forces of the United States or to promote the success of its enemies and whoever, when the Unites States is at war, shall willfully cause or attempt to cause insubordination, disloyalty, mutiny, or refusal of duty, in the military or naval forces of the United States, or shall willfully obstruct the recruiting or enlistment service of the United States, to the injury of the service of the United States, shall be punished by a fine of not more than $10,000 or imprisonment for not more than twenty years, or both.

Title XII

Section 1. Every letter, writing, circular, postal card, picture, print, engraving, photograph, newspaper, pamphlet, book, or other publication, matter or thing, of any kind, in violation of any of the provisions of this Act is hereby declared to be nonmailable matter and shall not be conveyed in the mails or delivered from any post office or by any letter carrier: *Provided*, That nothing in this Act shall be so construed as to authorize any person other than an employee of the Dead Letter Office, duly authorized thereto, or other person upon a search warrant by law, to open any letter not addressed to himself.

Section 2. Every letter, writing, circular, postal card, picture, print, engraving, photograph, newspaper, pamphlet, book, or other publication, matter or thing, of any kind containing any matter advocating or urging treason, insurrection, or forcible resistance to any law of the United States is hereby declared to be nonmailable.

Section 3. Whoever shall use or attempt to use the mails or Postal Service of the United States for the transmission of any matter declared by this title to be nonmailable shall be fined no more than $5,000 or imprisoned not more than five years, or both. Any person violating any provision of this title may be tried and punished either in the district in which the unlawful matter or publication was mailed or to which it was carried by mail for delivery according to the direction thereon, or in which it was caused to be delivered by mail to the person to whom it was addressed.

Sedition Act

Be it enacted by the Senate and House of Representatives of the United States of America in Congress assembled, that section three of title one of the Act entitled "An Act to punish acts of interference with the foreign relations, the neutrality, and the foreign commerce of the United States, to punish espionage, and better enforce the criminal laws of the United States, and for other purposes," approved June fifteenth, nineteen hundred and seventeen, be, and the same is hereby, amended so as to read as follows:

> Sec. 3. Whoever, when the United States is at war, shall willfully make or convey false reports or false statements with intent to interfere with the operation or success of the military or naval forces of the United States, or to promote the success of its enemies, or shall willfully make or convey false reports or false statements, or say or do anything except by way of bona fide and not disloyal advice to an investor or investors, with intent to obstruct the sale by the United States of bonds or other securities of the United States or the making of loans by or to the United States, and whoever, when the United States is at war, shall willfully cause or attempt to cause, or incite or attempt to incite, insubordination, disloyalty, mutiny or refusal of duty, in the military or naval forces of the United States, or shall willfully obstruct or attempt to obstruct the recruiting or enlistment service of the United States, and whoever, when the United States is at war, shall willfully utter, print, write or publish any disloyal, profane, scurrilous, or abusive language about the form of government of the United States, or the Constitution of the United States, or the military or naval forces of the United States, or the flag of the United States, or the uniform of the Army or Navy of the United States, or any language intended to bring the form of government of the United States, or the Constitution of the United States, or the military or naval forces of the United States, or the flag of the United

States, or the uniform of the Army or Navy of the United States into contempt, scorn, contumely, or disrepute, or shall willfully utter, print, write, or publish any language intended to incite, provoke or encourage resistance to the United States, or to promote the cause of its enemies, or shall willfully display the flag of any foreign enemy, or shall willfully by utterance, writing, printing, publication, or language spoken, urge, incite or advocate any curtailment of production in this country of any thing or things, product or products, necessary or essential to the prosecution of the war in which the United States may be engaged, with intent by such curtailment to cripple or hinder the United States in the prosecution of the war, and whoever shall willfully advocate, teach, defend, or suggest the doing of any of the acts or things in this section enumerated, and whoever shall by word or act support or favor the cause of any country with which the United States is at war or by word or act oppose the cause of the United States therein, shall be punished by a fine of not more than $10,000 or imprisonment for not more than twenty years, or both: *Provided*, That any employee or official of the United States Government who commits any disloyal act or utters any unpatriotic or disloyal language, and who, in an abusive and violent manner criticizes the Army or Navy or the flag of the United States shall be at once dismissed from the service. Any such employee shall be dismissed by the head of the department in which the employee may be engaged, and any such official shall be dismissed by the authority having power to appoint a successor to the dismissed official.

Note

1 Source: *Statutes at Large of the United States of America*, Vol. 40, Part 1, 217, 553 (Washington: Government Printing Office, 1919).

Appendix B

Sections 1, 2 and 3 of Title I of the Alien Registration Act

Following is the full text of sections 1, 2 and 3 of Title I of the Alien Registration Act of June 28, 1940:[1]

Section 1

A It shall be unlawful for any person, with intent to interfere with, impair, or influence the loyalty, morale, or discipline of the military or naval forces of the United States –

1 to advise, counsel, urge, or in any manner cause insubordination, disloyalty, mutiny, or refusal of duty by any member of the military or naval forces of the United States; or
2 to distribute any written or printed matter which advises, counsels, or urges insubordination, disloyalty, mutiny, or refusal of duty by any member of the military or naval forces of the United States.

B For the purposes of this section, the term "military or naval forces of the United States" includes the Army of the United States, as defined in section 1 of the National Defense Act of June 3, 1916, as amended (48 Stat. 153; U. S. C., title 10, sec. 2), the Navy, Marine Corps, Coast Guard, Naval Reserve, and Marine Corps Reserve of the United States; and, when any merchant vessel is commissioned in the Navy or is in the service of the Army or the Navy, includes the master, officers, and crew of such vessel.

Section 2

A It shall be unlawful for any person –

1 to knowingly or willfully advocate, abet, advise, or teach the duty, necessity, desirability, or propriety of overthrowing or destroying any government in the United States by force or violence, or by the assassination of any officer of any such government;

2 with the intent to cause the overthrow or destruction of any government in the United States, to print, publish, edit, issue, circulate, sell, distribute, or publicly display any written or printed matter advocating, advising, or teaching the duty, necessity, desirability, or propriety of overthrowing or destroying any government in the United States by force or violence;

3 to organize or help to organize any society, group, or assembly of persons who teach, advocate, or encourage the overthrow or destruction of any government in the United States by force or violence; or to be or become a member of, or affiliate with, any such society, group, or assembly of persons, knowing the purposes thereof.

B For the purposes of this section, the term "government in the United States" means the Government of the United States, the government of any State, Territory, or possession of the United States, the government of the District of Columbia, or the government of any political subdivision of any of them.

Section 3

It shall be unlawful for any person to attempt to commit, or to conspire to commit, any of the acts prohibited by the provisions of this title.

Note

1 Source: *Statutes at Large of the United States of America*, Vol. 54, Part 1, 670 (Washington: Government Printing Office, 1941).

Appendix C

Sections 1–15 of Title I and relevant sections of Title II of the Internal Security Act

Following is the full text of sections 1–15 of Title I and of relevant sections of Title II the Internal Security Act of 1950:[1]

Title I – Subversive Activities Control

Section 1

A This title may be cited as the "Subversive Activities Control Act of 1950."

B Nothing in this Act shall be construed to authorize, require, or establish military or civilian censorship or in any way to limit or infringe upon freedom of the press or of speech as guaranteed by the Constitution of the United States and no regulation shall be promulgated hereunder having that effect (b) For the purposes of this section, the term "military or naval forces of the United States" includes the Army of the United States, as defined in section 1 of the National Defense Act of June 3, 1916, as amended (48 Stat. 153; U. S. C., title 10, sec. 2), the Navy, Marine Corps, Coast Guard, Naval Reserve, and Marine Corps Reserve of the United States; and, when any merchant vessel is commissioned in the Navy or is in the service of the Army or the Navy, includes the master, officers, and crew of such vessel.

Necessity for Legislation

Section 2

As a result of evidence adduced before various committees of the Senate and House of Representatives, the Congress hereby finds that –

1 There exists a world Communist movement which, in its origins, its development, and its present practice, is a world-wide revolutionary movement whose purpose it is, by treachery, deceit, infiltration into other groups (governmental and otherwise), espionage, sabotage,

terrorism, and any other means deemed necessary, to establish a Communist totalitarian dictatorship in the countries throughout the world through the medium of a world-wide Communist organization.

2 The establishment of a totalitarian dictatorship in any country results in the suppression of all opposition to the party in power, the subordination of the rights of individuals to the state, the denial of fundamental rights and liberties which are characteristic of a representative form of government, such as freedom of speech, of the press, of assembly, and of religious worship, and results in the maintenance of control over the people through fear, terrorism, and brutality.

3 The system of government known as a totalitarian dictatorship is characterized by the existence of a single political party, organized on a dictatorial basis, and by substantial identity between such party and its policies and the government and governmental policies of the country in which it exists.

4 The direction and control of the world Communist movement is vested in and exercised by the Communist dictatorship of a foreign country.

5 The Communist dictatorship of such foreign country, in exercising such direction and control and in furthering the purposes of the world Communist movement, establishes or causes the establishment of, and utilizes, in various countries, action organizations which are not free and independent organizations, but are sections of a world-wide Communist organization and are controlled, directed, and subject to the discipline of the Communist dictatorship of such foreign country.

6 The Communist action organizations so established and utilized in various countries, acting under such control, direction, and discipline, endeavor to carry out the objectives of the world Communist movement by bringing about the overthrow of existing governments by any available means including force if necessary, and setting up Communist totalitarian dictatorships which will be subservient to the most powerful existing Communist totalitarian dictatorship. Although such organizations usually designate themselves as political parties, they are in fact constituent elements of the world-wide Communist movement and promote the objectives of such movement by conspiratorial and coercive tactics, instead of through the democratic processes of a free elective system or through the freedom-preserving means employed by a political party which operates as an agency by which people govern themselves.

7 In carrying on the activities referred to in paragraph (6), such Communist organizations in various countries are organized on a secret, conspiratorial basis and operate to a substantial extent through organizations, commonly known as "Communist fronts", which in

most instances are created and maintained, or used, in such manner as to conceal the facts as to their true character and purposes and their membership. One result of this method of operation is that such affiliated organizations are able to obtain financial and other support from persons who would not extend such support if they knew the true purposes of, and the actual nature of the control and influence exerted upon, such "Communist fronts".

8 Due to the nature and scope of the world Communist movement, with the existence of affiliated constituent elements working toward common objectives in various countries of the world, travel of Communist members, representatives, and agents from country to country facilitates communication and is a prerequisite for the carrying on of activities to further the purposes of the Communist movement.

9 In the United States those individuals who knowingly and willfully participate in the world Communist movement, when they so participate, in effect repudiate their allegiance to the United States, and in effect transfer their allegiance to the foreign country in which is vested the direction and control of the world Communist movement.

10 In pursuance of communism's stated objectives, the most powerful existing Communist dictatorship has, by the methods referred to above, already caused the establishment in numerous foreign countries of Communist totalitarian dictatorships, and threatens to establish similar dictatorships in still other countries.

11 The agents of communism have devised clever and ruthless espionage and sabotage tactics which are carried out in many instances in form or manner successfully evasive of existing law.

12 The Communist network in the United States is inspired and controlled in large part by foreign agents who are sent into the United States ostensibly as attaches of foreign legations, affiliates of international organizations, members of trading commissions, and in similar capacities, but who use their diplomatic or semidiplomatic status as a shield behind which to engage in activities prejudicial to the public security.

13 There are, under our present immigration laws, numerous aliens who have been found to be deportable, many of whom are in the subversive, criminal, or immoral classes who are free to roam the country at will without supervision or control.

14 One device for infiltration by Communists is by procuring naturalization for disloyal aliens who use their citizenship as a badge for admission into the fabric of our society.

15 The Communist movement in the United States is an organization numbering thousands of adherents, rigidly and ruthlessly disciplined. Awaiting and seeking to advance a moment when the United States may be so far extended by foreign engagements, so far divided in counsel, or so far in industrial or financial straits, that overthrow

of the Government of the United States by force and violence may seem possible of achievement, it seeks converts far and wide by an extensive system of schooling and indoctrination. Such preparations by Communist organizations in other countries have aided in supplanting existing governments. The Communist organization in the United States, pursuing its stated objectives, the recent successes of Communist methods in other countries, and the nature and control of the world Communist movement itself, present a clear and present danger to the security of the United States and to the existence of free American institutions, and make it necessary that Congress, in order to provide for the common defense, to preserve the sovereignty of the United States as an independent nation, and to guarantee to each State a republican form of government, enact appropriate legislation recognizing the existence of such worldwide conspiracy and designed to prevent it from accomplishing its purpose in the United States.

Definitions

Section 3

For the purposes of this title –

1 The term "person" means an individual or an organization.

2 The term "organization" means an organization, corporation, company, partnership, association, trust, foundation, or fund; and includes a group of persons, whether or not incorporated, permanently or temporarily associated together for joint action on any subject or subjects.

3 The term "Communist-action organization" means –

- a any organization in the United States (other than a diplomatic representative or mission of a foreign government accredited as such by the Department of State) which (i) is substantially directed, dominated, or controlled by the foreign government or foreign organization controlling the world Communist movement referred to in section 2 of this title, and (ii) operates primarily to advance the objectives of such world Communist movement as referred to in section 2 of this title; and
- b any section, branch, fraction, or cell of any organization defined in subparagraph (a) of this paragraph which has not complied with the registration requirements of this title.

4 The term "Communist-front organization" means any organization in the United States (other than a Communist-action organization as defined in paragraph (3) of this section) which (A) is substantially

directed, dominated, or controlled by a Communist-action organization, and (B) is primarily operated for the purpose of giving aid and support to a Communist-action organization, a Communist foreign government, or the world Communist movement referred to in section 2 of this title.

5 The term "Communist organization" means a Communist-action organization or a Communist-front organization.

6 The term "to contribute funds or services" includes the rendering of any personal service and the making of any gift, subscription, loan, advance, or deposit, of money or of anything of value, and also the making of any contract, promise, or agreement to contribute funds or services, whether or not legally enforcible.

7 The term "facility" means any plant, factory or other manufacturing, producing or service establishment, airport, airport facility, vessel, pier, water-front facility, mine, railroad, public utility, laboratory, station, or other establishment or facility, or any part, division, or department of any of the foregoing. The term "defense facility" means any facility designated and proclaimed by the Secretary of Defense pursuant to section 5 (b) of this title and included on the list published and currently in effect under such subsection, and which is in compliance with the provisions of such subsection respecting the posting of notice of such designation.

8 The term "publication" means any circular, newspaper, periodical, pamphlet, book, letter, post card, leaflet, or other publication.

9 The term "United States", when used in a geographical sense, includes the several States, Territories, and possessions of the United States, the District of Columbia, and the Canal Zone.

10 The term "interstate or foreign commerce" means trade, traffic, commerce, transportation, or communication (A) between any State, Territory, or possession of the United States (including the Canal Zone), or the District of Columbia, and any place outside thereof, or (B) within any Territory or possession of the United States (including the Canal Zone)., or within the District of Columbia.

11 The term "Board" means the Subversive Activities Control Board created by section 12 of this title.

12 The term "final order of the Board" means an order issued by the Board under section 13 of this title, which has become final as provided in section 14 of this title.

13 The term "advocates" includes advises, recommends, furthers by overt act, and admits belief in; and the giving, loaning, or promising of support or of money or anything of value to be used for advocating any doctrine shall be deemed to constitute the advocating of such doctrine.

14 The term "world communism" means a revolutionary movement, the purpose of which is to establish eventually a Communist totalitarian

dictatorship in any or all the countries of the world through the medium of an internationally coordinated Communist movement.

15 The terms "totalitarian dictatorship" and "totalitarianism" mean and refer to systems of government not representative in fact, characterized by (A) the existence of a single political party, organized on a dictatorial basis, with so close an identity between such party and its policies and the governmental policies of the country in which it exists, that the party and the government constitute an indistinguishable unit, and (B) the forcible suppression of opposition to such party.

16 The term "doctrine" includes, but is not limited to, policies, practices, purposes, aims, or procedures.

17 The giving, loaning, or promising of support or of money or any other thing of value for any purpose to any organization shall be conclusively presumed to constitute affiliation therewith; but nothing in this paragraph shall be construed as an exclusive definition of affiliation.

18 "Advocating the economic, international, and governmental doctrines of world communism" means advocating the establishment of a totalitarian Communist dictatorship in any or all of the countries of the world through the medium of an internationally coordinated Communist movement.

19 "Advocating the economic and governmental doctrines of any other form of totalitarianism" means advocating the establishment of totalitarianism (other than world communism) and includes, but is not limited to, advocating the economic and governmental doctrines of fascism and Nazism.

Certain Prohibited Acts

Section 4

A It shall be unlawful for any person knowingly to combine, conspire, or agree with any other person to perform any act which would substantially contribute to the establishment within the United States of a totalitarian dictatorship, as defined in paragraph (15) of section 3 of this title, the direction and control of which is to be vested in, or exercised by or under the domination or control of, any foreign government, foreign organization, or foreign individual: *Provided, however*, That this subsection shall not apply to the proposal of a constitutional amendment.

B It shall be unlawful for any officer or employee of the United States or of any department or agency thereof, or of any corporation the stock of which is owned in whole or in major part by the United States or any department or agency thereof, to communicate in any manner or by any means, to any other person whom such officer or employee knows or has reason to believe to be an agent or representative of any foreign government or an officer or member of any Communist organization as defined in paragraph (5) of section 3 of this title, any information of a kind which shall have been classified by the President (or by the head of any such department, agency, or corporation with the approval of the President) as affecting the security of the United States, knowing or having reason to know that such information has been so classified, unless such officer or employees shall have been specifically authorized by the President, or by the head of the department, agency, or corporation by which this officer or employee is employed, to make such disclosure of such information.

C It shall be unlawful for any agent or representative of any foreign government, or any officer or member of any Communist organization as defined in paragraph (5) of section 3 of this title, knowingly to obtain or receive, or attempt to obtain or receive, directly or indirectly, from any officer or employee of the United States or of any department or agency thereof or of any corporation the stock of which is owned in whole or in major part by the United States or any department or agency thereof, any information of a kind which shall have been classified by the President (or by the head of any such department, agency, or corporation with the approval of the President) as affecting the security of the United States, unless special authorization for such communication shall first have been obtained from the head of the department, agency, or corporation having custody of or control over such information.

D Any person who violates any provision of this section shall, upon conviction thereof, be punished by a fine of not more than $10,000, or imprisonment for not more than ten years, or by both such fine and such imprisonment, and shall, moreover, be thereafter ineligible to hold any office, or place of honor, profit, or trust created by the Constitution or laws of the United States.

E Any person may be prosecuted, tried, and punished for any violation of this section at any time within ten years after the commission of such offense, notwithstanding the provisions of any other statute of limitations: *Provided*, That if at the time of the commission of the offense such person is an officer or employee of the United States or of any department or agency thereof, or of any corporation the stock of which is owned in whole or in major part by the United States or any department or agency thereof, such person may be prosecuted, tried, and punished for any violation of this section at any time within ten years after such person has ceased to be employed as such officer or employee

F Neither the holding of office nor membership in any Communist organization by any person shall constitute per se a violation of subsection (a) or subsection (c) of this section or of any other criminal statute. The fact of the registration of any person under section 7 or section 8 of this title as an officer or member of any Communist organization shall not be received in evidence against such person in any prosecution for any alleged violation of subsection (a) or subsection (c) of this section or for any alleged violation of any other criminal statute.

Employment of Members of Communist Organizations

Section 5

A When a Communist organization, as defined in paragraph (5) of section 3 of this title, is registered or there is in effect a final order of the Board requiring such organization to register, it shall be unlawful –

1 For any member of such organization, with knowledge or notice that such organization is so registered or that such order has become final –

a in seeking, accepting, or holding any nonelective office or employment under the United States, to conceal or fail to disclose the fact that he is a member of such organization; or
b to hold any nonelective office or employment under the United States; or
c in seeking, accepting, or holding employment in any defense facility, to conceal or fail to disclose the fact that he is a member of such organization; or
d if such organization is a Communist-action organization, to engage in any employment in any defense facility.

2 For any officer or employee of the United States or of any defense facility, with knowledge or notice that such organization is so registered or that such order has become final –

a to contribute funds or services to such organization; or
b to advise, counsel or urge any person, with knowledge or notice that such person is a member of such organization, to perform, or to omit to perform, any act if such act or omission would constitute a violation of any provision of subparagraph (1) of this subsection.

B The Secretary of Defense is authorized and directed to designate and proclaim, and from time to time revise, a list of facilities, as defined in paragraph (7) of section 3 of this title, with respect to the operation of which he finds and determines that the security of the United States requires the application of the provisions of subsection of this section. The Secretary shall cause such list as designated and proclaimed, or any revision thereof, to be promptly published in the Federal Register, and shall promptly notify the management of any facility so listed; whereupon such management shall immediately post conspicuously, and thereafter while so listed keep posted, notice of such designation in such form and in such place or places as to give reasonable notice thereof to all employees of, and to all applicants for employment in, such facility.

C As used in this section, the term "member" shall not include any individual whose name has not been made public because of the prohibition contained in section 9 (b) of this title.

Denial of Passports to Members of Communist Organizations

Section 6

A When a Communist organization as defined in paragraph (5) of section 3 of this title is registered, or there is in effect a final order of the Board requiring such organization to register, it shall be unlawful for any member of such organization, with knowledge or notice that such organization is so registered or that such order has become final –

1 to make application for a passport, or the renewal of a passport, to be issued or renewed by or under the authority of the United States; or

2 to use or attempt to use any such passport.

B When an organization is registered, or there is in effect a final order of the Board requiring an organization to register, as a Communist-action organization, it shall be unlawful for any officer or employee of the United States to issue a passport to, or renew the passport of, any individual knowing or having reason to believe that such individual is a member of such organization.

C As used in this section, the term "member" shall not include any individual whose name has not been made public because of the prohibition contained in section 9 (b) of this title.

Registration and Annual Reports of Communist Organizations

Section 7

A Each Communist-action organization (including any organization required, by a final order of the Board, to register as a Communist-action organization) shall, within the time specified in subsection

(c) of this section, register with the Attorney General, on a form prescribed by him by regulations, as a Communist-action organization.

B Each Communist-front organization (including any organization required, by a final order of the Board, to register as a Communist-front organization) shall, within the time specified in subsection (c) of this section, register with the Attorney General, on a form prescribed by him by regulations, as a Communist-front organization.

C The registration required by subsection (a) or (b) shall be made –

1 in the case of an organization which is a Communist-action organization or a Communist-front organization on the date of the enactment of this title, within thirty days after such date;
2 in the case of an organization becoming a Communist-action organization or a Communist-front organization after the date of the enactment of this title, within thirty days after such organization becomes a Communist-action organization or a Communist-front organization, as the case may be; and
3 in the case of an organization which by a final order of the Board is required to register, within thirty days after such order becomes final.

D The registration made under subsection (a) or (b) shall be accompanied by a registration statement, to be prepared and filed in such manner and form as the Attorney General shall by regulations prescribe, containing the following information:

1 The name of the organization and the address of its principal office.
2 The name and last-known address of each individual who is at the time of filing of such registration statement, and of each individual who was at any time during the period of twelve full calendar months next preceding the filing of such statement, an officer of the organization, with the designation or title of the office so held, and with a brief statement of the duties and functions of such individual as such officer.
3 An accounting, in such form and detail as the Attorney General shall by regulations prescribe, of all moneys received and expended (including the sources from which received and the purposes for which expended) by the organization during the period of twelve full calendar months next preceding the filing of such statement.
4 In the case of a Communist-action organization, the name and last-known address of each individual who was a member of the organization at any time during the period of twelve full calendar months preceding the filing of such statement.
5 In the case of any officer or member whose name is required to be shown in such statement, and who uses or has used or who is

or has been known by more than one name, each name which such officer or member uses or has used or by which he is known or has been known.

E It shall be the duty of each organization registered under this section to file with the Attorney General on or before February 1 of the year following the year in which it. registers, and on or before February 1 of each succeeding year, an annual report, prepared and filed in such manner and form as the Attorney General shall by regulations prescribe, containing the same information which by subsection (d) is required to be included in a registration statement, except that the information required with respect to the twelve-month period referred to in paragraph (2), (3), or (4) of such subsection shall, in such annual report, be given with respect to the calendar year preceding the February 1 on or before which such annual report must be filed.

F (1) It shall be the duty of each organization registered under this section to keep, in such manner and form as the Attorney General shall by regulations prescribe, accurate records and accounts of moneys received and expended (including the sources from which received and purposes for which expended) by such organization.

(2) It shall be the duty of each Communist-action organization registered under this section to keep, in such manner and form as the Attorney General shall by regulations prescribe, accurate records of the names and addresses of the members of such organization and of persons who actively participate in the activities of such organization.

G It shall be the duty of the Attorney General to send to each individual listed in any registration statement or annual report, filed under this section, as an officer or member of the organization in respect of which such registration statement or annual report was filed, a notification in writing that such individual is so listed; and such notification shall be sent at the earliest practicable time after the filing of such registration statement or annual report. Upon written request of any individual so notified who denies that he holds any office or membership (as the case may be) in such organization, the Attorney General shall forthwith initiate and conclude at the earliest practicable time an appropriate investigation to determine the truth or falsity of such denial, and, if the Attorney General shall be satisfied that such denial is correct, he shall thereupon strike from such registration statement or annual report the name of such individual. If the Attorney General shall decline or fail to strike the name of such individual from such registration statement or annual report within five months after receipt of such written request, such individual may file with the Board a petition for relief pursuant to section 13 (b) of this title.

H In the case of failure on the part of any organization to register or to file any registration statement or annual report as required by this section, it shall be the duty of the executive officer (or individual performing the ordinary and usual duties of an executive officer) and of the secretary (or individual performing the ordinary and usual duties of a secretary) of such organization, and of such officer or officers of such organization as the Attorney General shall by regulations prescribe, to register for such organization, to file such registration statement, or to file such annual report, as the case may be.

Registration of Members of Communist-Action Organizations

Section 8

A Any individual who is or becomes a member of any organization concerning which (1) there is in effect a final order of the Board requiring such organization to register under section 7 (a) of this title as a Communist-action organization, (2) more than thirty days have elapsed since such order has become final, and (3) such organization is not registered under section 7 of this title as a Communist-action organization, shall within sixty days after said order has become final, or within thirty days after becoming a member of such organization, whichever is later, register with the Attorney General as a member of such organization.

B Each individual who is or becomes a member of any organization which he knows to be registered as a Communist-action organization under section 7 (a) of this title, but to have failed to include his name upon the list of members thereof filed with the Attorney General, pursuant to the provisions of subsections (d) and (e) of section 7 of this title, shall, within sixty days after he shall have obtained such knowledge, register with the Attorney General as a member of such organization.

C The registration made by any individual under subsection (a) or (b) of this section shall be accompanied by a registration statement to be prepared and filed in such manner and form, and containing such information, as the Attorney General shall by regulations prescribe.

Keeping of Registers; Public Inspection; Reports to President and Congress

Section 9

A The Attorney General shall keep and maintain separately in the Department of Justice –

1 a "Register of Communist-Action Organizations", which shall include (A) the names and addresses of all Communist-action

organizations registered under section 7, (B) the registration statements and annual reports filed by such organizations thereunder, and (C) the registration statements filed by individuals under section 8; and

2 a "Register of Communist-Front Organizations", which shall include (A) the names and addresses of all Communist-front organizations registered under section 7, and (B) the registration statements and annual reports filed by such organizations thereunder.

B Such registers shall be kept and maintained in such manner as to be open for public inspection: Provided, That the Attorney General shall not make public the name of any individual listed in either such register as an officer or member of any Communist organization until sixty days shall have elapsed after the transmittal of the notification required by section 7 (g) to be sent to such individual, and if prior to the end of such period such individual shall make written request to the Attorney General for the removal of his name from any such list, the Attorney General shall not make public the name of such individual until six months shall have elapsed after receipt of such request by the Attorney General, or until thirty days shall have elapsed after the Attorney General shall have denied such request and shall have transmitted to such individual notice of such denial, whichever is earlier.

C The Attorney General shall submit to the President and to the Congress on or before June 1 of each year (and at any other time when requested by either House by resolution) a report with respect to the carrying out of the provisions of this title, including the names and addresses of the organizations listed in such registers and (except to the extent prohibited by subsection (b) of this section) the names and addresses of the individuals listed as members of such organizations.

D Upon the registration of each Communist organization under the provisions of this title, the Attorney General shall publish in the Federal Register the fact that such organization has registered as a Communist-action organization, or as a Communist-front organization, as the case may be, and the publication thereof shall constitute notice to all members of such organization that such organization has so registered.

Use of Mails and Instrumentalities of Interstate or Foreign Commerce

Section 10

It shall be unlawful for any organization which is registered under section 7, or for any organization with respect to which there is in effect a final order of the Board requiring it to register under section 7, or for any person acting for or on behalf of any such organization –

1 to transmit or cause to be transmitted, through the United States mails or by any means or instrumentality of interstate or foreign commerce, any publication which is intended to be, or which it is reasonable to believe is intended to be, circulated or disseminated among two or more persons, unless such publication, and any envelope, wrapper, or other container in which it is mailed or otherwise circulated or transmitted, bears the following, printed in such manner as may be provided in regulations prescribed by the Attorney General, with the name of the organization appearing in lieu of the blank: "Disseminated by________, a Communist organization"; or
2 to broadcast or cause to be broadcast any matter over any radio or television station in the United States, unless such matter is preceded by the following statement, with the name of the organization being stated in place of the blank: "The following program is sponsored by________, a Communist organization".

Denial of Tax Deductions and Exemptions

Section 11

A Notwithstanding any other provision of law, no deduction for Federal income-tax purposes shall be allowed in the case of a contribution to or for the use of any organization if at the time of the making of such contribution (1) such organization is registered under section 7, or (2) there is in effect a final order of the Board requiring such organization to register under section 7.
B No organization shall be entitled to exemption from Federal income tax, under section 101 of the Internal Revenue Code, for any taxable year if at any time during such taxable year (1) such organization is registered under section 7, or (2) there is in effect a final order of the Board requiring such organization to register under section 7.

Subversive Activities Control Board

Section 12

A There is hereby established a board, to be known as the Subversive Activities Control Board, which shall be composed of five members, who shall be appointed by the President, by and with the advice and consent of the Senate. Not more than three members of the Board shall be members of the same political party. Two of the original members shall be appointed for a term of one year, two for a term of two years, and one for a term of three years, but their successors shall be appointed for terms of three years each, except that any individual chosen to fill a vacancy shall be appointed only for the unexpired term of the member whom he shall succeed. The President shall designate one member to serve as Chairman of the Board. Any member of the Board may be removed by the President, upon notice and hearing, for neglect of duty or malfeasance in office, but for no other cause.

B A vacancy in the Board shall not impair the right of the remaining members to exercise all the powers of the Board, and three members of the Board shall, at all times, constitute a quorum. The Board shall have an official seal which shall be judicially noticed.

C The Board shall at the close of each fiscal year make a report in writing to the Congress and to the President stating in detail the cases it has heard, the decisions it has rendered, the names, salaries, and duties of all employees of the Board, and an account of all moneys it has disbursed.

D Each member of the Board shall receive a salary of $12,500 a year, shall be eligible for reappointment, and shall not engage in any other business, vocation, or employment.

E It shall be the duty of the Board –

1 upon application made by the Attorney General under section 13 (a) of this title, or by any organization under section 13 (b) of this title, to determine whether any organization is a "Communist-action organization" within the meaning of paragraph (3) of section 3 of this title, or a "Communist-front organization" within the meaning of paragraph (4) of section 3 of this title; and

2 upon application made by the Attorney General under section 13 (a) of this title, or by any individual under section 13 (b) of this title, to determine whether any individual is a member of any Communist-action organization registered, or by final order of the Board required to be registered, under section 7 (a) of this title.

F Subject to the civil-service laws and Classification Act of 1949 the Board may appoint and fix the compensation of a chief clerk and such examiners and other personnel as may be necessary for the performance of its functions.

G The Board may make such rules and regulations, not inconsistent with the provisions of this title, as may be necessary for the performance of its duties.

H There are hereby authorized to be appropriated to the Board such sums as may be necessary to carry out its functions.

Proceedings Before the Board

Section 13

A Whenever the Attorney General shall have reason to believe that any organization which has not registered under subsection (a) or subsection (b) of section 7 of this title is in fact an organization of a kind required to be registered under such subsection, or that any individual who has not registered under section 8 of this title is in fact required to register under such section, he shall file with the Board and serve upon such organization or individual a petition for an order requiring such organization or individual to register pursuant to such subsection or section, as the case may be. Each such petition shall be verified under oath, and shall contain a statement of the facts upon which the Attorney General relies in support of his prayer for the issuance of such order.

B Any organization registered under subsection (a) or subsection (b) of section 7 of this title, and any individual registered under section 8 of this title, may not oftener than once in each calendar year make application to the Attorney General for the cancellation of such registration and (in the case of such organization) for relief from obligation to make further annual reports. Within sixty days after the denial of any such application by the Attorney General, the organization or individual concerned may file with the Board and serve upon the Attorney General a petition for an order requiring the cancellation of such registration and (in the case of such organization) relieving such organization of obligation to make further annual reports. Any individual authorized by section 7 (g) of this title to file a petition for relief may file with the Board and serve upon the Attorney General a petition for an order requiring the Attorney General to strike his name from the registration statement or annual report upon which it appears.

C Upon the filing of any petition pursuant to subsection (a) or subsection (b) of this section, the Board (or any member thereof or any examiner designated thereby) may hold hearings, administer oaths and affirmations, may examine witnesses and receive evidence at any place in the United States, and may require by subpena the attendance and testimony of witnesses and the production of books, papers, correspondence, memoranda, and other records deemed relevant, to the matter under inquiry. Subpenas may be signed and issued by any member of the Board or any duly authorized examiner. Subpenas shall be issued on behalf of the organization or the individual who is a party to the proceeding upon request and upon a statement or showing of general relevance and reasonable scope of the evidence sought. Such attendance of witnesses and the production of such documentary evidence may be required from any place in the United

States at any designated place of hearing. Witnesses summoned shall be paid the same fees and mileage paid witnesses in the district courts of the United States. In case of disobedience to a subpena, the Board may invoke the aid of any court of the United States in requiring the attendance and testimony of witnesses and the production of documentary evidence. Any of the district courts of the United States within the jurisdiction of which such inquiry is carried on may, in case of contumacy or refusal to obey a subpena issued to any person, issue an order requiring such person to appear (and to produce documentary evidence if so ordered) and give evidence relating to the matter in question; and any failure to obey such order of the court may be punished by such court as a contempt thereof. All process in any such case may be served in the judicial district whereof such person is an inhabitant or wherever he may be found. No person shall be held liable in any action in any court, State or Federal, for any damages resulting from (1) his production of any documentary evidence in any proceeding before the Board if he is required, by a subpena issued under this subsection, to produce the evidence; or (2) any statement under oath he makes in answer to a question he is asked while testifying before the Board in response to a subpena issued under this subsection, if the statement is pertinent to the question.

D (1) All hearings conducted under this section shall be public. Each party to such proceeding shall have the right to present its case with the assistance of counsel, to offer oral or documentary evidence, to submit rebuttal evidence, and to conduct such cross-examination as may be required for a full and true disclosure of the facts. An accurate stenographic record shall be taken of the testimony of each witness, and a transcript of such testimony shall be filed in the office of the Board.

(2) Where an organization or individual declines or fails to appear at a hearing accorded to such organization or individual by the Board pursuant to this section, the Board may, without further proceedings and without the introduction of any evidence, enter an order requiring such organization or individual to register or denying the application of such organization or individual, as the case may be. Where in the course of any hearing before the Board or any examiner thereof a party or counsel is guilty of misbehavior which obstructs the hearing, such party or counsel may be excluded from further participation in the hearing.

E In determining whether any organization is a "Communist-action organization", the Board shall take into consideration –

1 the extent to which its policies are formulated and carried out and its activities performed, pursuant to directives or to effectuate the policies of the foreign government or foreign organization

in which is vested, or under the domination or control of which is exercised, the direction and control of the world Communist movement referred to in section 2 of this title; and

2 the extent to which its views and policies do not deviate from those of such foreign government or foreign organization; and

3 the extent to which it receives financial or other aid, directly or indirectly, from or at the direction of such foreign government or foreign organization; and

4 the extent to which it sends members or representatives to any foreign country for instruction or training in the principles, policies, strategy, or tactics of such world Communist movement; and

5 the extent to which it reports to such foreign government or foreign organization or to its representatives; and

6 the extent to which its principal leaders or a substantial number of its members are subject to or recognize the disciplinary power of such foreign government or foreign organization or its representatives; and

7 the extent to which, for the purpose of concealing foreign direction, domination, or control, or of expediting or promoting its objectives, (i) it fails to disclose, or resists efforts to obtain information as to, its membership (by keeping membership lists in code, by instructing members to refuse to acknowledge membership, or by any other method); (ii) its members refuse to acknowledge membership therein; (iii) it fails to disclose, or resists efforts to obtain information as to, records other than membership lists; (iv) its meetings are secret; and (v) it otherwise operates on a secret basis; and

8 the extent to which its principal leaders or a substantial number of its members consider the allegiance they owe to the United States as subordinate to their obligations to such foreign government or foreign organization.

F In determining whether any organization is a "Communist-front organization", the Board shall take into consideration –

1 the extent to which persons who are active in its management, direction, or supervision, whether or not holding office therein, are active in the management, direction, or supervision of, or as representatives of, any Communist-action organization, Communist foreign government, or the world Communist movement referred to in section 2; and

2 the extent to which its support, financial or otherwise, is derived from any Communist-action organization, Communist foreign government, or the world Communist movement referred to in section 2; and

3 the extent to which its funds? resources, or personnel are used to further or promote the objectives of any Communist-action organization, Communist foreign government, or the world Communist movement referred to in section 2; and
4 the extent to which the positions taken or advanced by it from time to time on matters of policy do not deviate from those of any Communist-action organization, Communist foreign government, or the world Communist movement referred to in section 2.

G If, after hearing upon a petition filed under subsection (a) of this section, the Board determines –

1 that an organization is a Communist-action organization or a Communist-front organization, as the case may be, it shall make a report in writing m which it shall state its findings as to the facts and shall issue and cause to be served on such organization an order requiring such organization to register as such under section 7 of this title; or
2 that an individual is a member of a Communist-action organization (including an organization required by final order of the Board to register under section 7 (a)), it shall make a report in writing in which it shall state its findings as to the facts and shall issue and cause to be served on such individual an order requiring him to register as such under section 8 of this title.

H If, after hearing upon a petition filed under subsection (a) of this section, the Board determines –

1 that an organization is not a Communist-action organization or a Communist-front organization, as the case may be, it shall make a report in writing in which it shall state its findings as to the facts; issue and cause to be served upon the Attorney General an order denying his petition for an order requiring such organization to register as such under section 7 of this title; and send a copy of such order to such organization; or
2 that an individual is not a member of any Communist-action organization, it shall make a report in writing in which it shall state its findings as to the facts; issue and cause to be served upon the Attorney General an order denying his petition for an order requiring such individual to register as such member under section 8 of this title; and send a copy of such order to such individual.

I If, after hearing upon a petition filed under subsection (b) of this section, the Board determines –

1 that an organization is not a Communist-action organization or a Communist-front organization, as the case may be, it shall

make a report in writing in which it shall state its findings as to the facts; issue and cause to be served upon the Attorney General an order requiring him to cancel the registration of such organization and relieve it from the requirement of further annual reports; and send a copy of such order to such organization; or

2 that an individual is not a member of any Communist-action organization, or (in the case of an individual listed as an officer of a Communist-front organization) that an individual is not an officer of a Communist-front organization, it shall make a report in writing in which it shall state its findings as to the facts; issue and cause to be served upon the Attorney General an order requiring him to (A) strike the name of such individual from the registration statement or annual report upon which it appears or (B) cancel the registration of such individual under section 8, as may be appropriate; and send a copy of such order to such individual.

J If, after hearing upon a petition filed under subsection (b) of this section, the Board determines –

1 that an organization is a Communist-action organization or a Communist-front organization, as the case may be, it shall make a report in writing in which it shall state its findings as to the facts and shall issue and cause to be served on such organization an order denying its petition for the cancellation of its registration and for relief from the requirement of further annual reports; or

2 that an individual is a member of a Communist-action organization, or (in the case of an individual listed as an officer of a Communist-front organization) that an individual is an officer of a Communist-front organization, it shall make a report in writing in which it shall state its findings as to the facts and shall issue and cause to be served on such individual an order denying his petition for an order requiring the Attorney General (A) to strike his name from any registration statement or annual report on which it appears or (B) to cancel the registration of such individual under section 8, as the case may be.

K When any order of the Board requiring registration of a Communist organization becomes final under the provisions of section 14 (b) of this title, the Board shall publish in the Federal Register the fact that such order has become final, and publication thereof shall constitute notice to all members of such organization that such order has become final.

Judicial Review

Section 14

A The party aggrieved by any order entered by the Board under subsection (g), (11), (i), or (j) of section 13 may obtain a review of such order by filing in the United States Court of Appeals for the District of Columbia, within sixty days from the date of service upon it of such order, a written petition praying that the order of the Board be set aside. A copy of such petition shall be forthwith served upon the Board, and thereupon the Board shall certify and file in the court a transcript of the entire record in the proceeding, including all evidence taken and the report and order of the Board. Thereupon the court shall have jurisdiction of the proceeding and shall have power to affirm or set aside the order of the Board; but the court may in its discretion and upon its own motion transfer any action so commenced to the United States Court of Appeals for the circuit wherein the petitioner resides. The findings of the Board as to the facts, if supported by the preponderance of the evidence, shall be conclusive. If either party shall apply to the court for leave to adduce additional evidence, and shall show to the satisfaction of the court that such additional evidence is material, the court may order such additional evidence to be taken before the Board and to be adduced upon the proceeding in such manner and upon such terms and conditions as to the court may seem proper. The Board may modify its findings as to the facts, by reason of the additional evidence so taken, and it shall file such modified or new findings, which, if supported by the preponderance of the evidence shall be conclusive, and its recommendations, if any, with respect to action in the matter under consideration. If the court shall set aside an order issued under subsection (j) of section 13 it may, in the case of an organization, enter a judgment canceling the registration of such organization and relieving it from the requirement of further annual reports, or in the case of an individual, enter a judgment requiring the Attorney General (A) to strike the name of such individual from the registration statement or annual report on which it appears, or (B) cancel the registration of such individual under section 8, as may be appropriate. The judgment and decree of the court shall be final, except that the same shall be subject to review by the Supreme Court upon certiorari, as provided in title 28, United States Code, section 1254.

B Any order of the Board issued under section 13 shall become final –

1 upon the expiration of the time allowed for filing a petition for review, if no such petition has been duly filed within such time; or...

2 upon the expiration of the time allowed for filing a petition for certiorari, if the order of the Board has been affirmed or the

petition for review dismissed by a United States Court of Appeals, and no petition for certiorari has been duly filed; or

3 upon the denial of a petition for certiorari, if the order of the Board has been affirmed or the petition for review dismissed by a United States Court of Appeals; or

4 upon the expiration of ten days from the date of issuance of the mandate of the Supreme Court, if such Court directs that the order of the Board be affirmed or the petition for review dismissed.

Penalties

Section 15

A If there is in effect with respect to any organization or individual a final order of the Board requiring registration under section 7 or section 8 of this title –

1 such organization shall, upon conviction of failure to register, to file any registration statement or annual report, or to keep records as required by section 7, be punished for each such offense by a fine of not more than $10,000, and

2 each individual having a duty under subsection (h) of section 7 to register or to file any registration statement or annual report on behalf of such organization, and each individual having a duty to register under section 8, shall, upon conviction of failure to so register or to file any such registration statement or annual report, be punished for each such offense by a fine of not more than $10,000, or imprisonment for not more than five years, or by both such fine and imprisonment.

For the purposes of this subsection, each day of failure to register, whether on the part of the organization or any individual, shall constitute a separate offense

B Any individual who, in a registration statement or annual report filed under section 7 or section 8, willfully makes any false statement or willfully omits to state any fact which is required to be stated, or which is necessary to make the statements made or information given not misleading, shall upon conviction thereof be punished for each such offense by a fine of not more than $10,000, or by imprisonment for not more than five years, or by both such fine and imprisonment. For the purposes of this subsection –

1 each false statement willfully made, and each willful omission to state any fact which is required to be stated, or which is necessary to make the statements made or information given not misleading, shall constitute a separate offense; and

2 each listing of the name or address of any one individual shall be deemed to be a separate statement.

C Any organization which violates any provision of section 10 of this title shall, upon conviction thereof, be punished for each such violation by a fine of not more than $10,000. Any individual who violates any provision of section 5, 6, or 10 of this title shall, upon conviction thereof, be punished for each such violation by a fine of not more than $10,000 or by imprisonment for not more than five years, or by both such fine and imprisonment.

Title II – Emergency Detention

Section 100

This title may be cited as the "Emergency Detention Act of 1950".

Findings of Fact and Declaration of Purpose

Section 101

As a result of evidence adduced before various committees of the Senate and the House of Representatives, the Congress hereby finds that –

1 There exists a world Communist movement which in its origins, its development, and its present practice, is a world-wide revolutionary movement whose purpose it is, by treachery, deceit, infiltration into other groups (governmental and otherwise), espionage, sabotage, terrorism, and any other means deemed necessary, to establish a Communist totalitarian dictatorship in all the countries of the world through the medium of a world-wide Communist organization.

2 The establishment of a totalitarian dictatorship in any country results in the suppression of all opposition to the party in power, the complete subordination of the rights of individuals to the state, the denial of fundamental rights and liberties which are characteristic of a representative form of government, such as freedom of speech, of the press, of assembly, and of religious worship, and results in the maintenance of control over the people through fear, terrorism, and brutality.

3 The system of government known as a totalitarian dictatorship is characterized by the existence of a single political party, organized on a dictatorial basis, and by substantial identity between such party and its policies and the government and governmental policies of the country in which it exists.

4 The direction and control of the world Communist movement is vested in and exercised by the Communist dictatorship of a foreign country.

5 The Communist dictatorship of such foreign country, in exercising such direction and control and in furthering the purposes of the world Communist movement, establishes or causes the establishment of, and utilizes, in various countries, action organizations which are not free and independent organizations, but are sections of a world-wide Communist organization and are controlled, directed, and subject to the discipline of the Communist dictatorship of such foreign country.

6 The organizations so established and utilized in various countries, acting under such control, direction, and discipline, endeavor to carry out the objectives of the world Communist movement by bringing about the overthrow of existing governments and setting up Communist totalitarian dictatorships which will be subservient to the most powerful existing Communist totalitarian dictatorship. Although such Communist organizations usually designate themselves as political parties, they are in fact constituent elements of the world-wide movement and promote the objectives of such movement by conspiratorial and coercive tactics, and especially by the use of espionage and sabotage, instead of through the democratic processes of a free elective system or through the freedom-preserving means employed by a political party which operates as an agency by which people govern themselves.

7 In the United States those individuals who knowingly and willfully participate in the world Communist movement, when they so participate, in effect repudiate their allegiance to the United States and in effect transfer their allegiance to the foreign country in which is vested the direction and control of the world Communist movement; and, in countries other than the United States, those individuals who knowingly and willfully participate in such Communist movement similarly repudiate their allegiance to the countries of which they are nationals in favor of such foreign Communist country.

8 In pursuance of communism's stated objectives, the most powerful existing Communist dictatorship has, by the methods referred to above, already caused the establishment in numerous foreign countries of Communist totalitarian dictatorships, and threatens to establish similar dictatorships in still other countries.

9 The agents of communism have devised clever and ruthless espionage and sabotage tactics which are carried out in many instances in form or manner successfully evasive of existing law, and which in this country are directed against the safety and peace of the United States.

10 The experience of many countries in World War II and thereafter with so-called "fifth columns" which employed espionage and sabotage to weaken the internal security and defense of nations resisting totalitarian dictatorships demonstrated the grave dangers and fatal effectiveness of such internal espionage and sabotage.

11 The security and safety of the territory and Constitution of the United States, and the successful prosecution of the common defense, especially in time of invasion, war, or insurrection m aid of a foreign enemy, require every reasonable and lawful protection against espionage, and against sabotage to national-defense material, premises, forces and utilities, including related facilities for mining, manufacturing, transportation, research, training, military and civilian supply, and other activities essential to national defense.

12 Due to the wide distribution and complex interrelation of facilities which are essential to national defense and due to the increased effectiveness and technical development in espionage and sabotage activities, the free and unrestrained movement in such emergencies of members or agents of such organizations and of others associated in their espionage and sabotage operations would make adequate surveillance to prevent espionage and sabotage impossible and would therefore constitute a clear and present danger to the public peace and the safety of the United States.

13 The recent successes of Communist methods in other countries and the nature and control of the world Communist movement itself present a clear and present danger to the security of the United States and to the existence of free American institutions, and make it necessary that Congress, in order to provide for the common defense, to preserve the sovereignty of the United States as an independent nation, and to guarantee to each State a republican form of government, enact appropriate legislation recognizing the existence of such world-wide conspiracy and designed to prevent it from accomplishing its purpose in the United States.

14 The detention of persons who there is reasonable ground to believe probably will commit or conspire with others to commit espionage or sabotage is, in a time of internal security emergency, essential to the common defense and to the safety and security of the territory, the people and the Constitution of the United States.

15 It is also essential that such detention in an emergency involving the internal security of the Nation shall be so authorized, executed, restricted and reviewed as to prevent any interference with the constitutional rights and privileges of any persons, and at the same time shall be sufficiently effective to permit the performance by the Congress and the President of their constitutional duties to provide for the common

defense, to wage war, and to preserve, protect and defend the Constitution, the Government and the people of the United States.

Declaration of "Internal Security Emergency"

Section 102

A In the event of any one of the following:

1 Invasion of the territory of the United States or its possessions,
2 Declaration of war by Congress, or
3 Insurrection within the United States in aid of a foreign enemy, and if, upon the occurrence of one or more of the above, the President shall find that the proclamation of an emergency pursuant to this section is essential to the preservation, protection and defense of the Constitution, and to the common defense and safety of the territory and people of the United States, the President is authorized to make public proclamation of the existence of an "Internal Security Emergency".

B A state of "Internal Security Emergency" (hereinafter referred to as the "emergency") so declared shall continue in existence until terminated by proclamation of the President or by concurrent resolution of the Congress.

Detention during an Emergency

Section 103

A Whenever there shall be in existence such an emergency, the President, acting through the Attorney General, is hereby authorized to apprehend and by order detain, pursuant to the provisions of this title, each person as to whom there is reasonable ground to believe that such person probably will engage in, or probably will conspire with others to engage in, acts of espionage or of sabotage.

B Any person detained hereunder (hereinafter referred to as "the detainee") shall be released from such emergency detention upon –

1 the termination of such emergency by proclamation of the President or by concurrent resolution of the Congress;
2 an order of release issued by the Attorney General;
3 a final order of release after hearing by the Board of Detention Review, hereinafter established;
4 a final order of release by a United. States court, after review of the action of the Board of Detention Review, or upon a writ of habeas corpus.

Procedure for Apprehension and Detention

Section 104

A The Attorney General, or such officer or officers of the Department of Justice as he may from time to time designate, are authorized during such emergency to execute in writing and to issue –

1 a warrant for the apprehension of each person as to whom there is reasonable ground to believe that such person probably will engage in, or probably will conspire with others to engage in, acts of espionage or sabotage; and
2 an application for an order to be issued pursuant to subsection (d) of this section for the detention of such person for the duration of such emergency.

Each such warrant shall issue only upon probable cause, supported by oath or affirmation, and shall particularly describe the person to be apprehended or detained.

B Warrants for the apprehension of persons under this title shall be served and apprehension of such persons shall be made only by such duly authorized officers of the Department of Justice as the Attorney General may designate. A copy of the warrant for apprehension shall be furnished to any person apprehended under this title.
C Persons apprehended or detained under this title shall be confined in such places of detention as may be prescribed by the Attorney General. The Attorney General shall provide for all detainees such transportation, food, shelter, and other accommodation and supervision as in his judgment may be necessary to accomplish the purpose of this title.
D Within forty-eight hours after apprehension, or as soon thereafter as provision for it may be made, each person apprehended pursuant to this section shall be taken before a preliminary hearing officer appointed pursuant to the provisions of this section. Such hearing officer shall inform such person (1) of the grounds upon which application was made for his detention, (2) of his right to retain counsel, of his right to have a preliminary examination, (4) of his right to refrain from making any statement, and (5) of the fact that any statement made by him may be used against him. Such hearing officer shall allow such person reasonable time and opportunity to consult counsel. If such person waives preliminary examination, the hearing officer shall forthwith issue an order for the detention of such person, and furnish to him a copy of such order. If such person does not waive examination, the preliminary hearing officer shall hear evidence within a reasonable time. Such person may introduce evidence in his own behalf, and may cross-examine witnesses against him,

except that the Attorney General or his representative shall not be required to furnish information the revelation of which would disclose the identity or evidence of Government agents or officers which he believes it would be dangerous to national safety and security to divulge. Such hearing officer shall record all evidence offered by or on behalf of such person and all objections made by such person to his detention. If from the evidence it appears to the preliminary hearing officer that there is probable cause for the detention of such person pursuant to this title, such hearing officer shall forthwith issue an order for the detention of such person, furnish to him a copy of such order, and advise such person of his right to file with the Detention Review Board established by this title a petition for the review of such order. If from the evidence it appears to the preliminary hearing officer that probable cause for the detention of such person has not been shown, such officer shall issue an order discharging such person from detention, and shall furnish a copy of such order to such person. Upon the entry of such order, such person shall be released from custody by the Attorney General and by any subordinate officer or employee of the United States having custody of such person. Within seven days after the entry of any such order, the preliminary hearing officer shall prepare and transmit to the Attorney General, or such other officer as may be designated by him, (1) a report which shall set forth the result of such preliminary hearing, together with his recommendations with respect to the question whether any order issued for the detention of such person shall be continued in effect or revoked, and (2) any additional written representations or evidence which the detainee or his legal counsel may wish to file with the Attorney General. A copy of such report shall be served promptly upon the detainee or his legal counsel. Preliminary hearing officers may be appointed by the President, without regard to the civil service laws but subject to the Classification Act of 1949, in such numbers, and may serve at such places, as may be necessary for the expeditious consideration of cases involving persons apprehended pursuant to this section. No person who has, within the three years preceding the date of his appointment, served as an officer or employee of the Department of Justice shall be appointed as a preliminary hearing officer.

E The Attorney General, or such other officers of the Department of Justice as he may designate, shall upon request of any detainee from time to time receive such additional information bearing upon the grounds for the detention as the detainee or any other person may present in writing. If on the basis of such additional information received by the Attorney General or transmitted to him by such officers, he shall find there is no longer reasonable ground to believe that the detainee probably will engage in, or probably will conspire with others to engage in, acts of espionage or sabotage if released, the Attorney General is authorized to issue an order revoking the initial order or any final Board or court order of detention and to release such detainee. The Attorney General is also authorized to modify the order under which any detainee is detained and apply to such detainee such lesser restrictions in movement and activity as the Attorney General shall determine will serve the purposes of this title.

F In case of Board or court review of any detention order, the Attorney General, or such review officers as he may designate, shall present to the Board, the court, and the detainee to the fullest extent possible consistent with national security, the evidence supporting a finding of reasonable ground for detention in respect to the detainee, but he shall not be required to offer or present evidence of any agents or officers of the Government the revelation of which in his judgment would be dangerous to the security and safety of the United States.

G The Attorney General is authorized to prescribe such regulations, not inconsistent with the provisions of this title, as he shall deem necessary to promote the effective administration of this title. No such regulation shall require or permit persons detained under the provisions of this title to perform forced labor, or any tasks not reasonably associated with their own comfort and well-being, or to be confined in company with persons who are confined pursuant to the criminal laws of the United States or of any State.

H Whenever there shall be in existence an emergency within the meaning of this title, the Attorney General shall transmit bimonthly to the President and to the Congress a report of all action taken pursuant to the powers granted in this title.

Seperability of Provisions

Section 116

If any provision of this title, or the application thereof to any person or circumstance, is held invalid, the remaining provisions of this title, or the application of such provision to other persons or circumstances, shall not be affected thereby. Nothing contained in this title shall be construed to suspend or to authorize the suspension of the privilege of the writ of habeas corpus.

Note

1 Source: *Statutes at Large of the United States of America*, Vol. 64, Part 1, 987 (Washington: Government Printing Office, 1952).

Index

Note: Page numbers followed by "n" denote endnotes.

For Product Safety Concerns and Information please contact our EU representative GPSR@taylorandfrancis.com
Taylor & Francis Verlag GmbH, Kaufingerstraße 24, 80331 München, Germany

www.ingramcontent.com/pod-product-compliance
Ingram Content Group UK Ltd.
Pitfield, Milton Keynes, MK11 3LW, UK
UKHW022024061126
477531UK00002B/27
* 9 7 8 0 3 6 7 5 6 9 9 8 3 *